Laura Kuzia

Houseplants For Dummies®

Aaah! Scented Houseplants

The following plants have scented flowers or leaves. Some of them (notably the ~~corn plant~~, hyacinth, and snake plant) pack quite a perfumed punch when they are *in bloom*.

Calamondin orange *(× Citrofortunella microcarpa)*

Corn plant *(Dracaena fragrans)*

Hyacinth *(Hyacinthus)*

Narcissus *(Narcissus) trifasciata)*

Oleander *(Nerium oleander)*

Orchids (some varieties)

Peace lily *(Spathiphyllum wallisii)*

Scented geranium *(Pelargonium graveolens)*

Snake plant *(Sansevieria trifasciata)*

Wax plant *(Hoya carnosa)*

A Shorthand Guide to Keeping Your Plants Alive and Thriving

Buy your plants from a reputable nursery. Plants that spend time on department store or supermarket shelves sometimes don't get the care they need and may be already on a downward slide.

Buy plants listed in this book with the "Tuff 'n' Robust" icon. They're natural survivors and can thrive under less-than-great conditions.

Inspect plants closely before you buy them. Check for insects, disease, and signs of poor care, such as yellowing leaves. (Chapter 17 provides pointers on how to spot these problems.)

Make sure your plants are carefully wrapped before you leave the store. Exposing a plant to very hot or very cold outdoor air or intense direct sun can weaken the plant before you even have a chance to get it home.

Give them the light they need. The vast majority of all plants grow well under very bright light, with some protection from the midday sun; the remainder can thrive under medium light. No plant, even one with a "Low Light Plant" label, really likes low light.

Never let the potting medium dry out completely. Ninety-five percent of all plants should be watered thoroughly as soon as the top inch (2.5 centimeters) of their soil dries out. (See Chapter 9 for information on testing for dryness.) Don't wait until your plants are parched to water them.

Never let your plants soak in a water-filled saucer. Drain the saucer one half-hour after watering.

Use an air humidifier. Some plants don't mind dry air, but *all* plants like humid air.

Don't allow your plants to freeze or bake. Keep plants away from cold drafts and off of window sills that get the full force of the midday summer sun.

Repot your plants annually. A fresh batch of potting mix keeps your plants healthy while eliminating any soil that has become contaminated over time with excess mineral salts.

...For Dummies: Bestselling Book Series for Beginners

Houseplants For Dummies®

Cheat Sheet

Houseplant Resources on the Web

African Violets Online at `avsa.org`. The Web site of the African Violet Society of America, it has loads of information on growing African violets, a photo library, information on upcoming events, and a list of catalogues.

The Amateurs' Digest at `vvv.com/~amdigest/homepage.htm`. The online edition of the print magazine, *Amateurs' Digest,* offers lots of information on collecting and growing cacti and succulents, including the unusual ones.

American Gloxinia and Gesneriad Society at `www.aggs.org`. You can find information on growing all kinds of African violets and other gesneriads.

Bromeliad Society International at `www.bsi.org`. This site has a photo library and lots of sources for some of those hard-to-find bomeliads.

The Cactus and Succulent Plant Mall at `www.cactus-mall.com`. Simply one of the best houseplant Web sites of any kind. It has an excellent picture gallery and its many links are updated regularly.

Fern Resource Hub at `www.inetworld.net/~sdfern`. This Web site for the San Diego Fern Society has plenty of information on growing and identifying ferns, plus links to other sites on the subject of ferns.

House Plants Forum at `www.gardenweb.com/forums/houseplt`. This site has one of the better houseplant discussion groups. If you have a question on your plants, post it here and I guarantee you'll get a quick response.

International Bulb Society at `www.bulbsociety.com`. A good source of information on amaryllis, caladiums, and other indoor bulbs.

OrchidWeb at `www.pathfinder.com/vg/Gardens/AOS`. Published by the American Orchid Society, this is a particularly beautiful site with seemingly limitless illustrations and information on the topic of growing orchids.

Building Your Houseplant Vocabulary

Axil: The point at which a leaf meets the plant's stem.

Bract: A leaf-like appendage surrounding a plant's flowers that is often just as colorful (or even more so) than the actual blooms.

Chlorophyll: The green pigment that gives plants their color and allows them to absorb energy form the sun and convert it into food.

Corm: A plant structure that resembles a bulb, but which is actually formed from modified stem tissues. Crocuses and gladiolas are corms.

Cultivar: A plant developed by humans, either through natural mutation or by crossing different plants, as opposed to a wild plant species (from the term "cultivated variety").

Epiphyte: A plant that grows on trees rather than on the ground. Plants that live on or grow from the land are *terrestrial.*

Hybrid: The result of a cross between two different parent plants.

Node: The point at which a leaf joins a stem.

Petiole: A leaf stalk — the narrow part of a leaf that joins the blade to the stem.

Photosynthesis: The conversion of the sun's energy into sugars and starches, which supply a plant with food and allow it to grow.

Rhizome: A creeping underground stem.

Runner: A creeping or arching stem that produces baby plants. Also called a *stolon.*

Spadix: A flower spike surrounded by a leaf-like bract called a *spathe.*

Stomata: The pores through which a plant breathes. (A single pore is called a *stomate.*)

Tuber: A fleshy underground growth, similar to a bulb.

Variegation: Colorful patches or streaks appearing on a leaf or stem.

HOUSEPLANTS FOR DUMMIES®

**by Larry Hodgson
and the Editors of
The National Gardening Association**

IDG Books Worldwide, Inc.
An International Data Group Company

Foster City, CA ♦ Chicago, IL ♦ Indianapolis, IN ♦ New York, NY

Houseplants For Dummies®

Published by
IDG Books Worldwide, Inc.
An International Data Group Company
919 E. Hillsdale Blvd.
Suite 400
Foster City, CA 94404
www.idgbooks.com (IDG Books Worldwide Web site)
www.dummies.com (Dummies Press Web site)

Library of Congress Catalog Card No.: 98-86178

ISBN: 0-7645-5102-7

Printed in the United States of America

10 9 8 7 6 5 4 3 2 1

1E/RR/QY/ZY/IN

Distributed in the United States by IDG Books Worldwide, Inc.

Distributed by Macmillan Canada for Canada; by Transworld Publishers Limited in the United Kingdom; by IDG Norge Books for Norway; by IDG Sweden Books for Sweden; by Woodslane Pty. Ltd. for Australia; by Woodslane (NZ) Ltd. for New Zealand; by Addison Wesley Longman Singapore Pte Ltd. for Singapore, Malaysia, Thailand, Indonesia and Korea; by Norma Comunicaciones S.A. for Colombia; by Intersoft for South Africa; by International Thomson Publishing for Germany, Austria and Switzerland; by Toppan Company Ltd. for Japan; by Distribuidora Cuspide for Argentina; by Livraria Cultura for Brazil; by Ediciencia S.A. for Ecuador; by Ediciones ZETA S.C.R. Ltda. for Peru; by WS Computer Publishing Corporation, Inc., for the Philippines; by Unalis Corporation for Taiwan; by Contemporanea de Ediciones for Venezuela; by Computer Book & Magazine Store for Puerto Rico; by Express Computer Distributors for the Caribbean and West Indies. Authorized Sales Agent: Anthony Rudkin Associates for the Middle East and North Africa.

For general information on IDG Books Worldwide's books in the U.S., please call our Consumer Customer Service department at 800-762-2974. For reseller information, including discounts and premium sales, please call our Reseller Customer Service department at 800-434-3422.

For information on where to purchase IDG Books Worldwide's books outside the U.S., please contact our International Sales department at 650-655-3200 or fax 650-655-3297.

For information on foreign language translations, please contact our Foreign & Subsidiary Rights department at 650-655-3021 or fax 650-655-3281.

For sales inquiries and special prices for bulk quantities, please contact our Sales department at 650-655-3200 or write to the address above.

For information on using IDG Books Worldwide's books in the classroom or for ordering examination copies, please contact our Educational Sales department at 800-434-2086 or fax 317-596-5499.

For press review copies, author interviews, or other publicity information, please contact our Public Relations department at 650-655-3000 or fax 650-655-3299.

For authorization to photocopy items for corporate, personal, or educational use, please contact Copyright Clearance Center, 222 Rosewood Drive, Danvers, MA 01923, or fax 978-750-4470.

is a trademark under exclusive license to IDG Books Worldwide, Inc., from International Data Group, Inc.

About the Authors

Larry Hodgson first became interested in houseplants when he was 11 after his father gave him a terrarium. The turtle died, but the plants lived on, stimulating a life-long passion for everything that grows. Born in Toronto, Larry moved to Quebec City to study French and eventually settled there permanently. After trying his hand at various jobs from teaching to organizing blood donor clinics to translation, he decided to combine his communications skills with his favorite hobby and became a gardening writer.

Larry has authored or co-authored 15 gardening books and written for gardening magazines throughout Canada and the United States, and has served as editor-in-chief of *HousePlant Magazine, Fleurs, Plantes et Jardins, Houseplant Forum,* and *À Fleur de Pot* magazines and various plant society publications. He has written a garden column in the *Soleil* for 12 years, is a regular collaborator on several French- and English-language radio and television shows, lectures widely, and leads four or five garden tours every year that have taken him to more than 25 countries. Gardening remains his favorite pastime, with amateur theater a close second. Larry shares his life with his wife, his son, two stepchildren, a dog, a cat, and some 600 houseplants growing in every room of his house.

The **National Gardening Association** is the largest member-based, nonprofit organization of home gardeners in the U.S. Founded in 1972 (as "Gardens for All") to spearhead the community garden movement, today's National Gardening Association is best known for its bimonthly publication, *National Gardening* magazine ($18 per year). Reporting on all aspects of home gardening, each issue is read by some half-million gardeners worldwide. These publishing activities are supplemented by online efforts, such those on their World Wide Web site (www.garden.org) and on America Online (at keyword HouseNet). Other NGA activities include:

- **Growing Science Inquiry and GrowLab** (funded in part by the National Science Foundation) provides science-based curricula for students in kindergarten through Grade 8.

- Since 1972, the ***National Gardening Survey*** (conducted by the Gallup Company) has collected the most detailed research about gardeners and gardening in North America.

- **Youth Garden Grants.** Every year the NGA awards grants, each of which includes more than $500 worth of gardening tools and seeds, to schools, youth groups, and community organizations.

For more information about the National Gardening Association, write to 180 Flynn Ave., Butlington, VT 05401 USA.

ABOUT IDG BOOKS WORLDWIDE

Welcome to the world of IDG Books Worldwide.

IDG Books Worldwide, Inc., is a subsidiary of International Data Group, the world's largest publisher of computer-related information and the leading global provider of information services on information technology. IDG was founded more than 25 years ago and now employs more than 8,500 people worldwide. IDG publishes more than 275 computer publications in over 75 countries (see listing below). More than 90 million people read one or more IDG publications each month.

Launched in 1990, IDG Books Worldwide is today the #1 publisher of best-selling computer books in the United States. We are proud to have received eight awards from the Computer Press Association in recognition of editorial excellence and three from *Computer Currents'* First Annual Readers' Choice Awards. Our best-selling *...For Dummies®* series has more than 50 million copies in print with translations in 38 languages. IDG Books Worldwide, through a joint venture with IDG's Hi-Tech Beijing, became the first U.S. publisher to publish a computer book in the People's Republic of China. In record time, IDG Books Worldwide has become the first choice for millions of readers around the world who want to learn how to better manage their businesses.

Our mission is simple: Every one of our books is designed to bring extra value and skill-building instructions to the reader. Our books are written by experts who understand and care about our readers. The knowledge base of our editorial staff comes from years of experience in publishing, education, and journalism — experience we use to produce books for the '90s. In short, we care about books, so we attract the best people. We devote special attention to details such as audience, interior design, use of icons, and illustrations. And because we use an efficient process of authoring, editing, and desktop publishing our books electronically, we can spend more time ensuring superior content and spend less time on the technicalities of making books.

You can count on our commitment to deliver high-quality books at competitive prices on topics you want to read about. At IDG Books Worldwide, we continue in the IDG tradition of delivering quality for more than 25 years. You'll find no better book on a subject than one from IDG Books Worldwide.

John Kilcullen
CEO
IDG Books Worldwide, Inc.

Steven Berkowitz
President and Publisher
IDG Books Worldwide, Inc.

*Eighth Annual
Computer Press
Awards ➤1992*

*Ninth Annual
Computer Press
Awards ➤1993*

*Tenth Annual
Computer Press
Awards ➤1994*

*Eleventh Annual
Computer Press
Awards ➤1995*

IDG Books Worldwide, Inc., is a subsidiary of International Data Group, the world's largest publisher of computer-related information and the leading global provider of information services on information technology. International Data Group publishes over 275 computer publications in over 75 countries. More than 90 million people read one or more International Data Group publications each month. International Data Group's publications include: **ARGENTINA:** Buyer's Guide, Computerworld Argentina, PC World Argentina; **AUSTRALIA:** Australian Macworld, Australian PC World, Australian Reseller News, Computerworld, IT Casebook, Network World, Publish, Webmaster; **AUSTRIA:** Computerwelt Osterreich, Networks Austria, PC Tip Austria; **BANGLADESH:** PC World Bangladesh; **BELARUS:** PC World Belarus; **BELGIUM:** Data News; **BRAZIL:** Annuário de Informática, Computerworld, Connections, Macworld, PC Player, PC World, Publish, Reseller News, Supergamepower; **BULGARIA:** Computerworld Bulgaria, Network World Bulgaria, PC & MacWorld Bulgaria; **CANADA:** CIO Canada, Client/Server World, ComputerWorld Canada, InfoWorld Canada, NetworkWorld Canada, WebWorld; **CHILE:** Computerworld Chile, PC World Chile; **COLOMBIA:** Computerworld Colombia, PC World Colombia; **COSTA RICA:** PC World Centro America; **THE CZECH AND SLOVAK REPUBLICS:** Computerworld Czechoslovakia, Macworld Czech Republic, PC World Czechoslovakia; **DENMARK:** Communications World Danmark, Computerworld Danmark, Macworld Danmark, PC World Danmark, Techworld Denmark; **DOMINICAN REPUBLIC:** PC World Republica Dominicana; **ECUADOR:** PC World Ecuador; **EGYPT:** Computerworld Middle East, PC World Middle East; **EL SALVADOR:** PC World Centro America; **FINLAND:** MikroPC, Tietoverkko, Tietoviikko; **FRANCE:** Distributique, Hebdo, Info PC, Le Monde Informatique, Macworld, Reseaux & Telecoms, WebMaster France; **GERMANY:** Computer Partner, Computerwoche, Computerwoche Extra, Computerwoche FOCUS, Global Online, Macwelt, PC Welt; **GREECE:** Amiga Computing, GamePro Greece, Multimedia World; **GUATEMALA:** PC World Centro America; **HONDURAS:** PC World Centro America; **HONG KONG:** Computerworld Hong Kong, PC World Hong Kong, Publish in Asia; **HUNGARY:** ABCD CD-ROM, Computerworld Szamitastechnika, Internetto online Magazine, PC World Hungary, PC-X Magazin Hungary; **ICELAND:** Tolvulmemur PC World Island; **INDIA:** Information Communications World, Information Systems Computerworld, PC World India, Publish in Asia; **INDONESIA:** InfoKomputer PC World, Komputek Computerworld, Publish in Asia; **IRELAND:** ComputerScope, PC Live!; **ISRAEL:** Macworld Israel, People & Computers/Computerworld; **ITALY:** Computerworld Italia, Macworld Italia, Networking Italia, PC World Italia; **JAPAN:** DTP World, Macworld Japan, Nikkei Personal Computing, OS/2 World Japan, SunWorld Japan, Windows NT World, Windows World Japan; **KENYA:** PC World East African; **KOREA:** Hi-Tech Information, Macworld Korea, PC World Korea; **MACEDONIA:** PC World Macedonia; **MALAYSIA:** Computerworld Malaysia, PC World Malaysia, Publish in Asia; **MALTA:** PC World Malta; **MEXICO:** Computerworld Mexico, PC World Mexico; **MYANMAR:** PC World Myanmar; **NETHERLANDS:** Computer! Totaal, LAN Internetworking Magazine, LAN World Buyers Guide, Macworld Netherlands, Net, WebWereld; **NEW ZEALAND:** Absolute Beginners Guide and Plain & Simple Series, Computer Buyer, Computer Industry Directory, Computerworld New Zealand, MTB, Network World, PC World New Zealand; **NICARAGUA:** PC World Centro America; **NORWAY:** Computerworld Norge, CW Rapport, Datamagasinet, Financial Rapport, Kursguide Norge, Macworld Norge, Multimediaworld Norge, PC World Ekspress Norge, PC World Nettverk, PC World Norge, PC World ProduktGuide Norge; **PAKISTAN:** Computerworld Pakistan; **PANAMA:** PC World Panama; **PEOPLE'S REPUBLIC OF CHINA:** China Computer Users, China Computerworld, China InfoWorld, China Telecom World Weekly, Computer & Communication, Electronic Design China, Electronics Today, Electronics Weekly, Game Software, PC World China, Popular Computer Week, Software Weekly, Software World, Telecom World; **PERU:** Computerworld Peru, PC World Profesional Peru, PC World SoHo Peru; **PHILIPPINES:** Click!, Computerworld Philippines, PC World Philippines, Publish in Asia; **POLAND:** Computerworld Poland, Computerworld Special Report Poland, Cyber, Macworld Poland, Networld Poland, PC World Komputer; **PORTUGAL:** Cerebro/PC World, Computerworld/Correio Informático, Dealer World Portugal, Mac*In/PC*In Portugal, Multimedia World; **PUERTO RICO:** PC World Puerto Rico; **ROMANIA:** Computerworld Romania, PC World Romania, Telecom Romania; **RUSSIA:** Computerworld Russia, Mir PK, Publish, Seti; **SINGAPORE:** Computerworld Singapore, PC World Singapore, Publish in Asia; **SLOVENIA:** Monitor; **SOUTH AFRICA:** Computing SA, Network World SA, Software World SA; **SPAIN:** Communicaciones World España, Computerworld España, Dealer World España, Macworld España, PC World España; **SRI LANKA:** Infolink PC World; **SWEDEN:** CAP&Design, Computer Sweden, Corporate Computing Sweden, Internetworld Sweden, it.branschen, Macworld Sweden, MaxiData Sweden, MikroDatorn, Nätverk & Kommunikation, PC World Sweden, PCaktiv, Windows World Sweden; **SWITZERLAND:** Computerworld Schweiz, Macworld Schweiz, PCtip; **TAIWAN:** Computerworld Taiwan, Macworld Taiwan, NEW ViSiON/Publish, PC World Taiwan, Windows World Taiwan; **THAILAND:** Publish in Asia, Thai Computerworld; **TURKEY:** Computerworld Turkiye, Macworld Turkiye, Network World Turkiye, PC World Turkiye; **UKRAINE:** Computerworld Kiev, Multimedia World Ukraine, PC World Ukraine; **UNITED KINGDOM:** Acorn User UK, Amiga Action UK, Amiga Computing UK, Apple Talk UK, Computing, Macworld, Parents and Computers UK, PC Advisor, PC Home, PSX Pro, The WEB; **UNITED STATES:** Cable in the Classroom, CIO Magazine, Computerworld, DOS World, Federal Computer Week, GamePro Magazine, InfoWorld, I-Way, Macworld, Network World, PC Games, PC World, Publish, Video Event, THE WEB Magazine, and WebMaster; online webzines: JavaWorld, NetscapeWorld, and SunWorld Online; **URUGUAY:** InfoWorld Uruguay; **VENEZUELA:** Computerworld Venezuela, PC World Venezuela; and **VIETNAM:** PC World Vietnam.   5/7/98

Authors' Acknowledgments

From Larry:

My thanks to the many fine plant societies in North America that provided me with invaluable information used in the research and writing of this book.

I'd also like to thank Michael McCaskey and the staff of *National Gardening* magazine for inviting me to write this book and for their careful follow-up throughout the writing process. Thanks also to Bill Marken, the *...For Dummies* series editor for the National Gardening Association, and the project editor Nancy DelFavero of IDG Books Worldwide Inc., neither of whom, I believe, got more than a few hours sleep during the entire project. Thanks also go to the copy editor, Phil Worthington.

Finally, thanks to my wife Marie who took care of the plants and the entire garden (no small task!) while I was tied up with this book, and to my assistant Susanne who filtered all the calls and basically kept things running while I was immersed in the writing of this book.

From the National Gardening Association:

The NGA thanks the entire IDG Books Chicago team, one that we have relied so heavily — former Executive Editor Sarah Kennedy, Acquisitions Editor Holly McGuire, and Vice President and Publisher Kathy Welton. They are a great group to work with and we appreciate their support. The production team at IDG in Indianapolis deserves much credit, especially for their working with the demanding schedules. Many kudos also belong to the book's project editor extraordinaire Nancy DelFavero for her contributions to the title.

Thanks are also due to some folks at the NGA — President and Publisher David Els, Associate Publisher Larry Sommers, Editor-in-Chief Michael MacCaskey, *...For Dummies* Series Editor Bill Marken, Senior Horticulturist Charlie Nardozzi, and Assistant Editor Shila Patel.

Publisher's Acknowledgments

We're proud of this book; please register your comments through our IDG Books Worldwide Online Registration Form located at http://my2cents.dummies.com.

Some of the people who helped bring this book to market include the following:

Acquisitions, Development, and Editorial

Project Editor: Nancy DelFavero

Acquisitions Editor: Holly McGuire

Copy Editor: Phil Worthington

Technical Editors: Derek Burch, Richard Y. Evans

Editorial Manager: Mary C. Corder

Editorial Assistant: Paul E. Kuzmic

Production

Project Coordinator: Karen York

Layout and Graphics: Lou Boudreau, Linda M. Boyer, Maridee V. Ennis, Angela F. Hunckler, Jane E. Martin, Heather N. Pearson, Anna Rohrer, Brent Savage, Michael A. Sullivan

Proofreaders: Christine Berman, Kelli Botta, Sally Burton, Michelle Croninger, Rachel Garvey, Rebecca Senninger, Janet M. Withers

Indexer: Richard T. Evans

Illustrations: Ron Hildebrand, and Jody Litton

Photography: Thomas J. Creeden and Tropical Computers, Inc., John Glover

Special Help

Maureen F. Kelly, Paula Lowell, Jonathan Malysiak, Allison Solomon

General and Administrative

IDG Books Worldwide, Inc.: John Kilcullen, CEO; Steven Berkowitz, President and Publisher

IDG Books Technology Publishing: Brenda McLaughlin, Senior Vice President and Group Publisher

Dummies Technology Press and Dummies Editorial: Diane Graves Steele, Vice President and Associate Publisher; Mary Bednarek, Director of Acquisitions and Product Development; Kristin A. Cocks, Editorial Director

Dummies Trade Press: Kathleen A. Welton, Vice President and Publisher; Kevin Thornton, Acquisitions Manager

IDG Books Production for Dummies Press: Michael R. Britton, Vice President of Production and Creative Services; Beth Jenkins Roberts, Production Director; Cindy L. Phipps, Manager of Project Coordination, Production Proofreading, and Indexing; Kathie S. Schutte, Supervisor of Page Layout; Shelley Lea, Supervisor of Graphics and Design; Debbie J. Gates, Production Systems Specialist; Robert Springer, Supervisor of Proofreading; Debbie Stailey, Special Projects Coordinator; Tony Augsburger, Supervisor of Reprints and Bluelines

Dummies Packaging and Book Design: Robin Seaman, Creative Director; Jocelyn Kelaita, Product Packaging Coordinator; Kavish + Kavish, Cover Design

♦

The publisher would like to give special thanks to Patrick J. McGovern, without whom this book would not have been possible.

♦

Contents at a Glance

Cartoons at a Glance

By Rich Tennant

"...and this is my philodendron. She reacts badly to fungus, mealy bugs and the William Tell Overture."

page 31

"Look for angle parking — my plants won't survive this much southern exposure."

page 133

"I used to get fewer instructions when I looked after these people's children."

page 313

"Something's about to die in your cactus container."

page 281

"I never minded the watering and cleaning, but lately we've begun hearing drums at night."

page 221

"I never meant it to be a planter. It just hadn't been washed in so long, that stuff started growing out of it."

page 5

Fax: 978-546-7747 • E-mail: the5wave@tiac.net

Table of Contents

Part III: Growing Essentials 133

Chapter 8: Lighting Up Your Plant's Life 135

Chapter 9: Water, Water Everywhere 153

Introduction

● ●

*P*eople have been growing houseplants just about as long as they've been living in houses. Artifacts from ancient Egypt prove that the idea of bringing an outdoor plant indoors and potting it into a fancy container goes back at least 4,000 years. (The origin of the first macramé plant hanger is less certain, however.)

Houseplants are not only an inexpensive way to beautify your dwelling, they're good for you, too. Studies show that plants can help to purify polluted air without adding a penny to your electric bill. Plus, when you cultivate a plant indoors, you can watch it sprout, climb, and flower right before your very eyes.

But, before you charge out on a houseplant-buying spree, it pays to know what you can grow in your home environment and which plants are best suited to your taste and style. Then, after you have welcomed houseplants into your home, you need to know how to keep them alive and thriving with a minimum of fuss.

In *Houseplants For Dummies,* I introduce you to dozens of different foliage plants, flowering plants, cacti and other succulents, and even exotic varieties such as orchids that are easier to grow than you'd think. In addition, you can find essential houseplant growing techniques and loads of indoor gardening tips and tricks — some of which only the experts know. And, if you want to really want to show off your plants, Part V of this book is devoted entirely to the various ways you can display houseplants.

How to Use This Book

If you're already familiar with houseplant-growing basics, or if you're a seasoned indoor gardener, don't hesitate to head straight to the chapters that provide you with new information and topics of special interest. (For example, if your passion is flowering plants, turn to Chapter 5.) Or, you may be one of those who likes to get the most bang for your book-buying buck. In that case, I invite you to read from page to page. You may be surprised at the juicy bits of houseplant-growing advice that crop up along the way.

If you see a plant in the color insert's alphabetical listing that looks especially appealing, you can ask for it at your garden center by name — by either its common name or scientific name, which is the subject of the following segment of this introduction.

A Few Words about Botanical Names

I list each houseplant in this book by its most frequently used *common name,* which is not such a cut-and-dried matter. Some plants have more than a dozen common names. Therefore, each common name is followed by its *botanical* (or *scientific*) name.

Botanical names are in Latin or Latinate Greek and are sometimes difficult to pronounce and even harder to spell. (When you do refer to them in speech, just make sure you pronounce *all* the letters.) The nice thing about botanical names is that they are *truly* international and are used by every horticulturist the world over to identify particular plants.

Each botanical name has at least two parts: the *genus name,* which is capitalized and comes first, and the *species name,* which is listed second. The genus name is like a family name and can include several members. The genus *Ficus,* for example, also has several commonly grown members or *species*, including the creeping fig *(Ficus pumila),* rubber plant *(Ficus elastica),* and weeping fig *(Ficus benjamina).* To prevent confusion with the common names, botanical names are always shown in italics.

Occasionally, you'll see a multiplication sign, not in italics, included in a plant's botanical name. This indicates that the plant is a *hybrid.* For example, × *Citrofortunella microcarpa* is a manmade genus created by crossing *Citrus* with *Fortunella,* while *Caladium* × *hortulanum* is an artificial species resulting from crossing all sorts of types of Caladium together. By the way, you don't pronounce the multiplication sign when you're speaking of the plant's name.

Some plants also have a third part to their names. This is called their *cultivar* or *variety* name. By convention, the cultivar name is not shown in italics but is surrounded by single quotes. For example, the *Chamaedorea elegans* 'Bella' — which you may know as a "parlor palm" — is a special variety of the species *Chamaedorea elegans*.

I list most plants in this book by both their genus and species name, and the cultivar name where appropriate. In some cases, I use only the genus name — for example, Amaryllis *(Hippeastrum).* These plants are available in a wide variety of species and one pretty much equals the another as far as how they're grown and cared for.

How This Book Is Organized

The chapters of this book are divided into six easy-to-digest chunks arranged by subject matter.

Part I: The Root of the Matter: Houseplant Basics

Here, I explain what a houseplant is (if you've been trying to grow outdoor plants indoors, maybe that's why they never thrive). I also help you evaluate your home's environment and your own Plant Growing Profile to help you determine your best bets for houseplants. Then, I lead you to the best places to make wise houseplant purchases.

Part II: Houseplant Profiles from A to Z

This part of the book includes descriptions of more than 100 widely available houseplants, ranging from foliage plants to cacti to flowering plants and many others. The key to growing most houseplants is understanding their specific needs and how to supply them — this part of the book gives you that information.

Part III: Growing Essentials

In this part of the book, I cover all the essential ingredients you need to create the optimum environment for growing houseplants. I tell you how to combine light, water, humidity, fertilizer, temperature control, and potting mixes to get green-thumb results.

Part IV: Potted Plant Maintenance

Use this part of the book to discover how to keep your houseplants in the best possible shape, including how to get your plants home safely and how to acclimate outdoor plants to indoor conditions. I talk about how to groom your houseplants to keep them looking spiffy and how to ward off pests and diseases. I also show you how to multiply your plants by dividing them or by letting them "go to seed."

Part V: Houseplant Settings

You can be satisfied with simply stuffing your houseplants in green plastic pots and lining them up on your windowsill, or you can explore the many varieties of houseplant containers that are available and opportunities for decorating every room in your house with plants. This part of the book provides great ideas not just for indoor decorating, but also information on building the ultimate houseplant setting — a greenhouse.

Part VI: The Part of Tens

This section offers ten invaluable ideas for making sure your plants don't die of thirst while you're away from home and blasts ten common myths about houseplants right to smithereens.

Icons Used in This Book

 Stop here for houseplant-care tidbits that even very experienced indoor gardeners may not know.

 If you want to increase your houseplant word power, check out the definitions I supply next to this icon.

 This icon points out plants that are so tough even "black thumbs" can't seriously harm them.

 This icon flags some basic advice that every indoor gardener should live by.

 When you see this icon, it alerts you to products and practices that can potentially harm your plants.

 This icon identifies one of the dozens of plants featured in the color insert.

 Here, I suggest ways to save money.

Part I
The Root
of the Matter:
Houseplant Basics

The 5th Wave   By Rich Tennant

"I never meant it to be a planter. It just hadn't been washed in so long that stuff started growing out of it."

In this part . . .

You can begin to grow houseplants in one of two ways: Bring some home, scatter them around the house, and see how they do (a method that can be tough on the plants and hard on your wallet), or you can first do some homework on the subject, which will greatly improve your chances of success. In the opening part of this book, I give you the basic nitty-gritty on indoor plant growing.

First, I explain just what qualifies as a houseplant and what the average houseplant wants out of life. You also find out how your home stacks up for growing certain types of plants, and which plants to pick to suit your habits and lifestyle. Finally, I give you some tips on where and how to shop for the best houseplant specimens. Then you can start filling your home with the plants featured in Part II of this book.

Chapter 1

A Houseplant Primer (Or What Makes a Plant a Houseplant)

In This Chapter

▶ Distinguishing real houseplants from houseplant wannabes

▶ Knowing an ideal houseplant specimen when you see one

*F*or those of you in need of some houseplant preliminaries before you to move on to the "business end" of this book, you've turned to the right place. To begin with, just because a plant grows in a pot that doesn't necessarily make it a houseplant, and not all houseplants spend their entire lives indoors. I can give you the dictionary definition of the term *houseplant*, but I'm sure you want a more detailed explanation of what is and isn't a houseplant, which I gladly supply in the following pages.

Having Tropical Origins Helps

Perhaps you've had trouble in the past getting plants to flourish in your house (or at your workplace). The fact is, some plants make better houseplants than others.

Most houseplants — especially the easy-to-grow ones — originated in tropical or subtropical regions where they grow under the full shade of other plants, which makes them easy to adapt to growing under the "shade" of a roof. (*Tropical* climate regions never receive frost and *subtropical* regions experience brief dips below freezing only on rare occasions.)

Although you should never expose houseplants with tropical or subtropical origins to frost, most temperate weather plants are so well adapted to the cold that they not only can survive frost but *require* it in order to enjoy a full life cycle. (*Temperate* climates experience cold temperatures, often well below freezing in winter, sometimes for prolonged periods of time.)

Tropical and subtropical plants, therefore, make better houseplants than temperate climate ones because they can tolerate warm indoor temperatures year-round. Most temperate climate plants are, at best, temporary indoor guests. The occasional temperate climate plant that does survive indoors either can tolerate an unusually wide temperature range or can thrive indoors temporarily while in flower or in fruit.

If you eliminate plants with temperate climate origins from the list of potential houseplants, you still have a universe of possibilities. More than 90 percent of the world's 300,000 plant species originated in tropical or subtropical regions, so you're looking at hundreds of thousands of potential houseplant choices.

Oh, So That's a Houseplant

What makes a houseplant different from other plants? Most people would say that a houseplant is one that's planted in a pot. All houseplants *do* grow in some kind of container but dozens of strictly outdoor plants (for example, trees lining urban boulevards) also spend their entire lives in containers.

The dictionary will tell you that a houseplant is defined by *where* it lives — pick any plant that's grown indoors for an extended length of time (say, most of the year) and you've got yourself a houseplant. However, many houseplants spend their entire lives inside a covered structure other than someone's house (a nursery or greenhouse, for instance).

Some plants that people typically think of as houseplants actually spend much of the year outdoors and live indoors only in the colder months. Do they really qualify as houseplants? Sure — growing indoors is an essential part of their growth cycle.

It may be easier to define what a houseplant is by identifying those plants that have come by custom and tradition to be the plants we like to have in our homes. Many plants have developed into houseplants because they are relatively easy to grow, provide a touch of colorful decor, aren't too huge (or can be easily pruned down to size), and can be successfully grown in a relatively small container.

The list of potential indoor plants is a long one because far more plants can thrive indoors under controlled conditions than outdoors where the weather is unpredictable and sometimes ugly. Any of the following plant categories has houseplant potential:

✔ Trees and shrubs

✔ Perennials, biennials, and annuals

✔ Bulbs

✔ Cacti, succulents, and other arid-land residents

✔ Climbing and trailing plants

✔ Aquatic and semi-aquatic plants

✔ Plants grown for foliage or for flowers and fruits

✔ Container plants grown outside for the summer and brought indoors for the winter

Identifying the Ideal Houseplant

Having tropical or subtropical origins doesn't always guarantee that a plant is suited to be a domestic specimen. The following features make for the ideal houseplant (if not the ideal roommate):

✔ Tolerates dry indoor air

✔ Can live indoors for a prolonged period (meaning, at least a year for plants other than those brought in for temporary decoration)

✔ Grows relatively fast, yet tops out at ceiling height

✔ Easy to multiply (so you can share snips with Aunt Ida)

✔ Requires little pruning or pinching

✔ Looks good throughout all or most of the year, or goes so thoroughly dormant that you can hide it away in a closet until growing season

✔ Resistant to insects and disease

✔ Tolerates occasional abuse or neglect (such as your sometimes forgetting to water it, or when Rover's sledgehammer of a tail causes your plant to take a topple)

✔ Doesn't require extraordinary conditions for its survival, or if it's grown for its blossoms, doesn't require special conditions in order to flower

After applying the ideal-houseplants criteria, that eliminates a couple hundred thousand candidates in the vegetable kingdom, but leaves tens of thousands of interesting plants to choose from, not counting the hundreds of *hybrids* (man-made plants created by crossing two different plants) that are released annually.

They Get Around: Indoor/Outdoor Plants

Some plants are neither true houseplants nor true garden plants. Plants from this group are traditionally grown in containers, brought indoors during the colder months of the year, and then put back outdoors during warmer weather. Unlike *tender bulbs* (bulbs that can't tolerate hard frost), which spend the winter indoors in a dormant phase, indoor/outdoor plants remain in growth all year and often bloom both indoors or out.

Putting them outside for the summer

When you put indoor/outdoor plants outdoors for the summer, be sure to acclimate them first. Even plants grown directly in front of a sunny south window need time to adjust to direct outdoor sunlight because glass filters most of the UV rays that cause sunburn in both plants and humans. If you abruptly expose indoor plants to direct sun outdoors, they will *burn*.

Start them out in the shade, then move them gradually into brighter and brighter light over a two week period until they can tolerate full sun. Beware, too, of cool nights early in the season: If frost or cold threatens, bring them back indoors for a day or two. You can generally consider moving them outdoors when most nights are above 60°F (15°C).

When you grow potted plants outdoors, they need more attention paid to watering. Wind dries out plants in containers far more quickly than it does plants planted directly in the ground. In hot, dry weather you may need to water container plants as often as twice a day. Container plants also need more fertilizer outdoors than indoors. And keep them out of strong winds that can rip their foliage and knock them over.

To reduce the watering needs of container plants, simply bury the container in the garden! This results in less water loss and, therefore, less frequent waterings.

To keep the pot from becoming stained and the plant's roots from anchoring themselves into the soil (which greatly complicates digging them up again in the fall), just cover the pot with an old nylon stocking. When you need to bring the plants back inside, just dig up the pot and remove the stocking. The pot looks as good as new and no tough roots have wiggled out and anchored the plant into the garden.

Bringing them back indoors during the cold weather months

When temperatures drop again in the autumn, bring them back inside. In fact, most plants adapt better to the transition if you bring them back indoors *before* temperatures start to drop.

Before bringing them inside, give them a thorough cleanup. Remove any dead or dying leaves or flowers. Most plants grow during the summer, so you may need to repot them into larger pots with fresh potting mix. Also, prune any plants that have grown too large for your home environment (see Chapter 15 for pruning methods).

Spray all plants thoroughly with soap and water or an appropriate insecticide to help eliminate foliage insects before you bring the plants indoors. Then soak the entire root ball in a pail full of insecticidal soap, diluted to one-fifth the usual concentration (add one-fifth the amount soap or five times more water). Let it soak for two to three hours to eliminate any soil insects. These two insect control treatments work about 90 percent of the time, but to make sure that you account for the one in ten times that these methods don't catch all the foliage insects, always put the plants in quarantine for at least 40 days before putting them near your other houseplants.

Some popular indoor/outdoor plants

Gardeners commonly grow the following plants as container plants for both indoor and outdoor use. Some of the following plants are described in more detail in Chapter 5.

- Azalea *(Rhododendron simsii)*
- Bedding begonia *(Begonia × semperflorens-cultorum)*
- Bird of paradise *(Strelitzia regina)*
- Blue marguerite *(Felicia amelloides)*
- Browallia *(Browallia speciosa)*
- Coleus *(Coleus × hybridus* or *Solenostemon scutellarioides)*
- Dipladenia *(Mandevilla)*
- Fountain dracaena *(Cordyline australis* or *Cordyline indivisa)*
- Fuchsia *(Fuchsia* and cultivars)*
- Geranium *(Pelargonium hortorum* and *P. peltatum)*
- Heliotrope *(Heliotropium arborescens)*
- Impatiens *(Impatiens wallerana* and *I. × hawkeri)*

- Madagascar periwinkle *(Catharanthus roseus)*
- Marguerite *(Arygyranthemum frutescens)*
- Miniature rose *(Rosa* and cultivars)
- Oleander *(Nerium oleander)*
- Osteospermum *(Osteospermum barberae)*
- Polka-dot plant *(Hypoestes phyllostachya)*
- Potato vine *(Solanum jasminoides)*
- Scented geranium *(Pelargonium graveolens)*
- Transvaal daisy *(Gerbera jamesonii)*
- Winged pea *(Lotus berthelotii)*

Close, But No Cultivar

Some plants spend at least part of the year indoors but for one reason or another are *not* generally considered houseplants. For example, consider the following:

- **Tender bulbs (dahlias, cannas, gladiolus) brought indoors for the winter in colder climes.** You don't usually grow these flowering bulbs indoors; they just spend their dormant period in the house. Therefore, they don't really count as houseplants.

- **Annuals and vegetables started indoors from seeds.** These temporary indoor residents simply get their head start on the growing season by sprouting indoors, but actually finish their lives as strictly outdoor plants.

- **Plants on temporary indoor display.** You can bring an outdoor bonsai or hanging basket inside for a special occasion, but if you put it right back outside after your company leaves, it's not a houseplant.

- **Cut flowers.** The ultimate in temporary indoor residents, cut flowers aren't rooted and, therefore, don't really grow indoors. Technically speaking, they are plants, but are they houseplants? Nope.

- **Artificial plants.** No matter how good they look (plastic and silk plants are becoming more and more life-like all the time), they just ain't plants. You bought a book called *Houseplants For Dummies,* so I'm betting you want to try your hand at cultivating something that's alive. Leave plastic plants to collect dust and pollute the air — yep, they actually give off toxic substances, which makes them far inferior to live plants that filter the air and make it easier to breathe. When you have a choice, always go for living plants, all the time, everywhere.

Chapter 2

Analyzing Your Growth Potential

Growing houseplants is a two-way street. You can't just buy any type of plant and expect it to flourish without knowing what you have to offer it in return. A surprising number of beginning houseplant gardeners don't stop to analyze their living environments before charging out to buy up a bunch of indoor greenery. You'd never put a goldfish in a sand box, but many would-be houseplant gardeners do just that when they try to grow a fern in a room better suited to a cactus. Inevitably, the plant withers and dies, not out of neglect, but simply because it was stuck in the wrong place.

Evaluating how well suited your home's environment is to growing houseplants is the first step to having happy houseplants. For example, is your home (or parts of your home) cool, dark, and damp, or hot, sunny, and dry?

In this chapter, I tell you how to analyze your dwelling to determine how houseplant-friendly your home is and how to locate those special indoor "microclimates" that certain plants just love. I also help you examine your plant-care habits and how they can affect your ability to keep houseplants alive and healthy.

Relying on More than Dumb Luck for Success with Houseplants

Consider the first-time houseplant owner who buys a couple of plants that happen to be well adapted to the owner's living environment. As months go by, the plants not only don't die, but thrive. This houseplant owner, unaware of the source of his or her success in houseplant cultivation, just chalks it up to having that mysterious "green thumb." Then, one day that green thumb turns brown after the would-be gardener buys some plants that don't find the environment to be all that tremendous.

The air quality, temperature, and lighting conditions of your home may be fine for a great many types of houseplants. If you happen to purchase those plants, you'll look like you have the greenest thumb in town with barely lifting a finger. But, the key to success in cultivating a *variety* of plants is in providing the appropriate growing environment for *each* plant — a set of conditions that plants can not only tolerate, but also thrive under.

You can change any indoor environment to make it more suitable for a certain type of plant, without having to resort to extraordinary measures. For example, simply adding a room humidifier can open the door to a wide range of plants that don't grow in dry air (more information on air quality is in Chapter 10), or adding growlights can turn a dingy corner into a sunny alcove.

Analyzing Your Home's Environment

Pick a room in your house where you want to grow some plants. How would you characterize the room's overall environment? Chances are, you don't know how well suited an area of your home is to growing plants because you probably don't think of your home as an "environment." To help you take stock of your home's growing conditions, ask yourself the following questions:

✔ **Is the room sunny, dark, or partially lit?**

Lighting varies more widely than any other indoor environmental factor. How do you know if a room is sunny, dark, or in-between (bright but not much full sun)? How much light does it get in the summer? In the winter? If you're uncertain, use the "shadow test" I describe in Chapter 8 — it costs nothing and works just as well as the best light meters.

✔ **Is the room usually cold, cool, warm, or hot in winter? What about in summer?**

If you need to wear an extra layer of clothing in the room during the winter and you're not particularly sensitive to the cold, the room falls into the "cool in winter" category. If no one will sit in the room without wearing a heavy blanket, you know the room's definitely on the cold side. If you pull the blinds in summer to keep out the heat, you can consider the room hot in summer. If the room seems just right, in either season, as far as plants are concerned you have a warm room.

✔ **Is the air generally dry or moist in summer? In winter?**

Many houseplants depend on a specific humidity level. You can use a hygrometer (see Chapter 10) to measure the air's humidity, but why spend good money when you can easily determine your home's humidity at no expense?

Just assume that if you live in an arid climate your home is always dry. And if you heat your home in winter, you can safely assume that your home is dry during winter. The only humid places (by plant standards) in most homes are bathrooms, basements, and laundry rooms.

After you have a fairly good idea of your indoor environment, you have some extremely useful information to use when you go plant shopping. (I also encourage you to use the plant profiles in Part II of this book to help you choose the best plants to suit your indoor environment.)

Don't be shy about asking a clerk at your local nursery or garden center to for advice on picking out a few plants. And, don't forget to read the plant's label, which provides a brief rundown of the plant's requirements. If the tag says "Requires full sun" and you have little natural light in your home, don't be surprised if your new plant pal says "sayonara" after a few weeks or so.

Nothing can stop you — I repeat, *nothing* — from succeeding with houseplants if you pick out the right ones.

Identifying Indoor Microclimates

Horticulturalists define a *microclimate* as a "mini-climate" of sorts that varies in some way from the larger climate that immediately surrounds it. A microclimate can be hotter, cooler, drier, wetter, sunnier, or shadier than other parts of the "macroclimate."

Indoor environments have microclimates, too. Even though you may think of your living room as being sunny, hot, and humid in the summer, and shady, warm, and dry in the winter, different parts of the room get more or less sun, more or less heat, and even more or less humidity. In fact, just grouping your plants together can create a microclimate that's much more humid than the rest of the room (more on grouping plants can be found in Chapter 8).

A mostly bright or sunny room has some darker areas, usually to either side of a window or a distance away from it. A mostly dark room is often quite bright directly in front of a window, especially in the summer. Areas directly in front of or above heaters are always the hottest, driest spots in a room. So, if you buy a plant that needs full sun, but you want to add it to the decor of a mostly dark room, make sure to situate it in the brightest spot in the room.

Picking the Best Plants Based on Your Plant Growing Profile

After you have a clear picture of your home's global growing environment and the various microclimates in the rooms where you intend to grow houseplants, the next step is determining what kinds of plants to buy based on your personal style, spare time, and general domestic habits. I like to call this the "Plant Growing Profile" (or PGP) factor. In the following sections I identify the best plants to buy based on your PGP.

The Fickle-Fingered Gardener

Do you tend to jump gung-ho into projects only to lose interest after a short while? Pick only low-care plants, such as cacti, succulents, and some of the more stalwart foliage plants listed in Chapter 4 that carry the "Tuff 'n' Robust" icon. Then when your enthusiasm wanes, all you have to do is water the plants on occasion and your leafy decor still looks great.

Stick to the following plants if you're excited about loading your home with greenery, but you know you'll be moving on to a new passion sometime soon:

- Cast iron plant (*Aspidistra elatior*)
- Century plant (*Agave americana*)
- Cereus (*Cereus peruvianus*)
- Corn plant (*Dracaena fragrans*)
- Crown of thorns (*Euphorbia milii*)
- Donkey's tail (*Sedum morganianum*)
- Golden ball cactus (*Echinocactus grusonii*)
- Heartleaf philodendron (*Philodendron scandens oxycardium*)
- Old man cactus (*Cephalocereus senilis*)
- Parlor palm (*Chamaedorea elegans* 'Bella')
- Pony tail (*Beaucarnea recurvata* or *Nolina recurvata*)
- Pothos (*Epipremnum aureum*)
- Silver vase (*Aechmea fasciata*)
- Snake plant (*Sansevieria trifasciata*)
- Snowball cactus (*Mammillaria bocasana*)
- Spineless yucca (*Yucca elephantipes*)

The Absent-Minded Gardener

Are you well-intentioned but a bit neglectful? That's okay. Just stick to low-maintenance plants, especially those that can tolerate drought. That way, if you forget a watering or two, the plants are none the worse off for it. Consider the following:

- ✔ Arrowhead plant *(Syngonium podophyllum)*
- ✔ Bunny ears *(Opuntia microdasys)*
- ✔ Cast iron plant *(Aspidistra elatior)*
- ✔ Century plant *(Agave americana)*
- ✔ Cereus *(Cereus peruvianus)*
- ✔ Corn plant *(Dracaena fragrans)*
- ✔ Crown of thorns *(Euphorbia milii)*
- ✔ Donkey's tail *(Sedum morganianum)*
- ✔ Dumbcane *(Dieffenbachia)*
- ✔ Golden ball cactus *(Echinocactus grusonii)*
- ✔ Heartleaf philodendron *(Philodendron scandens oxycardium)*
- ✔ Jade plant *(Crassula argentea)*
- ✔ Old man cactus *(Cephalocereus senilis)*
- ✔ Pony tail *(Beaucarnea recurvata* or *Nolina recurvata)*
- ✔ Pothos *(Epipremnum aureum)*
- ✔ Silver vase *(Aechmea fasciata)*
- ✔ Snake plant *(Sansevieria trifasciata)*
- ✔ Snowball cactus *(Mammillaria bocasana)*
- ✔ Spineless yucca *(Yucca elephantipes)*
- ✔ Warneckei dracaena *(Dracaena deremensis* 'Warneckei')

The Overly Ardent Caregiver

Are you the kind of person who just can't pass by a plant without fussing with it? Do you like to primp and prune your greenery on a daily basis? If so, choose some of the more challenging plants — they love attention. Forget low-care plants, though; they actually prefer to be left alone once in a while. You can literally pamper some plants to death.

TIP

If you're an habitual waterer, forget cacti and succulents and stick with plants that don't mind soggy soil, such as the baby's tears plant and umbrella plants.

The following are some plants that just can't get enough coddling:

- African violet *(Saintpaulia ionantha)*
- Aluminum plant *(Pilea cadierei)*
- Azalea *(Rhododendron simsii)*
- Baby's tears *(Soleirolia soleirolii)*
- Bird's nest fern *(Asplenium nidus)*
- Bonsai (all kinds)
- Caladium *(Caladium × hortulanum)*
- Calamondin orange *(× Citrofortunella mitis)*
- China doll *(Radermachera sinensis)*
- Coleus *(Coleus × hybrida* or *Solenostemon scutellarioides)*
- Croton *(Codiaeum variegatum pictum)*
- Episcia *(Episcia cupreata)*
- Florist's gloxinia *(Sinningia speciosa)*
- Hibiscus *(Hibiscus rosa-sinensis)*
- Lady Jane Anthurium *(Anthurium × andreacola* 'Lady Jane')
- Nerve plant *(Fittonia verschaffeltii)*
- Peacock plant *(Calathea makoyana)*
- Polka-dot plant *(Hypoestes phyllostachya)*
- Purple passion plant *(Gynura aurantiaca* 'Purple Passion')
- Streptocarpus *(Streptocarpus × hybridus)*
- Umbrella plant *(Cyperus alternifolius)*
- Wandering Jew *(Zebrina pendula)*
- Zebra plant *(Aphelandra squarrosa* 'Dania')

TIP

If you're an overly ardent caregiver, you're among the rare people who find the normally difficult florist plants (plants usually offered in full bloom as gifts), such as the cineraria, pocketbook plant, and cyclamen, easy to grow. In fact, you may even be able to get some of them to rebloom whereas most of us count ourselves lucky just to keep them alive. (For more information on florist plants, see Chapter 5.)

The Collector

Then, you have The Collector. (I must confess that I belong to this category.) We want one of everything in the plant world and are willing to put in the extra effort to keep every plant happy, even if it means turning the bathroom into a soggy rain forest and the living room into a miniature Sahara. Aesthetics have no special influence on collectors — in fact, some collectors prefer quirky, odd-looking plants over ravishing beauties.

 If you feel this side of your personality bursting through, a word of advice: Look for miniature and dwarf varieties. You can find tiny versions of nearly all standard plants, and the smaller the plant, the more you can cram into a limited space.

Most of the following plants are available in hundreds of varieties, giving you an enormous selection from which to build your collection:

- African violet *(Saintpaulia ionantha)*
- Air plant *(Tillandsia)*
- Amaryllis *(Hippeastrum)*
- Bird of paradise *(Strelitzia regina)*
- Boston fern *(Nephrolepis exaltata)*
- Bougainvillea *(Bougainvillea)*
- Caladium *(Caladium × hortulanum)*
- Cattleya *(Cattleya)*
- Clivia *(Clivia miniata)*
- Coleus *(Coleus × hybrida* or *Solenostemon scutellarioides)*
- Columnea *(Columnea)*
- Croton *(Codiaeum variegatum pictum)*
- Crown of thorns *(Euphorbia milii)*
- Dipladenia *(Mandevilla)*
- Earth star *(Cryptanthus)*
- English ivy *(Hedera helix)*
- Episcia *(Episcia)*
- Florist's gloxinia *(Sinningia speciosa)*
- Flowering maple *(Abutilon × hybridum)*
- Hibiscus *(Hibiscus rosa-sinensis)*

- ✔ Holiday cactus *(Schlumbergera × buckleyi)*
- ✔ Lady's slipper *(Paphiopedilum)*
- ✔ Living stone *(Lithops)*
- ✔ Miniature sinningia *(Sinningia ×)*
- ✔ Moth orchid *(Phalaenopsis ×)*
- ✔ Oleander *(Nerium oleander)*
- ✔ Orchid cactus *(× Epicactus)*
- ✔ Orchids (most kinds)
- ✔ Scented geraniums *(Pelargonium)*
- ✔ Staghorn fern *(Platycerium bifurcatum)*
- ✔ Streptocarpus *(Streptocarpus × hybridus)*
- ✔ Wax plant *(Hoya carnosa)*
- ✔ Zonal geranium *(Pelargonium × hortorum)*

The Specialist

The Specialist is the collector's next-of-kin. Specialists love to collect, too, but whereas collectors like to grow just about anything, specialists zero in on select houseplant varieties favored only by a few indoor gardeners.

African violets, orchids, bromeliads, bonsais, and cacti are but a handful of the plant groups that tend to attract this type's attention — and usually only the newest and rarest plants are good enough. If you think you're a Specialist, check out the plants listed in Chapter 7.

The Split Personality

Will more than one person take care of your plants regularly? That can be a recipe for disaster, especially if your care habits differ. Office plants especially tend to suffer from the excess care of too many helping hands. Either everyone seems to think the plant needs water, so it's swimming in it, or they all assume someone else has done the watering, so the poor plant is totally parched.

If you're living in a collaborative plant-care situation, try to assign certain people to certain plants or to certain rooms. Better yet, decide who cares for which plants based on each individual's PGP (Plant Growing Profile). Remember, just as too many cooks can spoil the broth, too many gardeners can kill even the toughest houseplant.

Matching plant groups to indoor gardening profiles

After you've determined your PGP and the PGPs of those in your household or office, keep the following in mind about the major plant groups.

Flowering plants

These plants catch everyone's eye (you can read more about flowering plants in Chapter 5). However, they require careful attention and very specific conditions to get them to bloom well. Furthermore, their blooming period is often quite short.

If you buy a flowering plant as a decorative item, are you willing to put up with its prima donna personality? And do you have the conditions — and enough interest in meeting its needs — to get it to bloom again after it's lost its bloom once? If you don't care whether a flowering plant ever blooms again, just think of it as temporary guest that feeds the compost pile after it finishes blooming.

Foliage plants

Foliage plants are often, but not always, easier to grow than flowering plants and generally look good for months on end. And if you're looking for color, foliage plants come in loads of colors other than green. (I have plenty more to say about foliage plants in Chapter 4.)

Foliage plants often make the best choice for general room decor because they can become nearly permanent fixtures. When you have a nice foliage background, then you can add the occasional flowering plant for temporary color.

Cacti and succulents

Cacti and other succulents are great choices if you tend toward being neglectful. Remember, though, that most cacti and succulents do require lots and lots of light, if not full sun. The few shade-tolerant succulents, such as the snake plant, rank among the toughest of all houseplants and make great gifts for people who admit to having black thumbs.

Orchids and bromeliads

Orchids are another good choice for houseplant owners who don't always give plants their fullest attention. I know they have a reputation for being delicate but, trust me, they are tough as nails. Bromeliads, too, can hang in there under adverse conditions. I cover both in Chapter 7.

Indoor bonsai

Bonsai plants are ideal for extremely attentive indoor gardeners. They require care almost every day, as well as plenty of pruning, pinching, and pampering, just to stay alive. (I tell you more about growing bonsai in Chapter 7.)

If you're meticulous and aren't short on patience, buy a starter bonsai plant or even try growing one from seed. Some bonsai plants can take 15 years or more just to start looking the part! If you're meticulous but impatient, buy a mature bonsai and give it all the care you want.

Chapter 3

A Guide for the Smart Houseplant Shopper

In This Chapter

▶ Buying from specialty stores versus buying from just about anybody

▶ Saving money on your plant purchases

▶ Identifying signs of a less-than-terrific houseplant purchase

Ready to buy some plants and get growing, are you? First, you need to find out where to go shopping and how to get the best deals. Plus, you probably wouldn't mind some tips on how to spot healthy and not-so-healthy plants. With that in mind, I happily present Chapter 3 of *Houseplants For Dummies.*

I must warn you, though. This chapter won't do you much good if you don't know the Golden Rule of Houseplant Ownership: Know thy home environment and know which plants can hack living in it and which will wish they were back at the nursery. (For some help in analyzing your plant-growing environment, read Chapters 1 and 2. Then you can get back to the business of shopping for plants with barely skipping a beat.)

Before you spend your hard-earned cash on some foliage that catches your eye, how do you know that you're getting a quality plant or one that's on its last leaves? (I have actually seen *dead* bonsais for sale at a local department store — and they weren't even marked down!) As the old saying goes, *caveat emptor*, which can be translated to "empty out your wallet" if you rush out and buy houseplants without first knowing how to spot the keepers.

How Much Is That Dieffenbachia in the Window?

Commercial plant sales places fall quite neatly into two categories: the "know-nothings" and the "dens of green thumb wisdom."

Places that sell everything, including houseplants

The "know-nothings" typically (but not always) include department stores, hardware stores, supermarkets, and some florists. They receive shipments of plants with the goal of selling the plants quickly before they expire.

Although you may run into a retail clerk who is a storehouse of knowledge on houseplants (one of my great plant friends was a salesperson in the Plants and Pets Department of a well-known retail chain), more often than not the clerks at grocery stores and department stores know little about the plants they're selling other than their price. Many don't know even how to wrap a plant correctly (yes, there's a right way and a wrong way to wrap up a plant — you can read about that in Chapter 14).

The know-nothing florists are experts at wrapping plants up beautifully. They can even sound quite knowledgeable, spouting horticultural terminology as if they really understand it. But the main business of most florists is selling cut flowers, not plants. I once heard a florist tell another customer that you have to water a yucca in the center of the plant (the florist had the yucca, a succulent, confused with a bromeliad, which is entirely something else). Another time, I heard a salesperson very accurately explain to a customer how to fertilize a eucalyptus — the problem was, he wasn't selling a eucalyptus *plant,* he was selling some dried eucalyptus *branches* that were stuck in a pot.

Places that are in the business of selling houseplants and gardening items

The "dens of green thumb wisdom" typically include garden centers and nurseries as well as some florists (admittedly, I have no sure-fire way of separating the well-informed florists from the know-nothings). Not everyone who works at these places is super-knowledgeable about houseplants *per se,* but they usually know enough about plants in general to help you make a smart choice.

Some of the bigger nurseries and garden centers employ a "houseplants expert" who really does know a lot about growing houseplants, if not in a home environment then certainly in a greenhouse setting. If you find such an expert, latch on to that person to help you with your future purchases. Those folks are worth their weight in vermiculite.

Given the enormous disparity between know-nothings and dens of green thumb wisdom in terms of their expertise, level of of service, and product quality, why would anyone choose to buy from the former? Generally, it comes down to price.

Watch out for the loss-leader gambit

Department stores, hardware stores, and supermarkets often use houseplants as *loss leaders* — products sold far below market value in order to attract customers to the store or get them in a spending mode so that they buy other products at regular prices. Some loss-leader plants sell at wholesale prices or even less, prices almost impossible for other places to beat — unless another store sells the plants as loss leaders at even lower prices.

Department store prices generally are lower than those charged by garden centers, nurseries, and florist shops, even when the department store plants aren't on sale. If the price is right, you know the plant is healthy, and although not collector-grade it's suitable for a kitchen windowsill or office shelf, why not buy a plant from a grocer or discount department store? But, just make sure you keep all the caveats I mention in this chapter in mind.

Buying good plants at discount prices (and recognizing the leftovers)

What's the secret to getting healthy plants from a source that doesn't specialize in nursery or gardening items: Get there early!

Department stores, nurseries, and garden centers all use the same sources — wholesale growers who have the plants shipped from mostly subtropical and tropical regions — so the plants are of equivalent quality once they hit their retail destinations. If you want to get a bargain and still buy a good quality plant, get to the store shortly after the plants arrive, preferably within two or three days. To be sure you get there on time, ask the store manager when the next arrivals are due in.

If the plants have had poor care for even just a week, you're usually looking at a plant that's had seven full days of inadequate lighting and too much or too little watering, and possibly contact with insects and diseases left over from the previous shipment. A plant's quality can slide downhill *very* quickly.

Avoid reduced prices on obviously stressed plants — those that are wilted, have numerous yellow or brown leaves, visible insect damage, lean to one side, or exhibit other signs that that they've been abused. You can bet those plants are leftovers from a previous shipment. They're often in such poor condition that they may not even survive the trip home. Even if they do, who knows what undesirable little beasties their weakened stems and leaves may harbor?

Buying quality plants at good prices from those who know their stuff

Nurseries and garden centers also sell loss leaders. After all, they want to lure you into their stores just as much as any other commercial enterprise. To find a real bargain at garden centers and other specialty dealers, watch the newspaper ads, check the flyers deposited in your mailbox, or make a habit of dropping in regularly to your favorite nursery to see what's new. You do run the risk of visiting a store, being sucked in by the loss leader, and then falling for something at regular price. But look at it this way, if you add up the price of each plant and divide by two, you still bought both at a discount.

When nurseries and garden centers expect a new shipment, they sometimes reduce the prices on slow-selling plants from previous shipments. Whereas leftover plants sold by a department store are usually in such poor shape that they're barely bargains at all, those that reputable nurseries and garden centers sell are often still in top form because those stores almost always maintain their plants under ideal conditions.

Furthermore, you rarely see insect infestation in plants purchased from specialty stores because those stores immediately remove infested plants from their shelves at the first sign of problems. Also, unlike department stores and supermarkets, specialty stores have a reputation for maintaining good-quality plants, a reputation that they work to uphold because they want repeat business. They're far more likely, therefore, to destroy unsatisfactory plants than to reduce prices in the hopes of cutting their losses with a quick close-out sale. If one of these stores sells a plant, you can expect top quality, even if the price seems suspiciously low.

You can find most of the plants mentioned in this book at a local garden center or nursery. If you run up against a wall in trying to find a certain plant, consider sending for it by mail from one of the nurseries listed in Appendix B.

If You Can Stand the Wait, Start from Scratch or Get Them Young

You can save a considerable sum by buying young plants rather than full-size ones. You can often find excellent prices on seedlings or well-rooted cuttings, but whether those plants are truly bargains depends on your degree of patience as well as your plant-growing skills.

Are you willing to wait seven years for a small bird-of-paradise plant to mature to full size? Can you provide it with the conditions that it needs to reach flowering? That spectacular four-foot-wide golden barrel cactus may be worth every penny of the $150 asking price, when you consider that growing a three-inch one to that size can take more than 50 years.

The best bargains among small plants are the fast-growing ones. Why pay $20 for a full-grown coleus or polka-dot plant when you can buy a small one at $1.49 and grow it to full size in only two months? Now that's a bargain! The following plants grow so quickly that buying small means saving big:

- African violet *(Saintpaulia ionantha)*
- Aluminum plant *(Pilea cadierei)*
- Angelwing begonia *(Begonia* 'Lucerna'*)*
- Baby rubber plant *(Peperomia obtusifolia)*
- Baby's tears *(Soleirolia soleirolii)*
- Boston fern *(Nephrolepis exaltata)*
- China doll *(Radermachera sinensis)*
- Coleus *(Coleus × hybrida)*
- Creeping fig *(Ficus pumila)*
- Donkey's tail *(Sedum morganianum)*
- Dumbcane *(Dieffenbachia)*
- Dwarf schefflera *(Schefflera arboricola)*
- Emerald ripple peperomia *(Peperomia caperata)*
- English ivy *(Hedera helix)*
- Episcia *(Episcia cupreata)*

- Flowering maple *(Abutilon × hybridum)*
- Grape ivy *(Cissus rhombifolia)*
- Heartleaf philodendron *(Philodendron scandens oxycardium)*
- Hibiscus *(Hibiscus rosa-sinensis)*
- Jade plant *(Crassula argentea)*
- Mother-of-thousands *(Tolmiea menziesii)*
- Nerve plant *(Fittonia verschaffeltii)*
- Polka-dot plant *(Hypoestes phyllostachya)*
- Pothos *(Epipremnum aureum)*
- Prayer plant *(Maranta leuconeura)*
- Purple passion plant *(Gynura aurantiaca* 'Purple Passion'*)*
- Rose-scented geranium *(Pelargonium graveolens)*
- Spider plant *(Chlorophytum comosum)*
- Strawberry begonia *(Saxifraga stolonifera)*
- Streptocarpus *(Streptocarpus × hybridus)*
- Swedish ivy *(Plectranthus australis)*
- Umbrella plant *(Cyperus alternifolius)*
- Wandering Jew *(Zebrina pendula)*
- Zonal geranium *(Pelargonium × hortorum)*

Need another reason to buy a small plant rather than a full-size one? Small plants adapt better to change. That beautiful 4-foot (1.2-meter) croton you paid a full-day's salary for may die within weeks if it doesn't like the conditions in your living room. On the other hand, a tiny croton in a 4-inch (10-centimeter) pot can adapt to just about any growing conditions. It may take two or three years to reach full size, but when it does, you know it will continue to thrive.

Just about any full-size indoor tree is likely to suffer some shock when you move it from a greenhouse to your home. Two other plants especially renowned for their difficulty as mature plants in adapting to a new environment are the croton *(Codiaeum variegatum pictum)* and the weeping fig *(Ficus benjamina)*. Buy these plants small or don't buy them at all!

A Lesson in Houseplant Quality Control

Always give a plant a quick once-over, at the very least, before you make the purchase no matter where you're buying the plant. The following list tells you about the major signs of distress and disease in a plant (and you can follow along with Figure 3-1):

- **Wobbly plants:** Give the plant a quick shake. A plant that's unsteady in its pot may not be well-rooted. Shaking the plant also tells you whether the plant has whiteflies because the flies, which resemble dandruff, take off like a shot when you move the plant. (See Chapter 17 for more on these pests.)

- **Crowded roots:** Check the bottom of the pot for roots coming out of the drainage hole. Roots emerging from holes in the pot don't necessarily mean that the plant is underpotted, but it's frequently a first symptom. If in doubt, ask the clerk to remove the pot (if possible) so that you can see the roots. (Expect this kind of service only in a nursery, garden center, or florist shop.) If roots are wound around the base of the plant, you know it's underpotted and possibly stressed. Try to find another plant of the same kind that has a less-developed root ball. A healthy root ball holds together but doesn't have excess roots showing when you remove it from the pot.

- **Unhealthy roots:** If you've convinced the clerk to remove the pot to let you check for crowded roots, go ahead and check the plant's overall health as well. Roots come in all sizes, shapes, and colors, but they should always feel firm, not squishy, with the tips a paler color than the rest of the roots. Examine bits of white fluff among the roots with suspicion: You're quite possibly face to face with soil mealybugs. On the other hand, that white fluff may be nothing more than bits of *perlite,* a common medium for potting plants. A soggy growing medium also means bad news.

- **Signs of rot:** Sniff the potting mix. If it has a forest-after-a-spring-rain smell, all is well. If it has the sickly sweet smell of a rotting potato, put the plant down — more than likely, that plant has a bad case of root rot or stem rot.

- **Leaf spots:** Leaf spots can indicate disease — and I know you don't want to buy a diseased plant. Physical damage can generate leaf spots, too (garden center plants tend to get jostled around a bit). Damaged leaves never recover, however. Ask yourself whether you're willing to wait for the plant to produce new leaves. You may decide you prefer a healthier specimen.

- **Spindly, leggy plants or ones with brown leaf tips:** These symptoms indicate the plant has not been getting adequate care for quite some time.

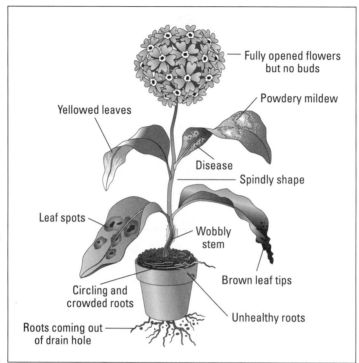

Fully opened flowers
but no buds

Powdery mildew

Yellowed leaves

Disease

Spindly shape

Leaf spots

Wobbly
stem

Figure 3-1:
Trouble
signs to
watch for
when
shopping
for plants.

Brown leaf tips

Circling and
crowded roots

Unhealthy roots

Roots coming out
of drain hole

✔ **Signs of insects or disease:** Make sure to look underneath the leaves and at the leaf *axils* (the point where the leaf meets the stem), two places where most pests hang out.

✔ **Yellowed leaves or abundant leaf loss:** A yellow leaf or two at the base of a plant is nothing to be alarmed about. If you see many yellow or fallen leaves, however, the plant's probably stressed and therefore not a good choice.

✔ **Lots of open flowers, but only a few unopened buds:** A flowering plant in full bloom can look spectacular but may be well past its prime and ready to stop blooming in short order. Buy a plant mostly in bud with just enough open blooms to let you see its eventual color. Then you know that you've yet to see the plant at its best.

Chrysanthemums and miniature roses are exceptions to the avoid-lots-of-opened-flowers rule: Chrysanthemum and rose buds not fully open may not open at all under home growing conditions unless you can give them full sun. Buy chrysanthemums and miniature roses already at their peak of bloom.

Part II
Houseplant Profiles
from A to Z

The 5th Wave — By Rich Tennant

"...and this is my philodendron. She reacts badly to fungus, mealy bugs and the William Tell Overture."

In this part . . .

Quick, what's the difference between a foliage plant and a flowering plant? And, how do their growing needs differ? Can a cacti live without water? And what the heck is a epiphyte? All of those questions and more can be answered in the following four chapters that feature dozens of fact-filled profiles on foliage plants, flowering plants, cacti and succulents, and specialty plants. I'll tell you how to recognize the various kinds of houseplants (you can also check out the illustrations throughout these chapters and the color photos in this book) and I tell you about each plant's special needs so you can enjoy goof-proof growing.

Chapter 4

(Usually) Green, Leafy, and Built for Beginners: Foliage Plants

. . . .

In This Chapter

▶ Distinguishing a foliage plant from other plants

▶ Discovering how to use foliage plants in your home

▶ Checking out the profiles of 49 foliage plants

. . . .

*I*ndoor gardeners inevitably divide plants into two main categories — foliage plants and flowering plants — but both of these terms are misnomers when it comes right down to it. Almost all plants produce leaves (cacti and a few succulents being the main exceptions) and almost all indoor plants eventually flower (ferns being the exception here). Foliage plants sometimes *do* flower (and when they do, their blooms are often quite spectacular), and many flowering plants have very attractive leaves. Those "in the grow," however, understand that *foliage plants* are those that are grown mostly for their stems and foliage, whereas *flowering plants* are those appreciated mainly for their flowers.

In this chapter, I introduce you to a wide variety of foliage plants and the best way to care for them. But first, in the following sections, I offer some basic information on foliage plants and what makes them so popular.

The Brutes of the Houseplant World

Many indoor gardeners prefer to grow only foliage plants for one main reason — producing flowers requires a great deal more energy than producing leaves and not all indoor plants get enough light (their only source of energy) to bloom abundantly. Rather than owning flowering plants that don't bloom and whose leaves sometimes aren't that attractive, many growers simply stick to foliage plants, all of which look just great and are easy to grow.

Besides needing less light than other houseplant varieties, most foliage plants are inherently tough. That's no coincidence, either. Many generations of houseplant lovers have experimented with foliage plants, keeping and multiplying those that survive and tossing those that fail. The result is that today's foliage plants are a tough bunch indeed. They resist dry air, weak light, irregular waterings, varying temperatures . . . just about anything you can throw at them. That doesn't mean, however, that they enjoy mistreatment, but you can count on most foliage plants to last at least six months under even the most stressful conditions.

Besides their ability to tolerate lower light levels more so than flowering plants, most foliage plants are better at tolerating dry air, overwatering and underwatering, very hot or very cold temperatures, insufficient fertilizer, and, in general, simple neglect. If you tend to forget to tend to your plants, foliage plants are a wise choice.

Most foliage plants are easy to grow, but if you're just getting started with houseplants, look for those that I've marked with the icon at the left. These plants are practically indestructible.

Then, Why Did My Foliage Plant Just Up and Die One Day?

Many foliage plants are so inherently tough that their great tolerance of all conditions is their main flaw. Most flowering plants quickly let you know when they are unhappy with their growing conditions. They drop leaves and buds, stretch for the light, or wilt quite visibly — all signs that they want better treatment, right *now,* or else they're going to die.

Unfortunately for foliage plants, many are so long-suffering that they can (and do) survive for months, even years, under unacceptable conditions, barely showing their discomfort. They may not have grown much in all that time, often only a leaf or two, but at least they *seem* healthy. Then one day, out of the blue, the plant begins to drop leaves like crazy, leaving its owner totally perplexed. What went wrong?

What *was* wrong was that the plant was living on its reserves, energy it stored up back in the days when it was a happy young plant growing in a greenhouse or in the tropics. After 6 to 18 months without sufficient food (light energy), it simply gave up and died. More indoor plants suffer from a lack of light than from any other type of neglect. Never hesitate to improve the lighting conditions of even so-called low-light plants. And never figure you're succeeding with a foliage plant until it has managed to live for at least 18 months under your care.

Green, and then some

Many foliage plants have leaves that are marbled, striped, or speckled in tones of white, cream, pink, or yellow, in addition to the standard-issue green shades. This irregular coloration is called *variegation*, which is usually a product of genetic mutation. Other foliage plants are naturally colorful, with distinct patches of silver, red, pink, white, brown, and so forth, on the surface of their leaves. For example, the highly popular coleus (featured in this chapter) was already beautiful in the wild and hybridizers have made it even more attractive. Some plants feature entirely purple leaves or deep red leaves. Foliage leaves sometimes are so attractive that they outshine the most exotic flowers. You can find a bit of green somewhere on just about any foliage plant because every plant must have at least some cells that contain *chlorophyll* (a vital component in allowing plants to convert light energy into the sugars and starches they need to survive). And, many plants that are merely green truly are colorful. The shades of green found in houseplants vary from the palest chartreuse to an inky greenish-black.

Foliage Plant Profiles

The inherent toughness of foliage plants makes them the ideal choice for indoor decorating. Place them throughout the house, either singly or in groups, on the floor, or on a table or pedestal. Many also make great choices for hanging baskets. Think of foliage plants as your basic indoor greenery and good background plants; then add a few flowering plants here and there as highlights. (See Chapter 19 for more specific ideas on how to use plants in every room of the house.)

Despite countless plant labels that state otherwise, there is no such thing as a low-light houseplant. *All* indoor plants prefer good light at all times. Low-light plants are simply those that can tolerate lower light intensities without suffering too visibly. In the long run, though, keeping *any* plant alive under low light is a difficult proposition. Don't forget to move foliage plants to brighter light every few weeks if they're in a room with poor lighting conditions (see Chapter 8 for more on lighting). You can keep them going for years if you give them at least two weeks' worth of good conditions per month.

One term pops up now and again that you need to know. The word *cultivar* derives from the phrase "cultivated variety." These plants are genetic variations from the plant species in the wild, developed by man through natural mutation or by crossing two different plants.

In the following sections of this chapter, you can find information on 49 of the world's most popular foliage plants. If you're not sure what I mean with each of the care requirements, propagation options, and care ratings of each plant, see Appendix A of this book, the "Key to Plant Profile Descriptions," where I explain all.

Aluminum plant (Pilea cadierei)

This small but fast-growing plant reaches only 10 to 12 inches (25 to 30 centimeters) high and forms a mound of quilted green leaves with silvery markings on thin, watery stems. Its blooms are insignificant. To keep it looking its best, prune frequently or start over from cuttings annually.

Display: Table, terrarium

Requirements: Bright to medium light, drench and let dry, high to average humidity, normal room temperatures, all-purpose fertilizer, soilless mix

Propagation: Stem cuttings

Care Rating: Easy

Arrowhead plant (Syngonium podophyllum)

Sometimes sold as *Nephthytis afzelii,* its dark green leaves are arrowhead-shaped and often have white, cream, pink, or silver veins or shading. *Juveniles* (young plants) form clusters of upright stems with arrow-shaped leaves. As they mature, they start producing long trailing or climbing stems and larger leaves with three to seven lobes. If you prefer the denser appearance of the juvenile form, just prune out any trailing stems as they appear and the plant retains its youthful shape. The eventual size, ranging from 8 inches (20 centimeters) to 3 feet (90 centimeters) or more, depends on the *cultivar.* You can expect fast growth if you place an arrowhead plant in good light.

Display: Floor, hanging basket, table

Requirements: Bright to medium light, tolerates low light, drench and let dry, high to average humidity, normal room temperatures, all-purpose fertilizer, soilless mix

Propagation: Stem cuttings

Care Rating: Very easy

Asparagus fern (Asparagus densiflorus 'Sprengeri')

This fern-like plant produces new shoots that look like thin asparagus spears and long, trailing prickly stems that eventually reach more than 4 feet (120 centimeters) in length. The stems are covered with tiny, flattened, needle-like green growths. The occasional white, star-shaped flowers are followed by red berries. Expect fast growth if you place it in good light.

The aspargus fern forms thick, massive roots that soon take up all the space in the pot, destroying the potting mix's ability to store water. Watering from above or filling the saucer with water, therefore, may not work. You can achieve greater success rates if you just immerse the entire root ball in water for at least ten minutes.

Display: Hanging basket, table

Requirements: Bright to medium light, drench and let dry, average humidity, normal to cool temperatures, all-purpose fertilizer, soilless mix

Propagation: Seeds, division (you may need a hatchet for division — the roots are very tough)

Care Rating: Easy

Baby rubber plant (Peperomia obtusifolia)

This small, low-growing plant rarely reaches over a foot (30 centimeters) in height or width. It forms thick, succulent, upright stems that sometimes become trailing as they age and usually are well-covered with fleshy, glossy, spoon-shaped leaves in dark green. Several variegated clones have yellow, cream, or white markings. It occasionally produces rattail-shaped stalks capped with pale cream flowers.

Display: Table

Requirements: Bright to medium light, drench and let dry, average humidity, normal room temperatures, all-purpose fertilizer, soilless mix

Propagation: Stem cuttings

Care Rating: Easy

Baby's tears (Soleirolia soleirolii)

This fast-growing, moss-like, creeping plant displays thread-like trailing stems and tiny, rounded, deep-green leaves. It eventually forms a dense mound about 1/2-inch (1 centimeter) high, but can trail to 8 inches (20 centimeters) or more. Variegated and golden cultivars are also available.

The flowers, if any, are so tiny that you may need a microscope to view them. Although it makes great ground cover for terrariums, it does need some air circulation, so avoid closed containers. And, never let it dry out! To multiply it, simply press cuttings into a moist mix; they root almost overnight.

Display: Table, open terrarium

Requirements: Bright to medium light, keep moderately moist, high humidity, normal to cold temperatures, good air circulation, all-purpose fertilizer, soilless mix

Propagation: Stem cuttings, division

Care Rating: Fairly demanding

Banana-leaf fig (Ficus maclellandii)

Sold as *Ficus binnendijkii* in Europe, this indoor tree often serves as a substitute for its close cousin, the weeping fig (*Ficus benjamina*), because it is less subject to leaf loss under poor conditions. Its attractive beige stems and numerous thin branches are similar to those of the weeping fig, but its leaves — long, narrow, sword-like, and dark green — render it instantly recognizable.

Because it grows slowly under most indoor conditions, buy one that's already close to the size you need. Nevertheless, a banana-leaf fig still reaches the ceiling if you don't prune occasionally, so don't hesitate to cut it back if it threatens to take over. *Note:* It occasionally produces green berries.

Display: Floor, table

Requirements: Bright to medium light, drench and let dry, average humidity, normal room temperatures, all-purpose fertilizer, soilless mix

Propagation: Air layering, stem cuttings

Care Rating: Easy

Beefsteak begonia (Begonia 'Erythrophylla')

You are more likely to get a cutting of this old-fashioned *rhizomatous* begonia from a friend than to find this plant in a store. It produces huge heart-shaped leaves that are shiny olive green above and deep red below on thick, creeping *rhizomes*. The small light-pink flowers are borne in great numbers on tall stems in winter, but its foliage is this plant's main claim to fame.

Several variants of this plant have frilly leaves that sport spiraled centers that resemble a corkscrew. Literally thousands of other variants of rhizomatous begonias now exist, often smaller-sized and marked by green, marbled, or nearly black leaves. You can propagate most rhizomatous begonias through leaf cuttings or even leaf section cuttings (see Chapter 16 for more information), but the 'Erythrophylla' is an exception to the rule.

A *rhizome* is a creeping stem that grows underground or on the surface of the soil. *Rhizomatous* describes any plant that produces rhizomes.

Display: Floor, table

Requirements: Bright to medium light, drench and let dry, moderate to average humidity, normal to cool temperatures, all-purpose fertilizer, soilless mix

Propagation: Division, seed, rhizome cuttings

Care Rating: Very easy

Bird's nest fern (Asplenium nidus)

This distinctly unfern-like fern produces a deep rosette of apple green tongue-shaped fronds with a brown downy center. The fronds that emerge from the down look like green eggs at first, creating the "nest of eggs" appearance that gives the plant its common name. This plant often keeps to a quite compact size when grown in the home, owing to the typically low humidity found in most houses.

Under high-humidity conditions, it can attain heights exceeding 2 feet (60 centimeters). Place this plant where passersby can't brush up against it and damage its delicate fronds. Also, water the potting mix, not the center of the rosette; otherwise, rot can set in.

Display: Table, slab

Requirements: Bright to medium light, keep evenly moist, high to moderate humidity, normal room temperatures, all-purpose fertilizer, soilless mix

Propagation: Spores

Care Rating: Demanding

Boston fern (Nephrolepis exaltata 'Bostoniensis')

The true Boston fern produces sword-shaped, apple-green fronds that consist of narrow, lightly toothed leaflets. The fronds arch down to 3 feet (90 centimeters) or more below the top of the pot. Many of its cultivars and hybrids have a more upright or smaller and denser growth pattern, are golden in color or have deeply cut, almost frilly, fronds.

The plant also produces thin, hairy runners with plants at their tips. In fact, they often root in neighboring pots! The plant looks particularly lovely on a pedestal, but remember to remove any faded or yellowed fronds. This fern is less sensitive to dry air than some.

A *runner* is a special creeping or arching stem that produces baby plants. You'll also see it called a *stolon*.

Display: Hanging basket, table

Requirements: Bright to medium light, keep evenly moist, high to moderate humidity, normal to cool room temperatures, all-purpose fertilizer, soilless mix

Propagation: Division, layering

Care Rating: Easy

Butterfly palm (Chrysalidocarpus lutescens)

Also sold as *Areca lutescens,* this popular indoor palm produces clusters of thick, yellowish-orange, reed-like stems with plantlets at its base. Its long, feathery, arching fronds with narrow medium-green leaflets give it an "indoor coconut palm" appearance: You can easily imagine stringing a hammock between two butterfly palm trunks. It grows slowly indoors, but eventually reaches 7 feet (2 meters) or more in height. Like most palms, it is subject to red spider mites (see Chapter 17 for more on these pests).

Display: Floor, table

Requirements: Full sun to bright light, tolerant of low light for short periods, drench and let dry, high humidity, warm to normal room temperatures, all-purpose fertilizer, soilless mix

Propagation: Seeds (rarely available), division

Care Rating: Easy at first, but short-lived under normal indoor conditions

Cast iron plant (Aspidistra elatior)

This old-fashioned houseplant was all the rage in Victorian days, so I'm happy to see it making a comeback. Its broad, oblong, dark-green leaves that are leathery in texture, pointed at the end, and arch outward on solid petioles from an underground rhizome are quite unmistakable — it looks like no other houseplant. Several of its cultivars have cream, white, or yellow spots or stripes, but many turn all green in poor light.

Growing conditions as much as genetics determine its size; depending on how you handle it, it can reach from 12 to 24 inches (30 to 60 centimeters) in height. Its spread is indefinite. As long as you keep supplying larger and larger pots, it gets wider and wider. It grows extremely slowly — underpotted plants in low light scarcely grow at all after ten years. The insignificant but very curious reddish-brown flowers appear at the plant's base, scarcely popping through the potting mix.

Display: Floor, table

Requirements: Bright to medium light, tolerant of low light, drench and let dry, average humidity, normal to cold temperatures, all-purpose fertilizer, soilless mix

Propagation: Division

Care Rating: Very easy

China doll (Radermachera sinica)

This shrubby, tree-like plant with compound, bright-green, wavy, holly-like leaves and a fern-like appearance has become a staple foliage plant over a relatively short period of time. Nurseries, garden centers, and the like inevitably treat it with a growth retardant to maintain a dense appearance. When the retardant wears off in 6 to 18 months, the plant suddenly becomes the medium-size tree nature intended and it heads straight for the ceiling. At this point, you have no choice but pinch it regularly if you want to maintain its dense growth pattern, because growth retardants are not commercially available (see Chapter 15 for more on pinching plant stems).

Professional nurserypeople use growth retardants on many houseplants (China doll, hibiscus, geraniums, and others) to keep them short and compact after sale. However, because of possible health risks during their application, growth redardants are not available to the average consumer.

Display: Floor, table

Requirements: Bright light, keep moderately moist, average humidity, normal room temperatures, all-purpose fertilizer, soilless mix

Propagation: Seed, stem cuttings

Care Rating: Fairly demanding

Chinese evergreen (Aglaonema 'Silver Queen')

A very popular plant owing to its reputation for being able to survive for months under low light, it has large, pointed, dark-green, leathery leaves that are heavily marbled in silver and thick, upright stems. It occasionally produces, pale-green, barely opened, calla-like flowers followed by long-lasting, bright-red berries. It grows extremely slowly, eventually reaching 3 feet (90 centimeters) high. As it ages, it loses its lower leaves, becoming spindly. Cut it back to produce dense growth. Other cultivars of Chinese evergreen feature various silvery patterns, white marbling, or all-green leaves.

Display: Floor, table

Requirements: Bright to medium light, tolerant of low light, keep moderately moist, average humidity, normal room temperatures, all-purpose fertilizer, soilless mix

Propagation: Division, seed, stem cuttings

Care Rating: Very easy

Chinese fan palm (Livistona chinensis)

This slow-growing indoor palm has rounded, fan-shaped, bright-green leaves cut into segments at the tips and with hooked spines at their base. Young plants are stemless; older ones produce a short but thick trunk with a woody appearance. *Be forewarned:* This plant takes up 4 feet (120 centimeters) or more of horizontal space.

Display: Floor, table

Requirements: Full sun to bright light, tolerant of low light for short periods, drench and let dry, moderate humidity, normal to cool temperatures, all-purpose fertilizer, soilless mix

Propagation: Seeds (rarely available)

Care Rating: Very easy

Coleus (Coleus × hybrida)

The coleus is a shrub-like plant with square stems. Its highly colorful foliage can be any combination of yellow, cream, white, pink, orange, red, purple, or green. Its leaves come in a variety of shapes, ranging from heart-shaped, to narrow and fingerlike, to deeply cut and fringed. Its height varies as well, depending on the cultivar. Some never go beyond 6 inches (15 centimeters), others reach 7 feet (2 meters) or more. A few even have a trailing habit and look good in hanging baskets. Pinch this fast-growing plant often to control excessive growth. Remove any flower stalks that it may produce, as blooming weakens the plant.

Note: The botanical name for coleus recently changed to *Solenostemon scutellarioides*.

Display: Hanging basket, table

Requirements: Full sun to bright light, keep moderately moist, high to moderate humidity, normal to cool temperatures, all-purpose fertilizer, soilless mix

Propagation: Seed, stem cuttings

Care Rating: Fairly demanding

Corn plant (Dracaena fragrans)

The corn plant, shown in Figure 4-1, is an unbranched, tree-like plant usually clothed in leaves right to its base but sometimes purposely defoliated at the nursery to reveal its thick, woody trunk. The broad, sword-shaped, arching leaves are dark green or green with a broad cream-to-yellow stripe down the middle. It occasionally produces stalks of highly fragrant whitish flowers, but only after dark. Although slow-growing, it can eventually reach ceiling height. *Purchase with care:* Some plants sold have practically no root system!

Display: Floor, table

Requirements: Bright to medium light, tolerant of low light, drench and let dry, average humidity, normal room temperatures, all-purpose fertilizer, soilless mix

Propagation: Air layering, stem cuttings

Care Rating: Very easy

Figure 4-1:
Corn plant
(Dracaena
fragrans).

Creeping fig (Ficus pumila)

This trailing, creeping, or climbing plant has thin, wiry stems and tiny, puckered, heart-shaped, dark-green leaves, often variegated in white or cream. The stems have aerial roots that cling to upright supports or grow over moss-covered forms. Remove any and all green stems from variegated plants. And never let them go dry!

Display: Hanging basket, ground cover, table

Requirements: Bright to medium light, tolerant of low light, keep moderately moist, moderate humidity, normal to cool temperatures, all-purpose fertilizer, soilless mix

Propagation: Stem cuttings

Care Rating: Fairly demanding

Croton (Codiaeum variegatum pictum)

The croton is a popular tree-like indoor shrub that grows up to 7 feet (2 meters) in height with very colorful leaves marbled in yellow, orange, red, white, and green. The leaves vary considerably in shape, ranging from narrow to oval, lobed, or forked. On some cultivars, they even twist into a spiral or are curiously constricted in the middle, as if a second leaf had been tacked on as an afterthought. Try to give it the brightest light possible because its leaf color fades in poor light. Buy young plants if possible, too — mature specimens usually suffer serious leaf loss when you move them. It occasionally produces fluffy, cream-colored flowers.

Avoid contact with the plant's sap, which stains clothes permanently.

Display: Floor, table

Requirements: Full sun to bright light, keep moderately moist, high to moderate humidity, warm to normal room temperatures, all-purpose fertilizer, soilless mix

Propagation: Air layering, stem cuttings

Care Rating: Fairly demanding

Dumbcane (Dieffenbachia)

This indoor-plant staple produces a thick cane-like stem topped off by broad, fleshy, lance-shaped leaves that are lightly to heavily marbled in cream or white. It occasionally produces insignificant pale-green flowers that look like a rolled-up leaf. Although quite slow-growing, it does eventually reach ceiling height. You can air layer or take cuttings of tall plants to reduce their height (more on air layering is in Chapter 16). The dumbcane gets its name from its toxic sap, which can cause painful vocal loss to those who are silly enough to ingest it.

Display: Floor, table

Requirements: Bright to medium light, tolerant of low light, drench and let dry, average humidity, normal room temperatures, all-purpose fertilizer, soilless mix

Propagation: Air layering, stem cuttings

Care Rating: Very easy

Dwarf schefflera (Schefflera arboricola)

Also known as *Heptapleurum arboricola*, this indoor shrub reaches 7 feet (2 meters) or more in height if not pruned. Its thick branches are covered in compound leaves formed of small, dark-green leaflets set around the *petiole* (the narrow part of a leaf that joins the leaf blade to the stem) like spokes on a wheel. The leaflets usually are rounded or pointed, but occasionally are notched at the tip. Many variegated cultivars are variously splotched and mottled in yellow, cream, or white. Pinch occasionally to maintain even growth; this plant is reluctant to branch on its own.

It gets the name *dwarf schefflera* because its leaves are smaller than the regular schefflera, but the fact is that it's just as big as the regular schlefflera.

Display: Floor, table

Requirements: Bright to medium light, tolerant of low light, drench and let dry, average humidity, normal room temperatures, all-purpose fertilizer, soilless mix

Propagation: Air layering, stem cuttings

Care Rating: Very easy

Emerald ripple peperomia (Peperomia caperata)

The emerald ripple peperomia (see Figure 4-2) is a small mounding plant that grows up to 8 inches (20 centimeters) in height and width. It is composed of short stems heavily covered in heart-shaped, dark-green, deeply puckered leaves on pink to reddish petioles. It has several cultivars, some variegated in white and pink. It occasionally produces thin, cream-colored flower stalks in the shape of a mouse's tail.

Display: Table, terrarium

Requirements: Bright to medium light, drench and let dry, average humidity, normal room temperatures, all-purpose fertilizer, soilless mix

Propagation: Leaf cuttings, stem cuttings

Care Rating: Easy

Figure 4-2:
Emerald ripple peperomia (*Peperomia caperata*).

English ivy (Hedera helix)

A well-known trailing or climbing plant, English ivy has thin stems and glossy leaves in a variety of shapes: rounded, star-shaped, narrow, or irregularly cut and fringed. Its leaf color also varies, from dark green to golden, often with white, cream, or yellow mottling. Although normally grown as a hanging plant, you can also train it to grow on a support or on a moss-filled form. Some varieties are self-branching and require no more than an occasional pinching to remain full. Others produce long, open stems — pinch and prune them frequently to stimulate branching. This plant tends to get spider mites in dry air.

Display: Hanging basket, table, terrarium

Requirements: Bright to medium light, tolerant of low light, keep moderately moist, high humidity, normal to cold temperatures, all-purpose fertilizer, soilless mix

Propagation: Stem cuttings

Care Rating: Easy

False aralia (Dizygotheca elegantissima)

False aralia is an attractive indoor tree with woody stems and compound leaves featuring thin, brownish-green leaflets with a pale central vein and serrated edges. They're arranged around the petiole like fingers on a hand. You often see it sold several plants to a pot to create a denser appearance. Much broader adult leaves appear on plants more than 6 feet (180 centimeters) tall. Prune this plant as needed to control its height. It tends to drop leaves when you let the potting medium dry out.

Display: Floor, table

Requirements: Bright to medium light, drench and let dry, moderate humidity, warm to normal room temperatures, all-purpose fertilizer, soilless mix

Propagation: Seed, air layering, stem cuttings

Care Rating: Fairly demanding

Grape ivy (Cissus rhombifolia)

This popular trailing or climbing plant of unlimited height will, if allowed, clamber up nearby objects by means of its tendrils, but plant owners normally grow it as a hanging plant. Its shiny, dark green, compound leaves have heavily toothed leaflets. Pinch as needed to stimulate branching or allow it to climb up a support. It never blooms indoors.

Display: Hanging basket, table

Requirements: Bright to medium light, tolerant of low light, keep moderately moist, average humidity, normal to cool temperatures, all-purpose fertilizer, soilless mix

Propagation: Layering, stem cuttings

Care Rating: Very easy

Heartleaf philodendron (Philodendron scandens oxycardium)

Also sold as *P. cordatum,* this trailing or climbing plant has long, wandering stems that can attain 30 feet (9 meters) or more in length with glossy, dark green, heart-shaped leaves. You normally see it grown as a hanging plant, but some people train it up supports. Pinch to stimulate branching. One of the toughest of all houseplants!

Display: Hanging basket, table

Requirements: Bright to medium light, tolerant of low light, drench and let dry, average humidity, warm to normal temperatures, all-purpose fertilizer, soilless mix

Propagation: Layering, stem cuttings

Care Rating: Very easy

Holly fern (Cyrtomium falcatum)

This sturdy fern forms a flattened rosette of slightly arching fronds with large, shiny, dark, coarsely toothed leaflets that look like they've been dipped in wax. The result is a plant that looks more like holly than a true fern. The base of the plant is covered with silvery to brown "fur." The underside of the fronds of mature plants bear numerous brown spore cases. The entire plant rarely reaches over 18 inches (45 centimeters) in diameter. The holly fern is one of the toughest ferns, because its thick fronds are immune to the dry air that plagues other ferns.

Display: Table, terrarium

Requirements: Bright to medium light, tolerates low light for short periods, keep evenly moist, moderate to average humidity, normal to cool room temperatures, good air circulation, all-purpose fertilizer, soilless mix

Propagation: Division, spores

Care Rating: Easy

Madagascar dragon tree (Dracaena marginata)

This slow-growing, tree-like plant reaches 7 feet (2 meters) or more in height and displays a woody gray trunk, often straight but sometimes exotically curved. Each stem ends in a dense cluster of narrow, sword-shaped, arching, dark-green leaves edged in red. It has several variegated and purple-leafed cultivars. If it gets too tall, either air layer it or take cuttings, or simply cut it right back to the base — it readily sprouts anew.

Display: Floor, table

Requirements: Bright to medium light, tolerant of low light, drench and let dry, average humidity, normal room temperatures, all-purpose fertilizer, soilless mix

Propagation: Air layering, stem cuttings

Care Rating: Very easy

Ming aralia (Polyscias fruticosa)

This tree-like plant has twisted, woody stems and branches and dark-green, deeply cut, fern-like leaves that make it look like a natural bonsai. It rarely attains more than 5 feet (1.5 meters) in height and can thrive at heights of less than 1 foot (30 centimeters) if you prune it regularly. Pinch it as needed to stimulate denser growth. It is often planted in bonsai pots.

Display: Floor, table

Requirements: Bright to medium light, tolerant of low light, drench and let dry, moderate humidity, normal room temperatures, all-purpose fertilizer, soilless mix

Propagation: Air layering, stem cuttings

Care Rating: Fairly demanding (subject to leaf drop, especially when exposed to low humidity)

Mother-of-thousands (Tolmiea menziesii)

This plant, also known as the *piggyback plant* (see Figure 4-3), forms a low-growing mound of foliage about 8 inches (20 centimeters) in height and 24 inches (60 centimeters) in diameter. The fuzzy, heart-shaped, apple-green leaves are produced on long, thin petioles. Each leaf bears a baby plant in its center that weighs the leaf down as it grows and makes the plant attractive in a hanging basket. Under cool conditions, it produces tall stalks of insignificant flowers that you may as well cut off. Yellow variegated cultivars are also common.

Figure 4-3:
Mother-of-thousands
(Tolmiea
menziesii).

Display: Hanging basket, table

Requirements: Bright to medium light, tolerant of low light, keep moderately moist, moderate humidity, cool to cold temperatures, all-purpose fertilizer, soilless mix

Propagation: Division, layering, leaf cuttings

Care Rating: Easy

Nerve plant (Fittonia verschaffeltii)

The nerve plant is a low-growing, creeping ground cover less than 3 inches (8 centimeters) high with oval, medium-green leaves about 2 inches (5 centimeters) in length. Its main charm comes from its leaves, which are heavily veined in pink or white. Dwarf varieties with much smaller leaves are also available. It blooms quite readily but the flower heads are insignificant. Pinch it often to stimulate dense growth. Like many fast-growing plants, it ages rapidly; for best results, rejuvenate it annually from cuttings.

Display: Hanging basket, table, terrarium

Requirements: Bright to medium light, tolerant of low light, keep moderately moist, high humidity, normal room temperatures, all-purpose fertilizer, soilless mix

Propagation: Division, stem cuttings

Care Rating: Fairly demanding

Norfolk Island pine (Araucaria heterophylla)

This excellent living Christmas tree is one of the rare indoor *conifers* (cone-bearing, often needled plants more commonly called *evergreens*). It is, as its name suggests, a native of Norfolk Island off the coast of Australia. It forms a tightly symmetrical upright tree of nearly unlimited height. Both its branches and the main stem are densely clothed in dark-green needles. On the downside, it readily drops its lower branches in dry air, excessive heat, or low light. You can't encourage it to regrow, because it reacts poorly to pruning of any kind. It is often sold several to a pot for a fuller appearance.

Display: Floor, table, terrarium (seedlings)

Requirements: Bright to medium light, tolerant of low light, keep moderately moist, moderate humidity, cool temperatures, all-purpose fertilizer, soilless mix

Propagation: Not possible in the average home

Care Rating: Fairly demanding

Parlor palm (Chamaedorea elegans 'Bella')

Perhaps the most popular indoor palm, this plant produces a single, short green trunk and very dark-green, arching, feather-like fronds. Although it often appears in clusters, that appearance is achieved by planting several plants to a pot — this palm never produces offsets. Very slow-growing, it reaches ceiling height only after several decades. It occasionally produces branching stalks of creamy yellow blooms indoors.

Seedlings of this species are often sold for dish garden and terrarium use. It's prone to getting red spider mites, although less so than most other palms.

Display: Floor, table, terrarium (seedlings)

Requirements: Bright to medium light, tolerant of low light, keep moderately moist, moderate humidity, warm to normal room temperatures, all-purpose fertilizer, soilless mix

Propagation: Seeds (rarely available)

Care Rating: Very easy

Peacock plant (Calathea makoyana)

This beauty is a nearly stemless clumping plant that grows up to 24 inches (60 centimeters) high. Its highly decorative leaves are oblong and partly translucent, have dark V-shaped markings, and are borne on long petioles. The leaves are nearly upright, so both the green upper parts and purplish lower parts are visible at the same time. When the sun shines through them, the effect is truly breathtaking! Its blooms are insignificant.

Display: Floor, table

Requirements: Bright to medium light, keep moderately moist, high to moderate humidity, normal room temperatures, all-purpose fertilizer, soilless mix

Propagation: Division

Care Rating: Fairly demanding

Polka-dot plant (Hypoestes phyllostachya)

This bushy, spreading plant reaches 15 inches (40 centimeters) or less in height and width. It has pointed, oval, medium-green leaves that are lightly to heavily dotted in white, pink, or red. It blooms readily, but the lilac flowers are small and insignificant. Pinch this plant often to stimulate dense growth and restart it annually from cuttings because the juvenile plants are more attractive than the older ones.

Display: Hanging basket, table, terrarium

Requirements: Bright to medium light, keep moderately moist, moderate humidity, normal to cool temperatures, all-purpose fertilizer, soilless mix

Propagation: Seed, division, stem cuttings

Care Rating: Easy

Pothos (Epipremnum aureum)

Pothos is a popular trailing or climbing plant with long, wandering stems of unlimited length. It produces shiny, medium-green, heart-shaped leaves much like those of the heartleaf philodendron, except that they are irregularly marbled with yellow or white. Although normally grown as a hanging plant, it can also be trained to grow up supports. Pinch it occasionally to stimulate branching.

It is often grown as a low-light plant, but it rarely thrives under such conditions. In fact, given intense light, its leaves increase considerably in size and it takes on a much more attractive appearance.

Display: Hanging basket, table

Requirements: Bright to medium light, tolerant of low light, drench and let dry, average humidity, warm to normal temperatures, all-purpose fertilizer, soilless mix

Propagation: Layering, stem cuttings

Care Rating: Very easy

Prayer plant (Maranta leuconeura)

This well-known spreading plant has oblong olive-green leaves marked with darker veins and spots. Some cultivars have red veins and darker coloration. All cultivars occasionally produce insignificant pinkish flowers. Don't hesitate to prune back straggly stems to stimulate dense, compact growth. Its common name derives from the fact that its leaves fold together at night, like hands closed in prayer.

Display: Hanging basket, table

Requirements: Bright to medium light, keep moderately moist, moderate humidity, normal room temperatures, all-purpose fertilizer, soilless mix

Propagation: Division, stem cuttings

Care Rating: Easy

Purple passion plant (Gynura aurantiaca 'Purple Passion')

This fast-growing, irregularly spreading plant produces toothed leaves and stems reaching up, and then out, to about 2 feet (60 centimeters) in length. All parts of the plant (and especially new growth) are densely coated with purple "hair," giving it a rich, velvety appearance. Remove the ill-scented, orange flowers as they appear and prune back any straggly stems to maintain compact growth.

Display: Hanging basket, table

Requirements: Bright to medium light, drench and let dry, moderate humidity, normal to cool temperatures, all-purpose fertilizer, soilless mix

Propagation: Stem cuttings

Care Rating: Easy

Rubber plant (Ficus elastica)

The rubber plant (shown in Figure 4-4) is a starkly upright, indoor tree of unlimited height that bears large, oval dark-green leaves that are thick, leathery, and shiny. Many purplish and variegated cultivars are available and the sheath that covers the new leaves is bright red in some varieties.

Most people are afraid to touch such a strong-looking plant, but if you pinch it regularly to encourage branching, it maintains a much more attractive appearance. This plant *bleeds* abundantly when you prune it: Spray the cut with water or powder it with fine charcoal to stop the flow. By the way, the white latex given off by the wounds was once used to make rubber.

Display: Floor, table

Requirements: Full sun to medium light, tolerant of low light for short periods, drench and let dry, moderate humidity, normal room temperatures, all-purpose fertilizer, soilless mix

Propagation: Air layering, stem cuttings

Care Rating: Easy

Figure 4-4:
Rubber plant *(Ficus elastica).*

Schefflera (Schefflera actinophylla)

The schefflera (shown in Figure 4-5) is large indoor tree that has a thick, straight trunk reaching 7 feet (2 meters) or more in height. Its compound leaves that consist of large, dark-green leaflets positioned around a petiole like the spokes on a wheel are similar to those of the dwarf schefflera but are glossier and much larger. It loses its lower leaves as it ages, so prune it back harshly to stimulate new growth. Watch out for spider mites: They _love_ this plant!

Display: Floor, table

Requirements: Full sun to medium light, drench and let dry, average humidity, normal room temperatures, all-purpose fertilizer, soilless mix

Propagation: Air layering, seed

Care Rating: Easy

Figure 4-5:
Schefflera.
(Schefflera actinophylla).

Scented geranium (Pelargonium graveolens)

Also called the *rose geranium,* this is a tall, sturdy plant that reaches up to 4 feet (120 centimeters) high if not pruned. It has gray-green, deeply lobed leaves reminiscent of a cut-leaf maple, but much thicker. The leaves give off a distinct scent of roses, or lemons and roses depending on the cultivar, when touched or rubbed. It produces clusters of rose pink flowers, but only when grown in full sun. This plant is actually only one of nearly 100 scented geraniums of all sizes, shapes, and forms whose aromas include lemon, apple, ginger, coconut, chocolatey mint, and many more.

Of course, you may need to apply some degree of olfactory imagination to distinguish the exact scent of certain varieties; others, however, such as the rose geranium, come so close to smelling like the real thing that they serve as substitutes in perfumes and cooking. You can add dried leaves to sachets. Place it outdoors in the summer for best results.

Display: Floor, table

Requirements: Full sun to medium light, drench and let dry, average humidity, normal to cool temperatures, tomato fertilizer, soilless mix

Propagation: Cuttings, seed

Care Rating: Easy

Spider plant (Chlorophytum comosum)

This plant is so well known that describing it seems almost superfluous. For those few people who have never seen a spider plant, it produces rosettes of arching, grass-like, medium-green leaves, often with a cream-colored central stripe and hanging stems (or, *stolons*) that grow up to 3 feet (90 centimeters) or more in length. They bear insignificant white flowers as well as numerous plantlets that you can either remove and root into their own pot or leave to dangle, giving the plant a spidery appearance.

It forms thick roots that soon take up all the space in the pot, reducing the potting mix's ability to store water. Watering from above or filling the saucer with water may, therefore, fail to suffice. Instead, immerse the entire root ball in water for at least ten minutes at watering time. Increase its light if the plant fails to produce the required babies.

Display: Hanging basket, table

Requirements: Bright to medium light, keep moderately moist, moderate to average humidity, normal to cool temperatures, all-purpose fertilizer, soilless or alkaline mix

Propagation: Division, layering, plantlets

Care Rating: Very easy

Staghorn fern (Platycerium bifurcatum)

This definitely is one of the most unusual of all ferns and, indeed, of all houseplants. It produces two distinctly different types of fronds. Cup-shaped, pale-green sterile fronds form at the base of the plant. In the wild, this *epiphyte* (a plant that grows on trees) uses these fronds to attach itself to tree trunks and branches. They quickly turn golden brown. The other type of fronds arch out from the base and resemble antlers. They are covered with white "felt," giving the plant a silvery appearance. Although called *fertile fronds,* they only rarely produce spores in culture.

Don't even bother trying to center this plant in a pot, because it naturally grows to one side. To compensate for this oddity, plant two or three staghorn ferns back to back. Even better, grow this plant on a slab (see the coverage of slab culture in Chapter 5) or attach it to a piece of wood with wire. You can water plants grown in pots from above or below in the normal fashion; those grown on slabs or wood should either be sprayed regularly or dunked in a pail of tepid water.

Display: Table, terrarium

Requirements: Bright to medium light, drench and let dry, high to moderate humidity, normal to cool room temperatures, good air circulation, all-purpose fertilizer, soilless mix

Propagation: Division, spores

Care Rating: Easy

Strawberry begonia (Saxifraga stolonifera)

This plant forms a low rosette less than 3 inches (8 centimeters) in height. Its hairy, round leaves are olive green with silver marbling above and reddish-purple coloring underneath. It produces numerous thin and reddish *stolons* (creeping stems) like those of a strawberry plant, each tipped with a baby plant. They either crawl or hang almost straight down, making the plant a hit in a hanging basket. It sometimes produces tall spikes of tiny, white, star-shaped flowers.

Display: Hanging basket, table, terrarium

Requirements: Bright to medium light, keep moderately moist, moderate humidity, normal to cold temperatures, all-purpose fertilizer, soilless mix

Propagation: Division, layering, plantlets

Care Rating: Easy

Swedish ivy (Plectranthus australis)

This native Australian plant got its common name because it first gained popularity in Sweden. It is a creeping or trailing plant that has scalloped, leathery, bright-green leaves and square stems. The Swedish ivy can form a dense ball of foliage 3 feet (90 centimeters) across (if carefully pruned) or become an ungainly tangle of half-naked stems (if left unpruned). Its pale-lavender to white blooms are quite noticeable, but don't really add much to its charm — just pinch them off. The leaves may yellow in too much sun. Pinch this fast-growing plant frequently to keep it in form or start it over from cuttings annually.

Display: Hanging basket, table

Requirements: Bright to medium light, keep moderately moist, moderate humidity, normal room temperatures, all-purpose fertilizer, soilless mix

Propagation: Stem cuttings, layering

Care Rating: Very easy

Swiss cheese plant (Monstera deliciosa)

This truly striking plant has huge heart-shaped leaves up to 3 feet (90 centimeters) across, often deeply slashed and perforated with holes. Young plants look quite different from the adults, producing smaller leaves without holes that resemble those of the heartleaf philodendron. If your plant has large, deeply cut leaves when you buy it but thereafter grows only smaller leaves with fewer or no holes, you can assume that the plant lacks light. Increase the light for a plant manifesting this problem and it soon starts producing the big, bold leaves for which it is renowned.

The Swiss cheese plant is a trailing or climbing plant of unlimited height with long, winding stems. It produces long aerial roots that help anchor it to its support in the wild, but which you can cut off if you prefer. In good conditions, it produces rolled-up, calla-like flowers followed by edible fruit (which takes several months to mature).

Display: Floor, table

Requirements: Bright to medium light, tolerant of low light, drench and let dry, moderate humidity, normal room temperatures, all-purpose fertilizer, soilless mix

Propagation: Stem cuttings

Care Rating: Easy

Tree philodendron (Philodendron bipinnatifidum)

Although loosely related to the heartleaf philodendron, this large plant looks almost nothing like it. It produces enormous, shiny-green leaves that are deeply cut with finger-like indentations. It has long petioles a short, thick trunk that may eventually require staking. You may cut off the long aerial roots that it develops if you find them undesirable. This one needs lots of horizontal space. Under low light, it can attain a width of 7 feet (2 meters) on in only a year or so! Under bright light, it remains more compact.

Display: Floor, table

Requirements: Bright to medium light, tolerant of low light, drench and let dry, moderate humidity, normal room temperatures, all-purpose fertilizer, soilless mix

Propagation: Division, seed, stem cuttings

Care Rating: Very easy

Umbrella plant (Cyperus alternifolius)

Can't seem to pass by your plants without watering them? Try growing an umbrella plant. This semi-aquatic beauty just *loves* water. Just set it in a deep tray and water away to your heart's content! This unusual plant produces dense clusters of thin, upright, green stems from 18 to 48 inches (45 to 120 centimeters) in height. They are topped off by narrow green *bracts* (leaf-like appendages surrounding a floral cluster) arranged in a circle like spokes on a wheel. The insignificant green flowers that later turn brown appear among the bracts. Prune out old and yellowed stems as necessary. The umbrella plant likes to be kept soaking in water at all times. It is subject to spider mites in dry air.

Display: Floor, table

Requirements: Full sun to medium light, keep wet at all times, high to moderate humidity, normal to cool temperatures, all-purpose fertilizer, soilless mix

Propagation: Division, stem cuttings

Care Rating: Easy

Wandering Jew (Zebrina pendula)

Numerous long, trailing stems growing to 3 feet (90 centimeters) in length or more characterize this common houseplant. The pointed leaves are purplish green with broad silver bands above and rich purple coloring underneath. They attach directly to the stem with no petiole. Several variegated cultivars have pink, cream, or bronze stripes. All occasionally produce short-lived but attractive magenta flowers. Pinch the wandering Jew often to prevent straggly growth, or start it over annually from cuttings.

Display: Hanging basket, table

Requirements: Bright to medium light, drench and let dry, average humidity, normal room temperatures, all-purpose fertilizer, soilless mix

Propagation: Layering, stem cuttings

Care Rating: Very easy

Warneckei dracaena (Dracaena deremensis 'Warneckii')

This slow-growing, tree-like plant can eventually attain a height of 7 feet (2 meters) or more. It is usually abundantly clothed with leaves, but older specimens sometimes display a thick green stem at their base. The narrow, arching, sword-shaped, dark-green leaves are shiny with narrow white stripes. Numerous cultivars have all green leaves or leaves with broader white, chartreuse, or yellow stripes.

Display: Floor, table

Requirements: Bright to medium light, tolerant of low light, drench and let dry, average humidity, normal room temperatures, all-purpose fertilizer, soilless mix

Propagation: Air layering, stem cuttings

Care Rating: Very easy

Weeping fig (Ficus benjamina)

This highly popular indoor tree of unlimited height has an attractive beige trunk and numerous thin branches densely covered in small, pointed, shiny green leaves, often variegated white or cream. The weeping fig (shown in Figure 4-6) is sometimes sold with a curiously braided trunk. It grows fast in the greenhouses where it is produced, but grows very slowly indoors, especially in poor light. It occasionally produces small green berries that may turn red before they drop off.

Figure 4-6:
Weeping fig
*(Ficus
benjamina).*

This plant has a very bad reputation among indoor gardeners, because it tends to lose leaves under poor conditions, but that hasn't stopped it from being among the most popular of all foliage plants. Young plants adapt better to change than mature specimens and make a better choice for the average home, but you still need patience to grow a tall indoor tree from a tiny starter plant!

Display: Floor, table

Requirements: Bright to medium light, drench and let dry, moderate humidity, normal room temperatures, all-purpose fertilizer, soilless mix

Propagation: Air layering, stem cuttings

Care Rating: Fairly demanding

More foliage plants to know and grow

Didn't find your favorite foliage plant among the profiles here? Some plants that have attractive leaves also belong to other plant categories — flowering plants, cactus and succulents, and so on — that I cover in later chapters of this book. The following is a quick list of those types that can also do double duty as foliage plants, and where to find them in this book:

- Air plant *(Tillandsia ionantha)*. See Chapter 7.
- Angelwing begonia *(Begonia 'Lucerna')*. See Chapter 5.
- Caladium *(Caladium × hortulanum)*. See Chapter 7.
- Earth star *(Cryptanthus bivittatus)*. See Chapter 7.
- Episcia *(Episcia cupreata)*. See Chapter 5.
- Flaming sword *(Vriesea splendens)*. See Chapter 7.
- Peace lily *(Spathiphyllum wallisii)*. See Chapter 5.
- Pony tail *(Beaucarnea recurvata)*. See Chapter 6.
- Silver vase *(Aechmea fasciata)*. See Chapter 7.
- Snake plant *(Sansevieria trifasciata)*. See Chapter 6.
- Spineless yucca *(Yucca elephantipes)*. See Chapter 6.
- Zebra plant *(Aphelandra squarrosa)*. See Chapter 5.

Chapter 5

For the Budding Indoor Gardener: Flowering Houseplants

· ·

In This Chapter

▶ Finding out why flowering plants need special care

▶ Handling the short-lived "florist plants"

▶ Taking full advantage of the decorative possibilities of flowering plants

▶ Checking out profiles of 25 flowering plants

· ·

*T*he major difference between a flowering plant and a foliage plant is a simple one — one plant is grown mostly for its flowers and the other mostly for its leaves. If a foliage plant doesn't bloom, who's to know? But if a flowering plant doesn't bloom, you're going to wonder what the heck went wrong. When you grow flowering plants, the emphasis isn't just on keeping them alive and healthy, but also on getting them to bloom. Therein lies the focus of this chapter.

They're Demanding — But, Oh Those Blossoms!

Some flowering plants are almost as easy to grow as foliage plants, and many are considerably trickier. Generally, flowering plants require more skill — and effort — to grow than their leafy brethren.

You want to feel like you have a green thumb? Start with foliage plants (especially those listed in Chapter 4 with the "Tuff 'n' Robust" icon) and learn the ropes with the more rugged varieties. If you wait until after you get the hang of growing foliage plants, you're far less likely to get discouraged if you have less-than-spectacular results with flowering plants. A failure or two is almost inevitable the first time you try growing flowering plants.

By and large, flowering plants need exactly the same care as foliage plants —
just more of it. They usually require more light, more water, higher humidity,
more fertilizer, and, especially, more attention to what may seem at first to
be minor aspects of their *culture* (that is, the means by which they are
grown). You can heap a considerable amount of neglect on some foliage
plants without too many ill effects. When you treat flowering plants that
way, they refuse to bloom.

Blossoming plants require greater care because flowering consumes much
of a plant's energy resources. Most flowering plants can survive for years on
only modest resources as many foliage plants do. However, they won't
bloom under those conditions because they lack the necessary energy.
Improve their conditions, and then just try to stop them from flowering.

You have a flowering houseplant that looks healthy but refuses to bloom?
Try the following:

- ✔ Increase its light levels. Ninety percent of the time, it starts to bloom
  within two months or during the upcoming flowering season.

- ✔ Check whether it is one of the (fortunately, quite few) plants that
  require special long-day or short-day schedules in order to bloom (see
  Chapter 8 for more information). If it is such a plant, change its lighting
  timetable.

- ✔ Increase the air humidity. Dry air can cause flower buds to *blast* (dry
  up) before they even become visible.

- ✔ Check its temperature needs. Refer to the plant's individual profile in
  this chapter and, if necessary, correct the room temperature.

- ✔ Make sure that it isn't overpotted (see Chapter 13 for more on potting).
  Moderate underpotting may actually help it bloom better.

- ✔ Check its roots for signs of insects or disease (see Chapter 17).

- ✔ Try giving it a shot of complete fertilizer (see Chapter 11). Be sure to
  use no more than the recommended dose on the label (and preferably,
  dilute it to around half or less of what the label recommends).

Great Expectations: Sometimes Bloomers and Everbloomers

Many novice indoor gardeners expect flowering plants to stay in full bloom
all year long. That's not likely, unless your plants happen to be made of
plastic (in which case, don't waste any precious fertilizer on them). Just as
most garden plants have a specific flowering season, the average flowering

plant blooms for anywhere from two weeks to two months, generally during a certain time of year (the individual plant profiles in this chapter tell you what those times are). Very few plants bloom nonstop throughout the year — and then only under tip-top conditions.

A few houseplants *can* bloom at any time of the year, which means that, theoretically, they are potentially *everblooming*. The following *everbloomers* tend to bloom off and on throughout the year, with especially heavy flowering in the spring and summer.

- African violet *(Saintpaulia ionantha)*
- Columnea *(Columnea,* some cultivars)
- Crown of thorns *(Euphorbia milii)*
- Flowering maple *(Abutilon × hybridum)*
- Fuchsia *(Fuchsia)*
- Hibiscus *(Hibiscus rosa-sinensis)*
- Impatiens *(Impatiens wallerana)*
- Lady Jane Anthurium *(Anthurium × andreacola* 'Lady Jane')
- Peace lily *(Spathiphyllum wallisii)*
- Streptocarpus *(Streptocarpus × hybridus)*
- Zonal geranium *(Pelargonium × hortorum)*

If you want these plants to bloom nonstop, try growing them under artificial lighting at least 14 to 16 hours a day (see Chapter 8 for more on grow lights). Continuous "daylight" can stimulate many plants to bloom year-round by tricking them into thinking that it's always summer.

Floral for a Fleeting Moment: The So-Called Florist Plants

The term *florist plant* has taken on a special meaning in the houseplant world. You can buy just about any houseplant in a florist shop, but those in the know reserve the term *florist plant* strictly for plants sold in bloom that are not likely to rebloom under average home conditions. They're also often called *gift plants,* or, more rarely but more precisely, *ephemerals.* Like long-lived cut flowers, you buy them as they near their prime, enjoy them for a few weeks, but don't expect them to somehow miraculously bloom again.

The reasons so-called florist plants are not likely to bloom again depend partly on the plant, but also on your growing conditions. Some, like the cineraria (see Figure 5-1), for example, are annuals or biennials. Whether in the home, the garden, or the greenhouse, they simply die after blooming — no ifs, ands, or buds about it. Others, however, *could* bloom again if you re-create the conditions they need — cool to cold room temperatures and high humidity, often combined with short days. Maintaining these conditions is not likely unless, by some chance, you have a greenhouse that you keep barely heated.

Some florist plants are simply garden plants forced into early bloom in a greenhouse. You can save these plants if you have an outdoor garden. Just plant them outside after they finish blooming (if the ground is frozen, wait until spring or until the ground thaws). They eventually readapt to outdoor life. Don't expect to see these plants bloom again for at least a full year. After that, though, they should bloom annually. Forcing plants to bloom early weakens them, so they need time to recoup enough energy reserves to bloom again.

What's nice about florist plants is that you shouldn't expect them to bloom again. You don't have to feel guilty if you can't keep them alive because they're programmed to bloom and then quit. You can enjoy them while they last and suffer no qualms about throwing them into the compost heap when they stop blooming.

Figure 5-1:
The cineraria *(Senecio cruentus)* is a typical florist plant. You buy it in bloom and compost it later.

How to pick a florist plant that's in its prime

If you're looking for a florist plant, choose a plant that has plenty of flower buds showing color but only enough fully open flowers to indicate the plant's full color. Avoid getting a plant with buds that are still green because the buds may not open indoors. Avoid plants in full bloom because they're probably already headed toward the compost heap.

Buying plants that have plenty of buds on the verge of bursting open but only a few flowers ensures not only instant appeal, but the longest possible blooming period. The chrysanthemum is one of the rare exceptions to the "buy in bud, not in flower" rule. Its buds, even if they do show color, often fail to open in the home, so always buy a chrysanthemum in full bloom.

By all means do *compost* your over-the-hill plants. Just chop 'em up, root ball and all, into bits and pieces and toss them into your backyard compost pile. All parts of a dead plant, from its leaves to its roots to its potting mix, decompose quickly and return their minerals to the soil. You can then use the humus-rich organic compost in your garden.

In the following lists, I tell you which flowering plants are true flowering houseplants that you can encourage to flower repeatedly in the home and which are merely florist plants. I also tell you whether you should simply compost the spent florist plant after it finishes blooming or whether, and under what conditions, you can plant it outdoors so that it can bloom again.

> ✔ **Toss after blooming because they won't bloom again**

- Christmas pepper *(Capsicum annuum)*
- Cineraria *(Senecio cruentus)*
- Pocketbook plant *(Calceolaria herbeohybrida)*
- Poinsettia *(Euphorbia pulcherrima)*
- Florist primrose *(Primula malacoides* and *P. obconica)*

You *can* flower the poinsettia a second time, but the result is rarely worth the effort. If you want to try to keep it alive from year to year, or even to get it to bloom, check out the poinsettia plant profile section later in this chapter.

> ✔ **Plant outdoors in a cool climate; otherwise, toss it into the compost pile**

- Christmas holly *(Ilex aquifolium)*
- Chrysanthemum *(Dendranthema* × *grandiflora)*
- Easter lily *(Lilium longiflorum)*

- Garden primrose *(Primula × polyantha)*
- Hardy bulbs: anemones, crocus, daffodils, hyacinths, tulips, and so on
- Hortensia *(Hydrangea macrophylla)*
- Miniature rose *(Rosa)*

✔ **Plant outdoors in a frost-free climate, or toss in the compost heap**

- Chrysanthemum *(Dendrathema × grandiflora)*
- Easter lily *(Lilium longiflorum)*
- Freesia *(Freesia × hybrida)*
- Gardenia *(Gardenia jasminoides)*
- Hortensia *(Hydrangea macrophylla)*
- Transvaal daisy *(Gerbera jamesonii)*

✔ **Can recuperate and be used as a repeat-flowering houseplant**

- African violet *(Saintpaulia ionantha)*
- Amaryllis *(Hippeastrum)*
- Azalea *(Rhododendron simsii)*
- Calamondin orange *(× Citrofortunella mitis)*
- Cyclamen *(Cyclamen persicum)*
- Flaming Katy *(Kalanchoe blossfeldiana)*
- Flaming sword *(Vriesea splendens)*
- Florist's gloxinia *(Sinningia speciosa)*
- Fuchsia *(Fuchsia)*
- Guzmania *(Guzmania lingulata)*
- Hibiscus *(Hibiscus rosa-sinensis)*
- Holiday cactus *(Schlumbergera × buckleyi)*
- Orchids (all types)
- Poinsettia *(Euphorbia pulcherrima)*
- Reiger begonia *(Begonia hiemalis)*
- Silver vase *(Aechmea fasciata)*

If you like flowering plants around the house, you might want to stick to strictly florist plants, toss them into the compost after they finish blooming, and replace the spent plants on a regular basis with fresh ones. If you have a backdrop of permanent (and easy-to-grow) foliage plants and a single

INSIDE DIRT

Your own flowering houseplant nursery

Many serious indoor gardeners maintain a plant room where they let plants recuperate between bouts of flowering (any spare room or even a basement space with grow lights will do). When a flowering plant starts to bloom, it can be whisked into the living room or front hall. When it starts to fade, send it back to the nursery. A nursery is also the ideal space for starting plants from cuttings or seeds, treating sick plants, repotting plants, and storing fertilizer, pots, pesticides, potting mixes, and indoor gardening tools.

potted florist plant that you replace every two weeks or so throughout the year, you can create living decor that always looks its best. Or, you can use a spare room or corner room of your house as a nursery (see the nearby sidebar "Your own flowering houseplant nursery") to house your plants when they aren't in bloom.

Flowering Plant Profiles

So, you've decided to try your hand at growing a few flowering plants. In this section, I tell you about 25 flowering plants that you can grow with pride. To demystify the plant care notations, Appendix A of this book includes definitions of the terms that I use in giving the care requirements, propagation options, and care ratings for each plant listed in this chapter.

African violet (Saintpaulia ionantha)

This low-growing plant forms a flat, symmetrical rosette about 1 foot (30 centimeters) in diameter that consists of dark-green, oval, somewhat fuzzy leaves on long *petioles* (leaf stalks). It can flower year-round under good conditions, and even plants that receive barely enough light to survive will often bloom at least occasionally when light is especially intense, usually in the summer. The flowers are borne in clusters near the center of the rosette and come in a wide range of forms (single, double, semi-double, fringed, star-shaped, and so on) and colors, including various bicolor combinations.

You also can find miniature, trailing, and variegated African violets. As African violets grow, they lose their lower leaves and reveal a less-than-attractive naked trunk. See Chapter 15 for information on how to hide this unsightly development.

Display: Hanging basket (trailing types), table

Requirements: Bright to medium light, keep moderately moist, moderate to average humidity, warm to normal temperatures, flowering plant fertilizer, soilless mix

Propagation: Leaf cuttings, stem cuttings, division, seed

Care Rating: Easy

Angelwing begonia (Begonia 'Lucerna')

Begonia 'Lucerna' (also called *'Corallina de Lucerna')* is an old-fashioned begonia hybrid rarely available commercially, but which houseplant lovers have exchanged among themselves for more than a century. A vigorous plant, it reaches 6 feet (180 centimeters) tall and has green bamboo-like stems that turn brown as the plant ages. It branches little, but new stems sprout regularly from its base. The large ear-shaped leaves are green with silvery spots above and deep-red coloring underneath. It produces clusters of deep-pink flowers sporadically throughout the year. Angelwing begonias come in various shapes and sizes, some with larger or smaller leaves, dwarf or spreading tendencies, and flowers ranging from white to deep red.

Display: Floor, table

Requirements: Bright to medium light, drench and let dry, moderate to average humidity, normal to cool temperatures, all-purpose fertilizer, soilless mix

Propagation: Division, seed, stem cuttings

Care Rating: Very easy

Azalea (Rhododendron simsii)

This popular florist plant is among those that you *can* use as a repeat-flowering plant, but it's a very demanding one. It forms a dense bush of small, shiny green leaves covered with hordes of flowers in winter or early spring. It grows slowly to reach more than 4 feet (120 centimeters) high, but you can limit it to much smaller sizes by pruning it immediately after it blooms. The flowers are usually double or semi-double and come in various shades of white, pink, rose, lavender, and red, often with stripes or spots.

After the azalea blooms, place it outdoors in semi-shade and keep it well watered (this plant drinks like a fish). Leave it outdoors all summer, and after a few weeks of cool temperatures in the autumn, bring it back inside and enjoy the bloom. It often blooms less heavily when you grow it yourself, but over a much longer period of time.

Display: Floor, table

Requirements: Bright light, keep moderately moist, high to moderate humidity, cool to cold temperatures, acid fertilizer, acid potting mix

Propagation: Stem cuttings

Care Rating: Fairly demanding

Bird of paradise (Strelitzia reginae)

The bird of paradise is a typical indoor/outdoor plant. This huge container plant grows up to 5 feet (1.5 meters) high and has leathery, dark-green, oblong leaves on long, thick petioles. Out of bloom, it resembles a banana plant. The plant's huge crested flowers, produced in spring and summer, are spectacular — imagine a bright-orange bird's head with a large blue or purple bill. It grows very slowly and mature plants are expensive, so take your pick: Cough up the cash for a blooming plant, or start small and wait patiently during the six to ten years it takes to get a seedling or offset to bloom. Consider a summer spent outside a must — it rarely blooms unless it spends at least three months outside in full sun.

Display: Floor, table

Requirements: Full sun to bright light, drench and let dry, average humidity, cool temperatures, all-purpose fertilizer, soilless mix

Propagation: Seeds, division

Care Rating: Fairly demanding

Bougainvillea (Bougainvillea glabra)

The bougainvillea (see Figure 5-2) is a woody climbing shrub that often possesses hidden spines. Left to its own devices, it can fill a sizable portion of a room. You can, however, train it to assume a bushy form only 2 or 3 feet (60 to 90 centimeters) in height and diameter. The dark-green, oval leaves, sometimes variegated, are fairly sparse and often drop off in the winter. And, let me tell you, minus the flowers, this plant is no beauty! Fortunately, its blooms, usually in spring or summer, are abundant and spectacular. Dozens of papery *bracts* (leaf-like appendages surrounding the flowers) in white, pink, orange, yellow, red, magenta, or purple surround tiny, tubular, cream-colored flowers. The true blooms drop off after only a few days, but the bracts can last for months. Prune back harshly after blooming and keep quite dry during its dormant period.

Display: Table, hanging basket

Requirements: Full sun to bright light, drench and let dry, moderate humidity, cool temperatures, dormancy suggested, all-purpose fertilizer, soilless mix

Propagation: Cuttings

Care Rating: Demanding

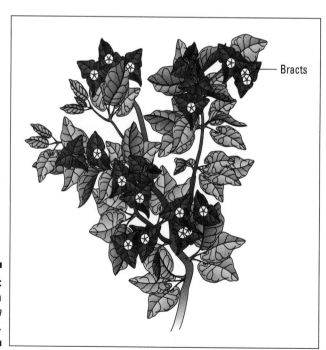
Bracts

Figure 5-2:
Bougainvillea
*(Bougainvillea
glabra).*

Calamondin orange (× Citrofortunella microcarpa)

This dwarf shrub with dense growth and shiny green leaves is among the rare flowering plants that is attractive year-round. Resulting from a cross between a Mandarin orange and a kumquat, it produces typical citrus flowers — white, clustered, and smelling of orange blossoms — and small round orange fruits about 1 inch (2.5 centimeters) in diameter. It blooms intermittently all year long and the fruits remain on the shrub for months. Even young cuttings barely rooted often start to bloom and produce fruit. It can reach up to 4 feet (120 centimeters) in height, but is generally pruned to a smaller size.

You can use the calamondin orange's sour fruit to make a very tasty marmalade.

Display: Floor, table

Requirements: Full sun to bright light, drench and let dry, moderate humidity, normal to cool temperatures, tomato fertilizer, soilless or acid mix

Propagation: Seeds, cuttings

Care Rating: Fairly demanding

Chrysanthemum (Dendranthema × grandiflora)

The florist plant *par excellence*, chrysanthemums are now available year-round and make ideal gifts for any occasion. The stiff stems are densely covered with oddly scented, irregularly lobed, dark-green leaves. Clusters of daisy-like single or double flowers in a wide range of colors, including white, cream, yellow, orange, pink, rose, bronze, purple, or red, top off each stem. When it's blooming, place it anywhere and keep it moist. Cooler night temperatures help extend its blooming to a month or longer.

Trying to get this plant to bloom again indoors is basically pointless. After it blooms once, compost it or cut it back severely and plant it outdoors. It may bloom again in autumn (its normal blooming season) and, in moderate climates, will even come back year after year.

Display: Floor

Requirements: Full sun to low light, keep moderately moist, moderate to average humidity, normal to cold temperatures, fertilizer not required, no need to repot

Propagation: Stem cuttings

Care Rating: Easy (as a temporary plant)

Clivia (Clivia miniata)

The clivia (see Figure 5-3) has thick lengths of dark-green foliage that's attractive all year long. It also sports wide stalks of vibrant, orange, bell-shaped flowers (usually in midwinter), although older plants tend to bloom a second or third time in spring or summer. It reaches only about 2 feet (60 centimeters) in height, but takes up considerable horizontal space — up to 4 feet (120 centimeters).

The clivia dislikes repotting, often refusing to bloom for a year or more after you transfer it to a new pot. Magnifying its sensitivity to repotting is the fact that it actually blooms better when root bound. Leave it in its pot until the container literally comes apart at the seams under the force of its thick fleshy roots! Although you may feel a strong urge to separate the young plants that appear at the base of the mother plant, you can remove them only by unpotting the mother and cutting them loose from among her roots and she may well show her dissatisfaction at such a disruption by refusing to bloom for another year or two.

Display: Floor, table

Requirements: Full sun to bright light, drench and let dry, average humidity, normal to cool temperatures, all-purpose fertilizer, soilless mix

Propagation: Seeds, division

Care Rating: Easy

Columnea (Columnea)

To look at it, this plant's relation to the African violet is scarcely evident, but it does share the latter's ability to flower abundantly and often almost constantly with only medium light. It is a shrubby plant of *epiphytic origin* (that is to say, it grows on trees). It usually produces hanging or trailing stems up to 3 feet (90 centimeters) in length with small, oval, opposing leaves that are sometimes smooth and sometimes hairy in texture. Tubular red, orange, pink, yellow, or bicolor flowers that flare at the tip are produced at the leaf *axils* (the point where the leaf meets the stem).

Some people claim the columnea looks like a fish and for that reason call it the *goldfish plant*. Many columneas are distinctly seasonal. If you want flowering all year long, ask for an everblooming clone, such as the 'Early Bird' or 'Mary Ann' varieties.

Display: Hanging basket, table

Requirements: Bright to medium light, keep moderately moist, moderate to average humidity, normal temperatures, flowering plant fertilizer, soilless mix

Propagation: Stem cuttings, division, seed

Care Rating: Easy

Figure 5-3:
Clivia *(Clivia miniata).*

Dipladenia (Mandevilla)

This increasingly popular indoor/outdoor plant is a woody, twining climber that can grow up a trellis or other support to over 7 feet (2 meters) high. If your space is limited, however, you can loop it around a foot-high trellis, or you can keep it pruned to a shrub-like form of any height. The stems bear pairs of smooth, glossy, dark-green leaves. From spring right through fall, it has huge white, pink, or red trumpet-shaped flowers, usually with a yellow throat. Pruning heavily after the last flower fades in autumn helps stimulate better bloom the following spring.

Beware: All parts of this plant can be deadly poisonous. So, keep it out of the reach of children and pets.

Display: Floor, hanging basket

Requirements: Bright light, drench and let dry, high to moderate humidity, normal to cool temperatures, all-purpose fertilizer, soilless mix

Propagation: Air layering, stem cuttings

Care Rating: Fairly demanding

Episcia (Episcia cupreata)

The episcia plant also sells under the names *flame violet* and *carpet plant.* If you've always thought of it more as a foliage plant than a flowering plant, you're forgiven. It's so attractive both in and out of flower that it easily fits in either category. It's basically a low-growing, rosette-forming plant whose leaves resemble those of its cousin, the African violet, but are distinctly more colorful. They come in all shades of green, bronze, pink, red, white, and brown, often with a metallic sheen and contrasting veins.

The plant also produces numerous creeping or hanging *stolons* that carry smaller plants at regular intervals, eventually forming a hanging curtain of strikingly colored foliage up to 3 feet (90 centimeters) long. It produces trumpet-shaped flowers, in red, pink, yellow, or lavender, sporadically throughout the year. Pinch off some or all of the stolons to increase bloom.

Display: Hanging basket, table, terrarium

Requirements: Bright to medium light, keep moderately moist, high to moderate humidity, warm to normal temperatures, flowering plant fertilizer, soilless mix

Propagation: Stem cuttings, leaf cuttings, layering, division, seed

Care Rating: Fairly demanding

Flowering maple (Abutilon × hybridum)

The flowering maple (see Figure 5-4) is a bushy shrub that grows to about 5 feet (1.5 meters) in height and diameter, generally with slightly downy, maple-like or heart-shaped medium-green leaves. It has several variegated *cultivars* (cultivated varieties). Those with yellow mottling bloom as abundantly as the all-green ones, but those with numerous white markings flower only weakly and qualify more as foliage plants. The large, single, bell-shaped, somewhat pendulous flowers usually appear from summer through autumn, but sometimes all year long. They come in various shades of white, cream, yellow, orange, pink, rose, and red. Prune at any time, but especially in spring, to keep this rather vigorous plant under control.

Display: Floor, table

Requirements: Full sun to bright light, drench and let dry, moderate humidity, normal to cool temperatures, all-purpose fertilizer, soilless mix

Propagation: Seeds, cuttings

Care Rating: Fairly demanding

Figure 5-4:
Flowering maple (Abutilon × hybridum).

Fuchsia (Fuchsia)

This highly popular indoor/outdoor plant is a soft-wooded shrub that has upright, spreading, or pendulous branches. Most varieties have short, red petioles and oval, serrated leaves. Some cultivars are variegated. The real charm of this plant, though, comes from the hanging flowers that give the plant the common name "Lady's Eardrops." The flowers usually are bicolored, with a colorful outer *calyx* (the outer part of the flower) whose segments curve upward in one shade and a skirt-shaped single or double *corolla* (the inner part, including the petals) hanging straight down in another color. The color range includes white, pink, red, salmon, magenta, and purple.

Given the wide range of hybrids of all sizes and shapes, you want to choose a fuchsia plant with care, according to your specific needs — miniature types for small spaces, trailing cultivars for hanging baskets, and so on. You can grow this plant in either of two ways: Force it into dormancy when you bring it inside for the cold season by pruning it back harshly and storing it in a dark, barely heated room until spring, or bring it back indoors early (before temperatures drop in the fall) and continue to supply bright light, regular waterings, and fertilizer. It may bloom all year if you use this second method. Watch out for whiteflies!

Display: Table, floor, hanging basket

Requirements: Bright light, drench and let dry, high to moderate humidity, normal to cold temperatures, all-purpose fertilizer, soilless mix

Propagation: Air layering, stem cuttings

Care Rating: Demanding

Hibiscus (Hibiscus rosa-sinensis)

The hibiscus is a vigorous, upright, spreading shrub that grows to 7 feet (2 meters) or more in height. It bears woody stems and large, glossy, dark-green, maple-shaped or heart-shaped leaves. Its white-marbled variegated cultivars sometimes flower only weakly. The saucer-shaped flowers are huge: up to 10 inches (25 centimeters) across, although most cultivars have flowers only half that size. The blooms last only one day or, in the case of double flowers two days, and come in a wide range of colors: white, pink, yellow, orange, and red, not to mention bicolors.

You can get the hibiscus to bloom nonstop under optimum conditions. It makes an interesting indoor/outdoor plant for the summer patio. Most cultivars grown today are treated with a growth retardant that nurseries use to keep them dense and compact. When the effect wears off after 6 to 18 months, the plant begins to grow rapidly and becomes ungainly. To control it without sacrificing flowers, prune it back by removing one older branch at a time. This plant is highly subject to spider mites.

Display: Floor, table

Requirements: Full sun to bright light, keep moderately moist, moderate humidity, warm to normal room temperatures, tomato fertilizer, soilless mix

Propagation: Cuttings

Care Rating: Fairly demanding

Impatiens (Impatiens wallerana)

This plant has come full circle. Long a popular indoor plant, it became one of the most popular garden annuals by the mid-20th century, and now is becoming popular again as a houseplant. It has a host of common names, from *Patient Lucy* to *Busy Lizzie,* which refer to its habit of waiting to expel its seeds in all directions until you touch the pod with your finger. A bushy, succulent-stemmed, everblooming plant, it rarely reaches more than 15 inches (45 centimeters) in height or diameter. Its medium-green to dark-green or bronze leaves are sometimes variegated, and its flat-faced flowers, which come in white, pink, salmon, red, orange, and bicolors, feature a spur at the back. It also comes in double-flowered varieties.

 Instead of bringing aging specimens of this popular indoor/outdoor plant inside from the garden come autumn, just take cuttings in late summer and root them indoors. Pinch and prune to keep them under control. Rinse this plant weekly under the tap to help prevent spider mites.

Display: Floor, table

Requirements: Bright to medium light, keep moderately moist, high to moderate humidity, warm to normal room temperatures, all-purpose fertilizer, soilless mix

Propagation: Cuttings, seeds

Care Rating: Fairly demanding

Lady Jane anthurium (Anthurium × andreacola 'Lady Jane')

This new arrival on the houseplant market doesn't exist in the wild. It is a complex hybrid resulting from crosses between some tough but not terribly exciting miniature anthuriums and the spectacular but difficult-to-grow flamingo flower (*A. andraeanum*). The result is a plant that blooms nonstop all year long (under good conditions, at least) and is no more difficult to care for than the average foliage plant. 'Lady Jane' (see Figure 5-5) produces smooth, shiny, dark-green leaves on long petioles. The flower head consists of a thin pink spike (or *spadix*) highlighted by a pinkish red leaf-like bract (or *spathe*). As the plant grows, it loses its lower leaves, so cover up the bare stem when you repot. Besides 'Lady Jane,' several other related anthuriums now come in white, pink, lavender, and red.

Display: Floor, table

Requirements: Bright to medium light, tolerates low light, keep moderately moist, moderate to average humidity, warm to normal room temperatures, all-purpose fertilizer, soilless mix

Propagation: Division

Care Rating: Easy

Figure 5-5:
Lady Jane
anthurium
(*Anthurium*
×
andreacola
'Lady Jane').

Lipstick plant (Aeschynanthus lobbianus)

The lipstick plant is an *epiphyte* (it grows on trees in the wild) that's related to the African violet. It produces trailing stems up to 2 feet (60 centimeters) long. It has dark-green leaves with a purplish edge that are distinctly waxy in appearance. The tubular, bright-red flower emerges from a narrow, blackish-purple *calyx* (the outer part of the flower). When the bud is just about to open, the effect is very similar to lipstick rising from a tube. Flowering tends to be seasonal (spring and summer) although newer cultivars may bloom sporadically all year long.

Display: Hanging basket, table

Requirements: Bright to medium light, keep moderately moist, moderate to average humidity, normal temperatures, flowering plant fertilizer, soilless mix

Propagation: Stem cuttings, division, seed

Care Rating: Easy

Oleander (Nerium oleander)

This popular indoor/outdoor plant prefers a summer outside to do well. It forms a large shrub with tall, upright stems with few branches and narrow, willow-like, medium-green leaves. Several variegated cultivars are available. It can reach 7 feet (2 meters) high or more, although its height is easy to control by pruning it after it blooms. Also, some dwarf varieties barely reach over 3 feet (90 centimeters) high. Its phlox-like clusters of deliciously perfumed white, pink, rose, yellow, or red single or double flowers appear at the tips of the branches throughout most of the summer.

All of its parts are extremely poisonous, so treat it with caution and wear long sleeves, gloves, and goggles when pruning or repotting an oleander. Wash well after working with it, and keep it out of the reach of kids and pets.

Display: Floor, table

Requirements: Full sun to bright light, keep moderately moist, moderate to average humidity, warm to normal room temperatures, all-purpose fertilizer, soilless mix

Propagation: Stem cuttings

Care Rating: Fairly demanding

Peace lily (Spathiphyllum wallisii)

This plant is probably the easiest to grow of all the flowering houseplants. And because its foliage is attractive (oblong, leathery, dark-green leaves that arch away from the plant's base), you might simply want to consider it a foliage plant that flowers every now and again. The flower head, held high above the foliage, consists of a narrow white stalk of tiny flowers set off by a large, white, leaf-like bract. It has a beautiful scent, but only at night when the flower is relatively fresh (it can stay in good shape for over a month, but the perfume may last only a week or two). The peace lily comes in dozens of varieties, ranging from only about 12 inches (30 centimeters) in height and diameter to well over 4 feet (120 centimeters).

Display: Floor, table

Requirements: Bright to medium light, tolerates low light, keep moderately moist, moderate to average humidity, normal room temperatures, all-purpose fertilizer, soilless mix

Propagation: Division

Care Rating: Very easy

Poinsettia (Euphorbia pulcherrima)

The poinsettia has become so synonymous with Christmas that displaying it in the home at any time other than December seems almost peculiar. It forms a branching shrub that has dark-green, oak-like leaves. Most modern cultivars rarely reach more than 18 inches (45 centimeters) in height or diameter. In winter (late December in the northern hemisphere), a cluster of colored bracts forms at the tip of each stem. They range in color from the traditional red to white, pink, salmon, lemon yellow, lime green (rare), and bicolor. Tiny, insignificant flowers appear among the bracts. Under good conditions, the bracts of hybrid poinsettias can remain in good shape for up to six months.

The poinsettia is a quintessential florist plant: Enjoy it while it blooms, then toss it — unless you live in a tropical climate where you can plant it outdoors. If you do keep it for the following year, don't expect it to bloom — but feel free to maintain it as a none-too-impressive foliage plant. If you insist on blooming yours a second time, start giving it 14 hours of darkness per day, starting in September.

Display: Floor, table

Requirements: Bright to medium light, tolerates low light, drench and let dry, moderate to average humidity, warm to normal room temperatures, all-purpose fertilizer, soilless mix

Propagation: Stem cuttings

Care Rating: Easy (as a temporary plant); demanding (if you intend to bloom it a second time)

Rieger begonia (Begonia hiemalis)

Hiemalis begonias have literally dozens of common names, depending on the name of the series of hybrids they belong to, but Rieger begonias and Eliator begonias (from the names of two series now rarely grown) are perhaps the most universal. Although experts consider them semi-tuberous because of their background, most hybrids show a bit of swelling at the base of the stem, but few other signs of their origins. Originally winter bloomers, the newer hybrids sell in bloom year-round as florist plants. In the home, they're likely to revert to their winter-flowering habits.

The plants can grow upright or trailing, with thick stems and bright-green to bronze asymmetrical leaves. The flowers, borne in clusters and often more than 2 inches (5 centimeters) in diameter, are single, semi-double, or double. They come in various shades of white, pink, yellow, orange, and red. After a bout of heavy blooming, new sprouts appear at the base of the plant — a sign that it's time to prune the old stems back. Keep the plants quite dry and on the cool side (under 65°F/18°C) during the period of slow growth that follows. As with many of the more difficult florist plants, you also can choose to simply toss the plant after its bloom passes.

Display: Hanging basket, table

Requirements: Bright light, drench and let dry, moderate to average humidity, cool temperatures, good air circulation, all-purpose fertilizer, soilless mix

Propagation: Division, seed, leaf cuttings, stem cuttings

Care Rating: Demanding

Streptocarpus (Streptocarpus × hybridus)

The streptocarpus, also called *cape primrose,* is a low-growing, stemless plant related to the African violet. It produces long, thick-textured, tongue-shaped leaves, each with its own set of roots. Although the plant seems to grow in a rosette, each leaf is actually an independent plant that you can separate and grow individually. The trumpet-shaped flowers are borne on upright stalks rising directly from the base of the leaf. They come in a vast array of colors, including shades of red, white, blue, purple, and pink, often with contrasting veins.

This cool-climate plant dislikes summer heat and may do better near a basement window during the hot season. When it likes its growing conditions, though, the streptocarpus can bloom nonstop all year long. Don't hesitate to trim back the long leaves if they turn brown at the tips. Completely remove any older leaves that no longer have any flower buds at their base.

Display: Table

Requirements: Bright to medium light, drench and let dry, moderate to average humidity, normal to cool temperatures, flowering plant fertilizer, soilless mix

Propagation: Leaf cuttings, division, seed

Care Rating: Fairly demanding

Wax plant (Hoya carnosa)

The wax plant twines or trails with long, twisting brown stems that often appear leafless at first (the leaves grow in later). The succulent, waxy, dark-green leaves appear in pairs on the stems. They are often variegated with white, cream, yellow, or pink patches, or spotted with silver. Some cultivars are curiously twisted, almost hiding the stem, giving the plant the name *Hindu rope plant.* The fragrant, star-like flowers in white or pink with a red center are borne in dense clusters in spring and summer, sometimes intermittently throughout the year.

When the flowers drop off, they leave a stub that you should not prune off, because the plant blooms again and again from the same spot. It can take several years for a wax plant to begin blooming after a repotting, but it usually blooms again after that — until you repot it. This is one plant worth keeping a bit pot-bound.

Display: Hanging basket, table

Requirements: Full sun to bright light, drench and let dry, moderate to average humidity, normal room temperatures, all-purpose fertilizer, soilless mix

Propagation: Stem cuttings

Care Rating: Easy

Zebra plant (Aphelandra squarrosa)

This stiffly erect plant, usually sold as a rooted cutting with a single thick stem (although mature plants do branch) features spectacular foliage — large, glossy, black-green leaves with striking ivory veins. If it weren't so beautiful in bloom, you could easily grow it as strictly a foliage plant. The "flower" is actually a dense spike of bright yellow bracts that form at the tip of the stem. The spike forms in summer or autumn and can remain in top shape for several months. The tubular yellow flowers, on the other hand, are short-lived.

The zebra plant isn't easy to grow, because it requires such high humidity to thrive. You may prefer to think of it as a florist plant, disposing of it after it blooms. If not, take cuttings after it blooms — young zebra plants are more attractive than older ones.

Display: Table

Requirements: Bright to medium light, keep moderately moist, high humidity, normal indoor temperatures, all-purpose fertilizer, soilless mix

Propagation: Stem cuttings

Care Rating: Demanding

Zonal geranium (Pelargonium × hortorum)

This popular indoor/outdoor plant produces thick, succulent stems and oddly scented, rounded leaves that often have a dark, horseshoe-shaped band. The single or double flowers are borne in dense, rounded heads. Two centuries of hybridization have resulted in many highly varied forms, including miniatures; plants with variegated and deeply cut leaves; rounded, narrow, or fringed flower petals; and a wide range of colors, including white, pink, salmon, orange, red, mauve, lavender, and purple. This plant is subject to rot and other fungal diseases, so pick off faded leaves and flowers routinely.

Display: Table

Requirements: Full sun to bright, drench and let dry, average humidity, normal to cool temperatures, tomato fertilizer, soilless mix

Propagation: Seed, stem cuttings

Care Rating: Easy

More flowering plants to know and grow

Some flowering plants also belong to other plant categories — cacti and succulents or orchids and bromeliads — therefore, I profile them under other groupings in this book.

- Amaryllis *(Hippeastrum)*. See Chapter 7.

- Cattleya *(Cattleya)*. See Chapter 7.

- Crown of thorns *(Euphorbia milii)*. See Chapter 6.

- Cyclamen *(Cyclamen persicum)*. See Chapter 7.

- Flaming Katy *(Kalanchoe blossfeldiana)*. See Chapter 6.

- Flaming sword *(Vriesea splendens)*. See Chapter 7.

- Florist's gloxinia *(Sinningia speciosa)*. See Chapter 7.

- Guzmania *(Guzmania lingulata)*. See Chapter 7.

- Holiday cactus *(Schlumbergera × buckleyi)*. See Chapter 6.

- Lady's slipper *(Paphiopedilum ×)*. See Chapter 7.

- Moth orchid *(Phalaenopsis ×)*. See Chapter 7.

- Orchid cactus *(× Epicactus)*. See Chapter 6.

- Silver vase *(Aechmea fasciata)*. See Chapter 7.

Chapter 6

In the Thick of Things: Cacti and Other Succulents

· ·

In This Chapter

▶ Distinguishing cacti from other succulents

▶ Meeting the special needs of these arid-climate plants

▶ Deciding whether your succulents need a dormant period in winter

▶ Perusing profiles of 21 interesting and easy-to-grow succulents

· ·

Many people consider succulents the easiest houseplants to grow. They really do seem to have a cast-iron constitution, as long as you meet their special but not-too-demanding needs. If you grow them under the right conditions, go easy on the watering, and, provide them with *lots* of light, they are, indeed, among the simplest plants to grow.

First, a Distinction: Not Every Succulent Is a Cactus

Succulents are plants that can store water and nutrients in visibly thickened stems or leaves. They developed this special capacity in order to cope with prolonged drought in their native climates. *Succulence,* as a survival pattern, evolved separately in many different plant families. The daisy and cucumber families, for example, both include members that are succulents. Some families, such as the crassula and cactus families, consist almost exclusively of succulents. Because succulents in different families have evolved to survive the same arid conditions, two different succulents that aren't at all related may require the same basic care.

Beware of impostors wearing dried flowers

Some plant sellers glue dried flowers onto cacti or poke live flowers into their stems — at best, an unfair commercial practice that permanently disfigures the plant; at worst, a technique that so severely damages the cactus that the plant simply dies a slow death. If you can't tell whether a cactus flower is real, touch it. Dried flowers are papery; real cactus flowers are soft.

Different plant species that evolve under similar conditions often end up looking very much alike. Some cacti from the arid regions of the western hemisphere and *euphorbias* from the arid regions of the eastern hemisphere look so similar that even experts have to look twice in order to tell them apart.

When most people see a plant with thick stems, spines, and no leaves they call it a *cactus,* period. But those in the know tend to be more precise in their descriptions. Any plant that has thick, water-storing stems or leaves is a *succulent,* whereas a cactus is just one type of succulent that belongs to a single family (the cactus family) of succulent plants. In short: All cacti are succulents, but not all succulents are cacti. If you're in doubt about whether a plant is a cactus, you can't go wrong by calling it a succulent.

All cacti have a number of features in common. For one, they're all *stem succulents;* that is, they store water in their stems rather than in their leaves (the majority, in fact, don't have any leaves or have rudimentary leaves that last for only a very short period of time). The vast majority of cacti also have *spines.* These similarities also apply to many other types of succulents, however. Cacti do have one common characteristic that makes them instantly distinguishable from all other succulents: All cacti have areoles.

Take a close look at a true cactus. Its spines, stems, and flowers all protrude from fuzzy, cushion-like organs called *areoles* (see Figure 6-1) and no other plant has them. Even plants that look incredibly cactus-like, such as certain euphorbias, do not have areoles. Checking to see whether the plant has areoles is the only real way to distinguish a cactus from other succulents.

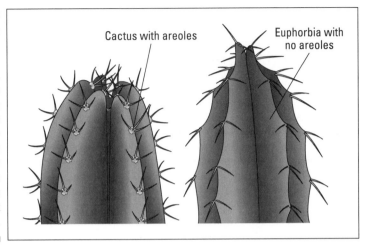

Figure 6-1:
Although otherwise very similar, the cactus section on the left has cushiony areoles while the euphorbia section on the right has none.

Cactus with areoles

Euphorbia with no areoles

Why Camels Have Humps and Succulents Have Tubers

Succulents are so closely identified with arid climates that many people assume all succulents live in deserts. In reality, though, you can find succulents in all sorts of environments, from true deserts to ocean beaches to tree tops. Each of these different environments is similar in one important way — they allow a succulent's roots to dry out thoroughly between periods of precipitation.

LEARNING THE LINGO

It is *not* a tumor! That's my crest

Some plants occasionally produce abnormally shaped stems that form a mass which more or less resembles the human brain. Plants with such growths are called *crested,* or *cristate,* plants. Other plants produce a multitude of growing points, known collectively as *monstrous growth,* which looks similar to a head of cauliflower. If you see these masses forming, the horticultural equivalent of cancerous tumors, in most plants you want to cut them off so that the plant can grow naturally.

Because leafless stems on succulents make such growths particularly visible, some plant owners actually welcome these anomalous growths on succulents and consider such plants collectibles. If you, too, like the appearance of cristate plants, be sure to prune off any *normal* stems that form. They grow much more quickly than the mutated stems and can quickly take over the entire plant.

Just remember to "drench and let *dry*" (with the emphasis on the dry part) and you're well on your way to providing succulents with the watering routine they need. Most plants dislike getting completely dry; succulents actually prefer it.

The vegetation in dry environments is not as lush as the vegetation in more-humid environments. This means that plants native to arid regions, such as succulents, rarely if ever receive protection against brilliant sunlight that overhanging shade tress and other foliage provide. Consequently, succulents had to evolve various ways of coping with the burning sun (ultraviolet rays are even more intense than usual in dry climates where cloud cover is sparse). Besides their thick leaves and stems, many succulents have developed one or more of the following characteristics (see Figure 6-2), all of which you can think of as the succulent's built-in "sun screen":

- *Bloom,* **a powdery or waxy whitish coating.** Bloom helps filter and reflect the sun, as well as reduce evaporation.

- **Thick "hair" or spines.** They help protect the plant from the sun while reducing evaporation. They also provide a multitude of surfaces where dew can condense at night, supplying extra water. Spines also help protect the plant from predators.

- **Fewer** *stomata* **(breathing pores) than other plants.** Open pores result in increased evaporation. Many succulents keep their stomata closed during the day (when hot air can steal moisture) and breathe only at night.

- *Tubers* **(swollen underground growths).** Many succulents also store water in their roots (you can think of them as underground thermoses).

- *Photosynthesis* **(energy conversion) via their stems.** Most plants carry out photosynthesis via their leaves, but succulents reduce the overall surface area exposed to the drying effect of the air by using only their stems for photosythesis.

- *Windows* **(translucent areas on their leaves).** Windows enable succulent plants to grow nearly underground with only their leaf tips exposed, which lets them stay cool and protects them from exposure to dry air.

- **Densely branching or low-growing profile.** Sticking close to the ground helps prevent evaporation.

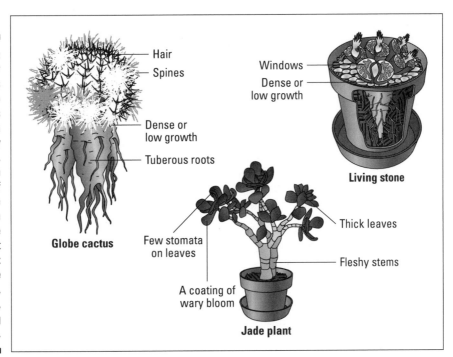

Figure 6-2:
A number of features help succulents survive in hot and dry climates. You can see some of those features in these three different succulents: the globe cactus, jade plant, and living stone.

Hair
Spines
Dense or low growth
Tuberous roots
Globe cactus

Windows
Dense or low growth
Living stone

Few stomata on leaves
A coating of wary bloom
Thick leaves
Fleshy stems
Jade plant

It's a jungle cactus up there

Not all cacti originated in arid climates. Several million years ago, a new branch evolved on the cactus family tree: the *jungle cactus*. These cacti learned to climb trees and grow as *epiphytes* (see Chapter 10 for more information about plants that live in trees, roots and all). As the jungle cacti evolved, most of them abandoned their sharp spines and thick, rounded stems and became trailing plants with thin, flattened branches. Epiphytes insist on the same good drainage as other cacti (little water accumulates on tree branches) but prefer a more humid atmosphere, warmer temperatures, and more frequent waterings. The holiday cactus (*Schlumbergera × buckleyi*) is a typical jungle cactus.

Are Succulents Really as Easy to Grow as They Say?

Are succulents as simple to grow as some people claim? It all depends on your growing conditions. The vast majority of succulents grow in nearly full sun in nature. Although they can tolerate somewhat less light indoors, if you can't supply at least bright light, you probably want to grow another type of plant. (See Chapter 8 to get an idea of how much light your home gets.)

Although succulents often go without water for months in the wild, they prefer more regular waterings when you grow them in pots. That's because succulents develop extensive root systems in the wild, capable of absorbing the slightest drop of water at considerable distances from the plant. Potted succulents, however, have restricted root systems and therefore can't draw on nearly the amount of water resources that wild succulents can.

The key to providing succulents with enough (but not too much) water is to water them thoroughly but then let the potting mix become dry to the touch before watering again. You may actually need to water them as often as any other type of plant during their growing season, but most succulents can go for at least several weeks without water during their rest period (see the nearby sidebar "After a long winter's nap, fabulous spring blossoms").

In a pinch, all succulents, even potted ones, can go for months without water (although they certainly don't look their best when that happens). Because they're the "camels" of the plant world, succulents make good choices for people who travel frequently.

You also can cut way back on fertilizer with succulents. Fertilize them lightly at most, using a complete fertilizer, and do it only during their growing season. Avoid nitrogen-rich fertilizers if possible: They produce rapid but weak growth. (See Chapter 11 for more information on fertilizers.)

Finally, don't worry about relative humidity if you grow only succulents: They can all tolerate dry air. Under very humid conditions, on the other hand, especially in a closed space with no air circulation, succulents may rot. *Never* grow succulents in a terrarium, for example.

After a long winter's nap, fabulous spring blossoms

Most succulents in nature go through at least a few months of hard drought each year and some, notably cacti, depend on this rest period (called *dormancy*) in order to bloom. Give them two or three months of colder conditions in winter, combined with reduced watering, and you may get stunning blooms the following spring or summer.

Exactly how cold or dry conditions must get for a succulent to go dormant depends on the specific plants you grow, but most succulents generally like a two-month rest period at about 50°F to 60°F (10°C to 15°C). Cacti want temperatures as low as 40°F to 50°F (4°C to 10°C) for three months. If temperatures remain below 50°F (10°C), don't even bother to water these plants during their dormancy. Just mist them occasionally to keep their stems from shriveling.

Cacti in culture (as opposed to cacti in nature) put up no objection to growing year-round, but they also rarely bloom without long periods of cold and drought. If you have no place in your house that is cool enough to invoke dormancy in your cactus, here are two ways to get them to bloom anyway:

✔ Put them outside for the summer and leave them there, even when nights are cool, and bring them in only if frost is forecast. In rainy climates, place them near a wall in the fall and lean an old window over them so that they receive plenty of sun but little precipitation. An autumn spent in cool, dry conditions often compensates for a lack of winter dormancy.

✔ Let them dry thoroughly and store them in a root cellar or unheated but frost-free basement or garage, the same as you do to get a gladiolus corm to bloom (see Chapter 7). As long as temperatures remain below 50°F (10°C) at all times, the plants stay fully dormant and don't need light. After three months, move them back into your home and begin watering again, but acclimatize them gradually over a two-week period to the strong light they normally prefer.

If you use either method, you can expect your cacti to bloom during the following spring or summer.

One other thing to keep in mind: Cacti do not bloom until they reach maturity. The maturation process can take only a year or so for some species, and more than 40 years for others. You do, however, have a surefire way to make sure that your cactus will bloom. Buy it already in flower. If you purchase a cactus that has no flowers, for all you know it may be years away from blooming. Give your flowering cactus the cool dormancy it needs and it will bloom year after year.

Profiles of Succulent Plants

The stark, architectural appearance of many succulents makes them interesting additions to your home decor, especially if your tastes lean to modern looks or Southwestern motifs. Keep in mind, however, that these supposedly easy-care plants are hard to maintain in any setting that does not receive a lot of sunlight. Like many other naturally slow-growing plants, cacti may look good for months under poor light, but after they consume the last of their energy reserves, they simply give up and die. You can still use succulents just about any place in your home, even under weak lighting, if you rotate them every two weeks between a sunny spot and their showcase spots.

In the following sections of this chapter, I list 21 cacti and succulents that you can grow with success. Many others besides these are available from most nurseries or florist shops.

See Appendix A for definitions of the terms that I use to describe each plant's requirements, propagation options, and care ratings. Most of the following succulents get a care rating of "easy," but remember: They're easy only if you furnish plenty of sunlight. If you don't, you can read that "easy" care rating as "very demanding" instead.

Bunny ears (Opuntia microdasys)

You can instantly recognize this true cactus by its flat beaver-tail-shaped pads that are heavily dotted with dense, rounded tufts of reddish, golden, or white areoles. It grows to 18 inches (45 centimeters) high or more by producing more pads on top of the existing ones. It also produces branches of pads, eventually taking on a tree-like appearance. Even mature bunny ears are reluctant to bloom indoors, but if they do, their large yellow flowers are spectacular.

Although the bunny ears cactus appears spineless, its areoles are actually covered in tiny spines, called *glochids,* that easily break off and penetrate the skin, prompting hours of itching and scratching. Therefore, handle this plant with care. If you do get glochids on your skin, rather than rub them, which only makes them penetrate even deeper, apply a piece of adhesive tape to the affected area and pull them off.

Requirements: Full sun to bright light, keep on the dry side, average humidity, normal to cold temperatures, tomato fertilizer, soilless or cactus mix

Propagation: Stem cuttings

Care Rating: Easy

Century plant (Agave americana)

Don't let the small size of the young plants of this noncactus succulent fool you. The century plant (see Figure 6-3) is an indoor giant, easily reaching 5 feet (150 centimeters) in diameter. Keep it pot-bound and you may manage to restrict its growth to half that. It forms a massive rosette of fleshy, gray-green, sharply toothed leaves, each ending in a needle-like spine (if you have young children in the home, I advise cutting the spines off for safety purposes). Most cultivars are beautifully striped in yellow or white.

Its common name comes from the fact that it was once thought to bloom only every 100 years. In fact, it can bloom after just 10 years or so — but then, only under ideal conditions. It may take 50 years or more in the average home! If yours does bloom, put it outside — the branching tree-like flower stalk can reach over 30 feet (9 meters) high. You should put your century plant outdoors in the summer anyway; it's an ideal indoor/outdoor plant. Unfortunately, all agaves die after blooming.

Figure 6-3:
Century
plant
*(Agave
americana).*

Note: Some people experience skin irritation when exposed to the century plant's sap.

Display: Floor, table

Requirements: Full sun to bright light, keep on the dry side, average humidity, normal to cold temperatures, tomato fertilizer, soilless or cactus mix

Propagation: Division, seed

Care Rating: Very easy

Cereus (Cereus peruvianus)

This tall, upright, columnar cactus has green to blue-green stems with distinct ribs marked with clusters of short brown spines arising from white cushiony areoles. When grown in bright light, it occasionally produces huge, sweet smelling, trumpet-shaped flowers that open only at night, followed by apple-like fruit. It can put up with low light for a year or more, but eventually rots if you don't place it in bright-light conditions. Several cristate or monstrous forms of this plant are available (see the sidebar "It is *not* a tumor! That's my crest" earlier in this chapter).

Display: Floor, table

Requirements: Full sun to bright light, tolerates low light for short periods, keep on the dry side, average humidity, normal to cool temperatures, tomato fertilizer, soilless or cactus mix

Propagation: Seed, stem cuttings

Care Rating: Very easy

Crown of thorns (Euphorbia milii)

You can't mistake this succulent for a cactus. Bright-green leaves cover its thick, gray, angular stems. They partially hide the numerous, inch-long (2.5-centimeter) spines that make repotting this plant such an effort. It grows relatively quickly for a succulent, forming a dense bush up to 4 feet (120 centimeters) tall, but you can easily keep it much shorter by pruning it. Clusters of flower heads composed of two thick, oval, red bracts and insignificant flowers appear at the ends of the stems.

The crown of thorns is one of the rare succulents capable of blooming year-round nonstop. To achieve this level of performance, keep this plant a bit moister than other succulents: If you let it dry out completely, it goes dormant and loses all its leaves and flowers. Besides the typical red-bracted crown of thorns, cultivars now have white, cream, lime-green, yellow, pink, and bicolor bracts. The sap is very irritating if it gets into the eyes or mouth, so watch where you put your fingers after working with a euphorbia.

Display: Floor, table

Requirements: Full sun to bright light, drench and let dry, average humidity, normal indoor temperatures, tomato fertilizer, soilless or cactus mix

Propagation: Stem cuttings

Care Rating: Easy

Donkey's tail (Sedum morganianum)

The donkey's tail is a succulent that forms long, trailing stems that hang straight down. They are covered with overlapping, blue-green, cylindrical leaves that fall off at the slightest touch. It blooms only rarely, with clusters of pink flowers at the tips of the stems. You can use any leaves that are knocked off to propagate the plant. This plant is so fragile that you should pot it up when it's young and then leave it completely alone except for watering. Some *cultivars* (cultivated varieties) have larger, longer leaves; others have shorter, thicker ones. The cultivars don't lose their leaves as readily as the main species, but all the same, I recommend against manipulating them any more than necessary.

Display: Hanging basket, table

Requirements: Full sun to bright light, keep on the dry side, average humidity, normal to cool temperatures, tomato fertilizer, soilless or cactus mix

Propagation: Leaf cuttings, stem cuttings

Care Rating: Easy (but fragile to the touch)

Echeveria (Echeveria elegans)

This succulent forms a short, dense, often stemless rosette up to 4 inches (10 centimeters) across. The rosette consists of fleshy, spoon-shaped, blue-gray leaves with translucent edges. Handle it as little as possible, because the leaves' bluish shading comes from a dusty powdering of waxy bloom that comes off when touched. Another reason to treat it with care is that the leaves break off easily. The echeveria readily produces pink stems with rosy pink and yellow flowers, notably in summer after a winter's rest. The flower stalk hooks downward as it forms, finally straightening out when the last flowers open. It produces offsets in abundance and a colony of smaller rosettes surround the main rosette. You can use any leaves that fall off to propagate the plant.

Display: Table

Requirements: Full sun to bright light, keep on the dry side, average humidity, normal to cool temperatures, tomato fertilizer, soilless or cactus mix

Propagation: Leaf cuttings, offshoots

Care Rating: Easy

Flaming Katy (Kalanchoe blossfeldiana)

Also known as *Christmas kalanchoe,* flaming Katy is one of the rare succulents grown strictly for its blooms. As the name suggests, the bloom normally appears in late December in the northern hemisphere. You can force it into bloom during any season simply by shortening the amount of daylight hours it gets. The plant is now commonly sold in flower year-round.

It forms a bushy growth of glossy, green, succulent leaves with scalloped edges. Each stem ends in a dense cluster of red, yellow, orange, pink, or white flowers that can last for months. Although growing this plant is easy enough, getting it to bloom a second time is quite challenging. I suggest treating it like a florist plant — toss it out after its first bloom or grow it thereafter just for its foliage. If you do want to get it to bloom, supply 14-hour nights for two months or until the flowers appear.

Display: Table

Requirements: Full sun to bright light, keep on the dry side, average humidity, normal temperatures, tomato fertilizer, soilless or cactus mix

Propagation: Seeds, stem cuttings

Care Rating: Fairly demanding

Golden ball cactus (Echinocactus grusonii)

The golden ball cactus, or *mother-in-law's cushion,* forms a single round globe that can reach enormous sizes — 4 feet (120 centimeters) or more in diameter (but only after many years). More often, though, you see the plant in sizes ranging from 4 to 12 inches (10 to 30 centimeters) in diameter. Hooked, yellow spines cover the plant's prominent ribs and thick, white, woolly hair tops it off. Only mature specimens bloom, producing yellow, cup-shaped flowers. This plant normally produces no offsets. Its reaction to poor conditions is so delayed that you may think that it's doing well, even in the shade, but the fact is that it doesn't grow at all without very bright light and eventually rots under low light.

Display: Floor, table

Requirements: Full sun to bright light, tolerates low light for short periods, keep on the dry side, average humidity, normal to cold temperatures, tomato fertilizer, soilless or cactus mix

Propagation: Seed

Care Rating: Very easy

Holiday cactus (Schlumbergera × buckleyi)

This cross between the winter-blooming Christmas cactus *(S. truncata)* and the autumn-blooming Thanksgiving cactus *(S. russelliana)* has inherited the best characteristics of both. Commercially, sellers force it to bloom in December in the northern hemisphere, but if you grow it on your own, you can expect it to bloom in the fall, and then again in midwinter. The holiday cactus is one of the rare so-called florist plants that actually improves with age! Newly purchased plants often lose many of their buds in transit. An established plant in the home, however, can produce literally hundreds of flowers over a long period.

Unlike most cacti, the holiday cactus is composed of arching chains of flattened, spineless, serrated, dark-green segments that many people mistake for leaves. The hanging flowers come in a wide range of colors, including red, purple, pink, orange, yellow, and white. To stimulate bloom, supply cool temperatures, long nights (14 hours or longer), and keep on the dry side in early autumn.

Display: Hanging basket, table

Requirements: Bright to medium light, tolerates low light for short periods, drench and let dry, average humidity, normal to cold temperatures, tomato fertilizer, soilless or cactus mix

Propagation: Cuttings

Care Rating: Easy

Jade plant (Crassula argentea)

This upright, tree-like succulent forms thick green stems that eventually turn brown and fleshy, and plump, spoon-shaped, jade-green leaves that become crimson-edged under exposure to full sun. It has several variegated cultivars. It can reach up to 4 feet (120 centimeters) in height and spread. Mature plants may bloom in winter, producing clusters of white to pink star-shaped flowers. Although the jade plant can tolerate relatively low light levels, its growth will be weak and will requires staking. Under full sun, however, it stands rigidly upright. To show off its naturally oriental appearance, grow it in a bonsai pot. You can use any leaves that get knocked off for propagation.

Display: Table, floor

Requirements: Full sun to bright light, tolerates low light, keep on the dry side, average humidity, normal to cool temperatures, tomato fertilizer, soilless or cactus mix

Propagation: Leaf cuttings, stem cuttings

Care Rating: Very easy

Living stone (Lithops)

Lithops is actually only one genus (albeit the best-known one) among the many living stones of southern Africa. These curious plants mimic the rocks among which they grow, taking on a fantastic range of colors, from grayish-green to solid gray, brown, red, or even purple, with each rounded or flattened leaf tip attractively marbled in a second shade. They produce a solitary, daisy-like flower in white, pink, yellow, or magenta in summer or early autumn. A stemless plant, lithops actually consists of two thick leaves pressed together. In the wild, they grow practically underground with only the leaf tips showing. Light penetrates the plant through translucent windows at the leaves' extremities.

Living stones tend to rot if you bury the leaves as deep as they grow in the wild, so plant them with only the base of the leaves underground. Because this plant is highly susceptible to rot, water it with the utmost care. Water only from spring until flowering; do not water in autumn and winter. The old leaves shrink as they supply all the moisture the new leaves need, and any excess water leads to rot. Also avoid fertilizing because it creates bloated, distorted growth.

Display: Table

Requirements: Full sun to bright light, keep on the dry side, average humidity, normal to cool temperatures, fertilizer not necessary, soilless or cactus mix

Propagation: Division, seed

Care Rating: Demanding

Madagascar palm (Pachypodium lamerei)

In its dormant phase, people often confuse this upright, tree-like succulent with a cactus because of the long, sharp spines that cover its thick, gray-green stems. You know that it isn't a cactus, of course, because it doesn't have areoles. Most of the time, however, it grows long, thin, shiny green leaves in abundance — a very uncactus-like characteristic. In many homes, it never goes entirely dormant and has leaves all year long. It can easily reach 7 feet (3 meters) or more in height, but you can prune it back, too. Specimens taller than 4 feet (120 centimeters) may produce star-shaped white flowers. It rarely produces offsets or branches, unless you prune it.

Display: Table, floor

Requirements: Full sun to bright light, tolerates low light for short periods, keep on the dry side, average humidity, normal to cool temperatures, tomato fertilizer, soilless or cactus mix

Propagation: Seed

Care Rating: Easy

Medicine plant (Aloe barbadensis)

This succulent is best known for the healing capacities of its sap, which people use to treat everything from burns to hair loss to constipation. It also makes an attractive houseplant, with its fleshy, gray-green, upward-curving foot-long (30-centimeter) leaves. The leaves are edged with soft "teeth" and marked by pale splotches. Young plants generally assume a fan-like shape, but adult plants form a rosette. Adult plants may also produce a tall, up-right, branching stalk of tubular yellow flowers.

To extract an aloe leaf's sap, peal off the bitter outer skin (the entire inner leaf is gelatinous). You can then apply the clear gel to your skin.

Display: Table, floor

Requirements: Bright to medium light, tolerates low light for short periods, keep on the dry side, average humidity, normal indoor temperatures, tomato fertilizer, soilless or cactus mix

Propagation: Division

Care Rating: Easy

Mistletoe cactus (Rhipsalis baccifera)

This spineless cactus originated in the jungle, rather than the desert, growing as an epiphyte in deep forests — hence, its very uncactus-like appearance. It produces long, thin, cylindrical stems that hang almost straight down (imagine green spaghetti). As the plant gets older, the stems increase in number and length until they form a thick curtain up to 7 feet (2 meters) long. The tiny, greenish-white, star-shaped flowers aren't very noticable, but translucent white berries resembling those on mistletoe plants show up later. The berries can remain on the mistletoe cactus for more than a year and add considerably to its attractiveness. The mistletoe cactus is one of the best cacti for people who aren't able to provide their plants with full sun.

Display: Hanging basket

Requirements: Bright to medium light, tolerates low light for short periods, drench and let dry, average humidity, normal to cool temperatures, tomato fertilizer, soilless or cactus mix

Propagation: Seed, stem cuttings

Care Rating: Very easy

Old man cactus (Cephalocereus senilis)

The old man cactus is a very slow-growing, upright, columnar cactus so densely covered in soft white hair that the stem is scarcely visible. Although it looks cuddly enough to hug, you'd do best to leave it alone — the hairs conceal dagger-sharp needles that are far from being furry to the touch. Although it can eventually reach ceiling height, it remains less than 18 inches (45 centimeters) tall during its first decade. It never blooms indoors.

Display: Floor, table

Requirements: Full sun to bright light, keep on the dry side, average humidity, cool to cold temperatures, tomato fertilizer, soilless or cactus mix

Propagation: Seed, stem cuttings

Care Rating: Easy

Orchid cactus (× *Epicactus*)

Often still sold under the name *Epiphyllum,* most orchid cacti (see Figure 6-4) are actually complex hybrids resulting from crosses between many large-flowered species of jungle cactus. These sizable, ungainly plants form long, irregular, notched stems that are equally likely to grow up, out, or down, and can reach 3 feet (90 centimeters) or more in length. Few people would grow them were it not for their flowers. The trumpet-shaped blooms are spectacular, as its common name suggests, and often measure 6 inches (15 centimeters) or more in diameter. The blooms come in a vast range of colors, including shades of red, pink, white, orange, yellow, mauve, and purple. The white-flowered varieties usually open only at night and emit an intense fragrance. Flowers normally appear in spring after a cool, dry winter.

Figure 6-4:
Orchid
cactus
(× *Epicatus).*

Display: Hanging basket

Requirements: Bright to medium light, drench and let dry, average humidity, normal to cool temperatures, tomato fertilizer, soilless or cactus mix

Propagation: Seed, stem cuttings

Care Rating: Fairly demanding

Pony tail palm (Beaucarnea recurvata)

People often mistake this tree-like plant for a palm, but actually it is more closely related to the yucca (see "Spineless yucca" later in the chapter). It produces a woody trunk with a fleshy, swollen base (giving it the common names *bottle palm* and *elephant's foot*) and a thick mop of long, strap-like leaves that twist and turn as they cascade all around the plant like a horse's tail. Although it can eventually reach ceiling height, this plant is so phenomenally slow growing that you should buy one already at the size you want. It may take years to grow only a few inches. This plant also goes by the botanical name *Nolina recurvata*.

Display: Floor, table

Requirements: Full sun to bright light, tolerates low light, keep on the dry side, average humidity, cool temperatures, tomato fertilizer, soilless or cactus mix

Propagation: Seed, stem cuttings

Care Rating: Very easy

Red ball cactus (Gymnocalycium mihanovichii friedrichii 'Rubra')

The popular red ball cactus is literally two plants in one. The red, ball-shaped part at the top is *Gymnocalycium mihanovichii friedrichii* 'Rubra,' a mutant, red-bodied cactus. It contains none of the green pigmentation that normally allows plants to absorb energy, so sellers always *graft* it onto an all-green cactus that can feed it. The grafting procedure basically involves cutting off the top of a green cactus and splicing a red offset onto the wound. These grafts rarely last more than a year or so. The green cactus usually chosen as a rootstock, *Hylocereus undatus,* is highly subject to rot, so don't expect a long lifespan out of your red ball cactus. It occasionally produces pink flowers, but only under optimum conditions. You can also buy orange, yellow, and multicolored versions of the red ball cactus.

Display: Table

Requirements: Full sun to bright light, keep on the dry side, average humidity, normal to cool temperatures, tomato fertilizer, soilless or cactus mix

Propagation: Grafting

Care Rating: Easy

Snake plant (Sansevieria trifasciata)

This popular succulent is probably the easiest houseplant to grow of all. About the only way you can kill it is to leave it outdoors in freezing weather or blast it in a microwave oven at full power. It produces tall, thick, pointed leaves up to 18 inches (45 centimeters) long that are heavily marbled in dark and light green. Many cultivars feature yellow or white striping. Although almost legendary for its capacity to put up with extremely low light, it actually barely grows at all under such conditions and really prefers bright light or full sun.

Under optimum conditions, it produces a spike of cream-colored flowers that emit a delicious perfume — although they emit the perfume only at night. You have to reproduce the variegated cultivars by division; leaf cuttings result in all-green plants. You also can find "bird's nest" versions of this plant: Their shortened, broadened leaves form a hollow rosette much like a nest.

Display: Floor, table

Requirements: Full sun to low light, keep on the dry side, average humidity, normal temperatures, tomato fertilizer, soilless or cactus mix

Propagation: Division, leaf cuttings

Care Rating: Very easy

Snowball cactus (Mammillaria bocasana)

A wide variety of mammillarias exists, and the snowball cactus is one of the most popular. Like its cousins, it is a low-growing, clustering cactus that forms many tiny, globular stems packed closely together in a dense clump. The stems are blue-green, but so densely covered in silky white hairs you scarcely notice their color. The hairs also hide sharp, yellow spines, so pay close attention when you handle it. It blooms abundantly from an early age, producing small yellow flowers about a half-inch (two centimeters) across in a circle near the top of the plant. After the flowers fade, bright red berries often take their place. A cool to cold winter dormancy is required to ensure blooming.

Display: Table

Requirements: Full sun to bright light, keep on the dry side, average humidity, cool to cold temperatures, tomato fertilizer, soilless or cactus mix

Propagation: Cuttings, division, seed

Care Rating: Easy

Spineless yucca (Yucca elephantipes)

Stores and nurseries sell this succulent in its juvenile form — a stemless, ground-hugging rosette — and in its adult form — a tall, tree-like plant with a thick woody trunk, often with several rosettes at the top. On older spineless yuccas, the base of the trunk swells up, much like that of its cousin, the pony tail palm. The arching leaves are 2 to 4 feet long (60 to 120 centimeters), sword-shaped, grass-green in color, and sometimes yellow striped.

The name "spineless yucca" derives from its comparison to its spiny brethren (other yuccas have dangerous thorns). The leaf tip of the *Yucca elephantipes* does have a soft spine and the leaf edges have tiny but sharp teeth. If possible, put this plant outside for the summer. Letting it live outdoors may encourage it to bloom. It can produce tall spikes of white, bell-shaped flowers.

Display: Floor, table

Requirements: Full sun to bright light, tolerates low light, keep on the dry side, average humidity, normal to cool temperatures, tomato fertilizer, soilless or cactus mix

Propagation: Stem cuttings

Care Rating: Very easy

Chapter 7

A Touch of the Exotic: Specialty Plants

- -

In This Chapter

▶ Discovering some secrets behind growing orchids

▶ Getting introduced to bromeliads and their aerial lifestyle

▶ Growing indoor plants from both hardy and tender bulbs

▶ Trying your hand at the art of bonsai

- -

*I*f you've perused the other three chapters in this part of the book, you know that most houseplants fall into one of the Big Three categories — foliage plants, flowering plants, and succulents. Within those categories are four houseplant subgroups — orchids, bromeliads, flowering bulbs, and bonsais — that merit special attention because of their beauty, charm, or sheer mystique. Many plant enthusiasts consider them the gems of the houseplant world deserving of collector's status.

With a little extra care, anyone can grow the collectible plants in these four groups. So, if you one day find yourself under the spell of the exotic orchid, the elegant amaryllis, or the mysterious bonsai, just consider yourself to be in good company. The follow sections tell you how to grow these specialty plants for your own enjoyment.

Growing Orchids

The orchid family is the largest in the vegetable kingdom (of which houseplants are a part), with well over 20,000 species in some 750 *genera* (a group of closely related species) and at least an equal number of hybrids. Although people tend to think of orchids as tropical plants, you can find orchids in just about every habitat, from the Arctic region to the jungle.

Picking apart an orchid

The most obvious similarity between the different types of orchids is in the way the flower is constructed (see Figure 7-1). Orchids generally have three *sepals* (outer flower parts) and three *petals.* One of the petals is called a *lip.* You can easily identify the lip because it's usually a different color and larger than the other petals.

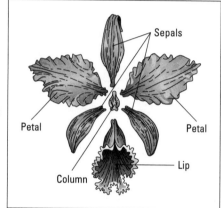

Figure 7-1:
A typical orchid flower and its parts.

Closer inspection reveals that an orchid's male and female reproductive organs are combined into a single organ, called a *column.* Also, unlike most plants, the orchid's pollen is stuck together in tight clusters, called *pollinia.*

One last characteristic of orchids is less obvious to the eye, but of vital importance. Orchids produce extremely small seeds (no bigger than dust particles) that lack any kind of stored energy. Furthermore, orchids typically can germinate in the wild only in the presence of a special kind of fungi. That means orchid seeds may travel widely but germinate only under very specific conditions. As a result, reproducing orchids from seeds is enormously difficult and is usually done only in laboratories.

Yes, orchids do grow on trees

Most orchids that people grow indoors are *epiphytes* (plants that grow on trees), although a few are *terrestrial* (plants that grow in soil). The orchid's aerial lifestyle has lead it to develop a unique system of stems and roots. Many orchids, for example, have *pseudobulbs* (see the next section, "Terminology time: Sympodial versus monopodial orchids") that help them store water between periods of rain. Also, most orchid roots are thick and absorb water rapidly. Orchids are so well-adapted to their aerial origins that when you plant them in a pot, they often refuse to stay within the potting mix and grow out into the air around them.

Terminology time: Sympodial versus monopodial orchids

Orchids grow in two main ways: as sympodial or monopodial plants.

Sympodial orchids (see Figure 7-2) produce a creeping *rhizome* (horizontal stem at the base of the plant) from which arises multiple *pseudobulbs* (bulb-like appendages). Each rhizome produces a new pseudobulb at each surge of growth, often only once a year but possibly more. After a pseudobulb flowers (and it flowers only once), it remains on the plant for several years, contributing its energy reserves to the plant's growth. Each plant, therefore, has a mixture of new, recently mature, and old pseudobulbs (the latter are called *backbulbs*) at any one time.

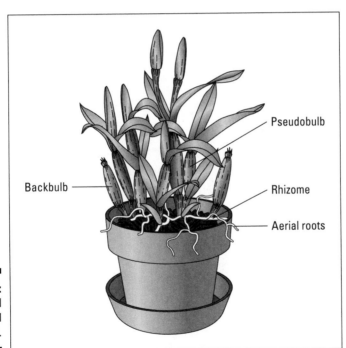

Figure 7-2:
A typical sympodial orchid.

To multiply sympodial orchids, you cut the clumps into two or more parts, each with at least three leafy pseudobulbs, and then repot them. Inserting a short stake into the potting mix helps to support the newly planted clumps. Another way to hold these plants in place is to use wire pot clips that orchid specialists sell. You can also cut off any backbulbs that are still green and pot them up on their own. They grow more slowly, but they do eventually sprout new growth.

Monopodial orchids (see Figure 7-3) grow upward from a single stem. Over time, the stem produces new leaves and flowers near its top, while older leaves and flowers drop off from its base. The same stem, therefore, can bloom repeatedly over many years.

You can propagate monopodial orchids in a couple of ways. One way is to take cuttings of the top growth when the plant becomes too tall (the old plant will sprout a new top). The other method involves removing the offsets that the plant occasionally produces from its base, along its stem, or sometimes from the flower stalk. (These offsets are called *keikis.*) Treat the cut top of the plant as you do any cutting (see Chapter 16 for more cuttings). Keikis usually already have a few roots when they are separated, so you can pot them up and treat them as adult plants.

Scientists can reproduce both sympodial and monopodial orchids in the laboratory through *meristem culture* (see Chapter 16 for more on that) or from seeds.

Not all orchids for sale in the average nursery grow well under normal home conditions, and orchids don't come cheap. Buying an orchid plant on a whim more often than not is little more than a way of uselessly parting with your money. If you're a novice, always ask an expert for advice. I list some addresses of orchid experts in Appendix B.

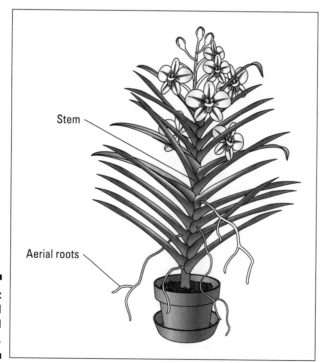

Stem

Aerial roots

Figure 7-3:
A typical
monopodial
orchid.

Slab culture: Imitating the orchid's natural habitat

You don't have to grow orchids in pots. In nature, most orchids grow on tree trunks with their roots fully exposed. You can imitate their natural setting by growing them on a slab of wood, cork, bark, or tree fern. Simply press a handful of moist sphagnum moss onto the slab and then set a recently divided orchid on it, attaching it solidly with wire, twine, or staples. A piece of old stocking makes for soft and unobtrusive tie material. Put the newly "potted" plant in a humid, lightly shaded spot for a few weeks, then return it to its normal spot. Most slabs last several years, but don't try for extra life by using "treated" wood. Most types of wood preservative are unfriendly to plant roots.

You can attach slabs to a wall or any upright surface. Because many epiphytes naturally grow on tree trunks, with their leaves arching outward, growing them on a slab gives them a natural appearance. The orchid often clasps onto the slab with its own aerial roots after a few months. You can then remove the wires or staples that hold it in place.

Because watering plants on slabs is difficult to do without getting your floor all wet, plunge them weekly into a bucket of tepid water, adding fertilizer at one-eighth the regular rate during the growing season. Let the plant soak for 15 minutes or so and then place it in the sink to drip until it dries out enough to hang back on its support. You also can water orchids on slabs by spraying them regularly and thoroughly.

Basic care and feeding of orchids

Orchids are really no more difficult to grow than any other flowering plant. They *do,* however, grow considerably slower. Additionally, reproducing them is relatively difficult, which accounts for their high price.

The needs of orchids do not significantly differ from the needs of other houseplants. Granted, their light, temperature, and fertilizer needs do vary according to the type of plant, but not all that much. Of course, they all prefer high relative humidity (at least 50 percent) and good air circulation (just like many other indoor plants). They do require a special potting mix (see Chapter 13), but that's the main difference between orchids and other plants. Finally, although you can get special containers for orchid *culture* (with extra holes for better aeration), ordinary clay and plastic pots generally are perfectly suitable.

Orchid experts tend to get into a tizzy over which pots are best for orchids, but here's a simple answer: Use clay pots if you have a humid atmosphere, plastic ones if your air is dry (less than 50 percent relative humidity).

Orchid profiles

Considering that you can choose from some 40,000-plus orchids, you should have no trouble finding one to suit your home's growing conditions. The following profiles are just a few examples of the kinds of orchids that you can grow in the average home.

If you're wondering about specifics on the care requirements, care ratings, and propagation options listed with each plant, turn to Appendix A where I explain them in more depth.

Cattleya (Cattleya)

Over the years, the term *Cattleya* has come to refer to the vast number of hybrids among the genus *Cattleya* and their other close relatives. It includes a wide range of orchids, from the tiny miniatures to the huge, ruffled corsage orchids of yesteryear. Cattleyas are sympodial and have distinct pseudobulbs, some rounded or spindle-shaped, others barely more than thickened stems. Each pseudobulb produces only one or two thick leaves but a large number of aerial roots.

Minus their blooms, cattleyas certainly aren't going to win any beauty prizes, but their flowers are spectacular and come in a wide variety of colors and color combinations, as well as a wide range of sizes. Most prefer a six-week period of drier conditions after flowering. Repot them every three to four years just after their rest period.

Display: Table, slab

Requirements: Bright light (a few require full sun), drench and let dry, high to moderate humidity, normal to cool temperatures, good air circulation, flowering plant fertilizer, orchid mix

Propagation: Division

Care Rating: Fairly demanding

Lady's slipper (Paphiopedilum)

Paphiopedilum is the only genus of terrestrial orchid commonly grown indoors, but it still prefers an orchid mix over ordinary soilless mix. Its growth pattern is sympodial but it lacks pseudobulbs. Each section forms a fan of strap-like, pointed leaves and produces a single stem, about 12 to 18 inches (30 to 45 centimeters) tall, that bears one or several large flowers. The waxy-textured blooms have a pouch-like lip, often in a color in contrast to the rest of the flower. Although its color range is vast, earthy colors tend to predominate. Each flower lasts up to 12 weeks. Repot every two to three years after the last flower fades. Paphiopedilums that have dark-green leaves prefer cool temperatures; those that have mottled leaves prefer normal indoor temperatures.

Display: Table

Requirements: Bright to medium light, drench and let dry, high to moderate humidity, normal to cool temperatures, flowering plant fertilizer, orchid mix

Propagation: Division

Care Rating: Fairly demanding

Moth orchid (Phalaenopsis)

The moth orchid is so well adapted to the average home that plant people often call it the beginner's orchid. Although monopodial, its stem is so short that you can hardly see it. It produces wide, leathery leaves and long, gray, aerial roots. The arching flower stalk produces up to 30 large, flat flowers in white, pink, red, purple, and yellow, often with a contrasting lip and veins. Each flower lasts about one month. After blooming, prune back the flower stalk to just below the lowest bloom; sometimes this encourages the plant to bloom a second time. This orchid has no significant rest period, but cooler temperatures for a few weeks in autumn can help stimulate bloom.

Display: Table, slab

Requirements: Bright to medium light, drench and let dry, high to moderate humidity, normal indoor temperatures, good air circulation, flowering plant fertilizer, orchid mix

Propagation: Keikis

Care Rating: Easy

Growing Bromeliads

Bromeliads are stemless, rosette-forming plants that people often grow as much for their attractive foliage as for their beautiful flowers. Most are epiphytes, although several terrestrial bromeliads are also popular.

They usually have short-lived flowers surrounded by colorful *bracts* (leaf-like appendages) that often last several months. Most bromeliads have upright, arching, or hanging flower stalks in a wide range of colors. Other bromeliads' flowers aren't as colorful. Often, the center of these bromeliads' rosettes, and sometimes even the entire plant, turns various brilliant shades at flowering time — red, orange, or yellow — to attract pollinators to their less-colorful flowers.

The downside of their long-lasting *inflorescence* (budding or flowering) is that bromeliads flower only once, then die. Most bromeliads, however, produce numerous offsets before they go. The offsets appear at the plant's base, among the lower leaves, or on its *stolons* (creeping stems) some distance from the mother plant.

Bromeliads come in three basic flavors:

- **Terrestrial:** These bromeliads have normal root systems and derive most of their moisture and nutrients from the soil. The center of terrestrial rosettes is often recessed, but it is not designed to hold water. Water them like any other houseplant. They usually have thick, spiny leaves that help protect them from predators.

- **Tank:** These bromeliads are mostly epiphytes, although a few are terrestrial. Their leaves are broad, sometimes spiny and sometimes smooth, and they form a central cup, or *tank,* that holds water. In the wild, the plant gets most of its moisture and nutrients from this cup. It collects a brownish liquid rich in nutrients derived from dead leaves and animal waste mixed with rainwater. Their roots serve mainly as anchors, attaching the plant to its host. When you grow tank bromeliads in pots, though, they usually develop normal root systems capable of absorbing water and nutrients.

- **Atmospheric:** These bromeliads form a small but highly successful group, all belonging to the genus *Tillandsia.* Essentially tree or rock dwellers, they require only modest supports on which to grow. Many go so far as to use telephone wires as a home. These plants have no central cup, but their thick, spineless, green to gray leaves absorb water and nutrients. In fact, the leaves of some atmospheric species absorb water so efficiently that the plants can survive on dew alone. Their roots often lose the capability to absorb water and nutrients and serve strictly as anchors. Green-leafed species can adapt to growing in pots and soon develop water-absorbing roots, but most of the gray-leafed varieties will rot in potting soil — you must grow them on bark or slabs.

Why, unlike the rest of us, bromeliads like rotten apples

Bromeliads normally bloom at maturity with no extra help on anyone's part. Depending on the species, it can take anywhere from nine months to ten years for a *pup* (the popular name for a bromeliad baby) to reach blooming size; however, two or three years is about average. If your bromeliad appears to be mature but shows no signs of blooming, put it in a plastic bag overnight with a rotting apple. Mature apples give off ethylene gas, a product that stimulates bloom. In this case, one rotten apple doesn't spoil a bunch of anything.

Making your own bromeliad tree

Much as many people like to grow orchids on slabs, owners often grow bromeliads on indoor "trees." Simply fix a solid branch in a large pot filled with plaster of paris or hold the branch upright by nailing it to a piece of wood. Attach bromeliad pups to the "trunk" by wrapping their base in sphagnum moss and holding them in place with wire or twine. Mist regularly to keep the moss moist. The plants soon form aerial roots and attach themselves to their support.

General care and feeding of bromeliads

Like orchids, bromeliads have an exotic appearance but their *culture* (growing enviroment) actually is quite similar to other houseplants, with the following few exceptions:

- ✔ Keep the cups of tank bromeliads filled with water. To prevent stains, avoid hard water or solutions that contain chemical fertilizers. Rainwater is a good alternative, and liquid seaweed fertilizer (see Chapter 11) makes a good nonstaining fertilizer.

- ✔ Empty out bromeliad cups once a month to prevent algae buildup. The cup develops quite a "stew" in nature, but unless you're a staunch purist, you probably don't want to harbor the stink and mess that it creates.

- ✔ To water atmospheric bromeliads, plunge them into a solution of water and nutrients once a week or mist them daily. Avoid hard water and chemical fertilizers.

- ✔ To multiply bromeliads, cut off their pups (as close as possible to their point of origin) when they reach one-third the size of the mother plant. If the pup has a root system, pot it up and treat it as an adult. If not, treat it as a cutting (see Chapter 16). When you remove all of a mother's pups, the plant usually produces more pups.

- ✔ Finally, like many other epiphytes, epiphytic bromeliads prefer good air circulation (see Chapter 10). Putting them outside for the summer often does wonders for their growth. If you grow them on slabs, simply attach them to a partly shaded wall or a tree trunk for the summer. If summer humidity is low and rains are rare, hose the plants down weekly.

Bromeliad profiles

In the following sections, I list a few examples of bromeliads that you can grow in the average home.

Air plant (Tillandsia ionantha)

Air plants are the most commonly available atmospheric bromeliads. A small, grass-like plant, its stiff, arching, silvery gray leaves rarely grow longer than 2 inches (5 centimeters). The entire plant turns a vivid rosy red at flowering time. The tubular, purple flowers rise directly from the center of the rosette. You must grow it on a slab, a bromeliad tree, or in orchid mix because it does not produce terrestrial roots and may rot in moist soil. Sellers often glue air plants onto statues or shells. Theoretically, they can grow on just about any object that doesn't move. Pups appear shortly after the plant blooms.

Display: Table, slab

Requirements: Bright to medium light, drench and let dry or spray, high to moderate humidity, normal indoor temperatures, good air circulation, flowering plant fertilizer, orchid mix

Propagation: Division, seed

Care Rating: Easy

Earth star (Cryptanthus bivittatus)

One of the terrestrial bromeliads, the earth star forms a ground-hugging, flat rosette of tough, pointed, rigid leaves with prickly edges. The species has greenish-brown leaves with lengthwise pinkish stripes. You also can find highly variegated *cultivars* (cultivated varieties) that are mostly a bright, shocking pink with only a hint of greenish-brown color. Unlike most bromeliads, the earth star doesn't change color at flowering time and doesn't have colored bracts. The flowers, which grow directly from the center of the plant, are small, white, and not very noticeable. Pups appear at blooming time.

Display: Table, terrarium

Requirements: Bright to medium light, drench and let dry or spray, high to moderate humidity, normal indoor temperatures, flowering plant fertilizer, orchid mix

Propagation: Division, seed

Care Rating: Easy

Flaming sword (Vriesea splendens)

PHOTO OP

The flaming sword (see Figure 7-4) forms a rosette of blue-green leaves with smooth edges with brown banding measuring about 2 feet (60 centimeters) across. The rosette has a distinct tank at its center. At maturity, after about two to three years' growth, a sword-shaped, bright-red flower stalk arises from the cup. When it reaches full height, it produces short-lived, yellow flowers from either side of the stalk for well over a month.

After the plant blooms, it usually produces only a single pup near its center. You can leave the pup on the plant (the mother then gradually fades away as the pup takes her place) or carefully cut it out and root it like a cutting. Cutting out the pups often pushes the mother plant to produce a few more pups.

Display: Table, slab

Requirements: Bright to medium light, drench and let dry or spray, keep the tank full of water, high to moderate humidity, normal indoor temperatures, good air circulation, flowering plant fertilizer, orchid mix

Propagation: Division, seed

Care Rating: Easy

Figure 7-4:
Flaming
sword
*(Vriesea
splendens).*

Guzmania (Guzmania lingulata)

This bromeliad produces a rosette of smooth, shiny, spineless, bright-green leaves with a deep tank. Different clones range from less than 1 foot to more than 3 feet (30 to 90 centimeters) across. Keep its tank filled with water. Around 18 months to 2 years after you separate the pup from the mother plant, the pup produces a long-lived, funnel-shaped flower stalk that consists of bright red bracts and short-lived, white flowers. Cultivars with yellow, pink, orange, and purple flower stalks are also available.

Display: Table, slab

Requirements: Bright to medium light, drench and let dry or spray, keep the tank full of water, high to moderate humidity, normal indoor temperatures, good air circulation, flowering plant fertilizer, orchid mix

Propagation: Division, seed

Care Rating: Easy

Silver vase (Aechmea fasciata)

This popular florist plant is usually sold in bloom. It forms a vase-like rosette of spiny, leathery, gray-green leaves with numerous silver bands about 2 feet (60 centimeters) high and 2 to 3 feet (60 to 90 centimeters) across. Some cultivars are almost entirely silver; others are variegated with cream-colored stripes. When the plant is mature, at about 3 to 4 years old, it produces a long-lived, cup-shaped flower stalk composed of spiny, bright-pink bracts and short-lived blue flowers that eventually turn bright red.

A blooming aechmea doesn't need special light conditions to stay in top shape for up to six months. Getting a silver vase pup to bloom, however, requires very bright light, even full sun. If the pup produces long, narrow, dark-green leaves instead of broad silvery ones, you know that you aren't providing it with enough light to bloom.

Display: Table, slab

Requirements: Full sun to bright light, drench and let dry or spray, keep the tank full of water, high to moderate humidity, normal indoor temperatures, good air circulation, flowering plant fertilizer, orchid mix

Propagation: Division, seed

Care Rating: Fairly demanding

Growing Plants from Bulbs

Many plants that come from climates where conditions change radically throughout the year adapt by developing an underground nutrient storage system. This system can take many forms and may have many names (bulb, corm, tuber, tuberous root, rhizome, and so on), but, to simplify matters, gardeners generally call this kind of setup a *bulb* — and so do I in this chapter.

Permanent versus temporary bulbs

Most bulbs are permanent, or at least maintain themselves from year to year by producing offsets. You can maintain this kind of bulbous plant, examples of which are the amaryllis and the florist's gloxinia (which I profile in this chapter), indefinitely as a permanent indoor plant.

Some bulbous plants, on the other hand, are temporary indoor residents referred to as *hardy bulbs*. They are *forced* into bloom for winter and spring color (see the following section for techniques to force bulbs to bloom). Growing them indoors in constant warm temperature wears bulbs out. Consequently, owners typically grow hardy bulbs indoors only for one season, then plant them back out in the garden or toss them into the compost after they finish blooming.

Most hardy bulbs perform poorly in tropical or subtropical climates, both indoors and out. Growing them on your own is difficult, so buy them in bloom — and if your climate is warm all year, don't even think of trying to plant them outside. Consider them as temporary plants and compost them after they bloom.

Forcing temporary hardy bulbs

You deploy the same basic procedures to force all hardy bulbs:

- ✔ Choose solid, unblemished bulbs. Spend a little more, if necessary, for larger sizes — they generate better results. Most bulbs for winter forcing arrive on the market in early autumn.

- ✔ Pot up the bulbs (see Chapter 13 for more on potting up) any time from early autumn to early winter. Early plantings result in midwinter blooms; later ones, spring flowers. Use ordinary soilless mix, placing the flat side down and leaving the tip exposed. Squeeze as many bulbs into the pot as it can hold.

✔ Water well and store in a cold (40°F to 50°F; 4°C to 10°C) and dark spot for 14 to 17 weeks. Good spots for storing bulbs include an outdoor trench covered in mulch or dead leaves, a root cellar, a refrigerator, or an unheated, frost-free (but cold) garage.

✔ Check the pots every two weeks and water as necessary to keep the soil evenly moist.

✔ When the pot is full of roots and distinct sprouts appear at the bulbs' tips, the bulbs are ready to force. Either proceed without delay or stagger the forcing, bringing out a pot every two weeks to prolong the flowering period.

✔ To force bulbs, remove them from cold storage and expose them to bright light but cool temperatures (about 55°F to 65°F; 13°C to 18°C). If you force bulbs at temperatures any higher than that, you may need to stake them.

✔ When the buds start to color up, usually in about two weeks, move the pots to a sunny window — and enjoy the show! If you can put the plants in a cool spot at night (less than 60°F; 16°C), the flowers can stay in top shape longer.

✔ If you live in a temperate or cold climate, plant them outside when the weather warms up enough. Do not try to force them a second time.

✔ If you live in a tropical or subtropical climate, planting hardy bulbs outdoors is pointless because they require a cold winter to thrive. Just compost them after their bloom ends.

You also can force bulbs without growing mix. Just pot them in a clear container using decorative stones to replace the soil. You also can use a specially designed hyacinth vase. Add water to the container until it reaches the base of the bulbs, then top it off regularly. Hyacinths and paperwhite narcissuses are ideal choices for soilless forcing.

For faster forcing times at normal home temperatures, use "prepared" hyacinths or tender narcissuses, such as the 'Paperwhite' and 'Grand Soleil D'Or' varieties. Just pot them following the instructions I just listed and place them in a dark cupboard at about 65°F (18°C) until the bulbs begin to sprout. The bulbs bloom in as little at five to eight weeks.

Finally, if you want to enjoy a floral display right now, you can also buy bulbs already forced and ready to bloom.

Popular temporary indoor bulbs

If you follow the instructions I provided in the previous section of this chapter, you can grow just about any temporary hardy bulbs. The following are some additional care and growing guidelines for a few of the most popular varieties.

Crocus (Crocus)

Crocuses need at least 14 (and preferably 15 to 16) weeks of cold storage. They are particularly susceptible to warm temperatures after you take them out of cold storage. If you can't provide temperatures below 60°F (16°C), I recommend that you choose a different kind of bulb.

Hyacinth (Hyacinthus)

Hyacinths are among the easiest bulbs to force. Prepared hyacinths can sprout even at temperatures barely below room temperature (65°F; 18°C), although they grow more compactly at lower temperatures — 50°F (10°C) is ideal. They bloom in as little as eight to ten weeks. Regular hyacinths need normal forcing temperatures (40°F to 50°F; 4°C to 10°C) and require about 13 to 15 weeks of cold temperatures.

Lily and Easter lily (Lilium)

Forcing lilies requires more skill than most other bulbs. I suggest making it easy on yourself and buying them as florist plants, in full bud, and ready to bloom.

Narcissus, jonquil, or daffodil (Narcissus)

A narcissus by any other name — narcissus, jonquil, or daffodil — is still botanically the same. Use whichever name you prefer. All narcissuses force well, but *tazetta* hybrids, such as 'Paperwhite' (white) and 'Grand Soleil D'Or' (yellow) bloom most rapidly (often in only five weeks) and at warmer temperatures. They are, however, tender bulbs and can thrive outdoors in frost-free climates only. The other narcissuses need the normal period (about 13 to 17 weeks) of cold temperatures, but in temperate and cold climates, you can recuperate them and grow them as outdoor bulbs. Try forcing dwarf varieties — they remain more compact and are less likely to require staking.

Tulip (Tulipa)

Not all tulips force well, so choose bulbs specifically recommended for forcing, such as early flowering tulips and dwarf varieties. Most tulips need a full 15 to 17 weeks of cold conditions.

Many other hardy bulbs, including *Anemone blanda, Anemone coronaria, Chionodoxa, Iris reticulata, Muscari,* and others, force readily if you follow the techniques I describe in this chapter.

Caring for permanent indoor bulbs

The most important thing to understand about bulbous plants (including both the hardy bulbs grown temporarily indoors and the permanant indoor bulbs of subtropical origin that can bloom over and over for many years) is that they go through a period of *dormancy*. The dormant period of bulbs is particularly striking, because most bulbs lose all of their leaves and disappear from sight for months on end, hiding out of sight in their underground storage organ. Many healthy but sleepy bulbs (notably those of florist plants) come to tragic ends in the trash because their owner mistakes them for dead when they're actually just dormant.

Remember that all permanent indoor bulbs can bloom again: Never toss them unless you're absolutely sure not only that the foliage has faded but that the bulb has rotted away, too. If in doubt, dig the bulb up and scratch lightly through its outer layer with your finger nail. If it is white or pale green inside, all is well.

You can buy permanent bulbous houseplants as dry bulbs or bulbs that are in full bloom.

Dry bulbs

Dry bulbs usually are sold either loose (pick the largest ones) or in a kit that includes the bulb, a pot, and some potting mix. Pot them up into a pot no more than 1 to 2 inches (2.5 to 5 centimeters) larger than the bulb's diameter. Most permanent bulbs prefer a somewhat *rootbound* living arrangement. If you can't find your indoor bulb among the plant profiles I list in this chapter, just assume that it requires basic bulb care, as follows:

1. **Plant it one bulb per pot, leaving its tip exposed.**

2. **Give it bright light and normal indoor temperatures and humidity.**

3. **Fertilize it regularly during the growing season.**

4. **Water only lightly the first two or three times. As the bulb's growth increases, water as you would any other houseplant.**

Bulbs in full bloom

If you buy a bulbous houseplant in full bloom (and many are popular florist plants), simply keep watering and fertilizing it and provide it with the light levels and temperatures described in the individual plant profiles.

What to do when the bloom is off the bulb

Do *not* cut off the bulb's foliage immediately after it finishes blooming or it may die! It needs to recuperate its energy in order to bloom again — and for that, it needs its leaves. Instead, keep watering and fertilizing them while exposing them to as much light as they can handle.

After three to six months of culture, bulbs begin to show signs of weakening (regardless of whether you bought them dormant or in bloom) — yellowed leaves, no new growth, and such. When you see these signs, you know that the bulbs are ready to go dormant. Simply stop watering and when their leaves dry up cut the leaves off entirely.

Store the dormant bulb, pot and all, in a dry, dark spot, such as a basement or cupboard. Temperatures slightly below normal are best, but you can also store them at room temperature. During their dormant period, lightly spray the potting mix with water once a month or so, just to keep the bulb from drying out entirely.

How long bulbs remain dormant depends on the type of bulb and its growing conditions. It can be anywhere from two to six months. Fortunately, the bulb lets you know when it is ready to break dormancy. It begins to sprout on its own, even if you haven't watered it for months.

The appearance of a sprout, however, only indicates that the bulb is ready to begin to grow, not that you necessarily need to begin watering it immediately. In nature, these bulbs patiently await the return of rains that often are slow in coming. You can prolong your bulb's dormancy by not watering it for up to six months after it begins sprouting. You can use this technique to stagger the blooming period of your bulbs over several months.

Before you begin watering a bulb coming out of dormancy, consider whether you need to repot or divide it (see Chapter 16 for dividing techniques).

Most permanent indoor bulbs dislike any root disturbance. Only repot a bulb if it takes up most of the space in the pot or if you have not repotted it for four or five years. If you do need to repot, put the bulb into a pot that's about 1 to 2 inches (2.5 to 5 centimeters) larger than the bulb's diameter.

If several bulbs have developed over time, you can divide them (see Chapter 16) before you repot. Simply separate the bulbs that have developed and plant each one in its own pot. Then all you have left to do to begin the cycle anew is to start watering and fertilizing again.

Profiles of permanent indoor bulbs

All of the following bulbs are available in bloom as florist plants, and often also as dry bulbs ready for potting. Note that the care rating refers to how easy they are to get to bloom. As with all so-called florist plants, if you buy them already in flower or bud, they're easy to maintain throughout the duration of their first flowering.

Amaryllis (Hippeastrum)

Plant this huge bulb with the top half of it exposed. Look for a large bulb that already shows the tip of the emerging flower stalk. If you see two tips, that guarantees double the number of flowers! An amaryllis takes only a few weeks to bloom. The tall stalk is hollow and may require staking. Each stalk produces four to six trumpet-shaped flowers, often more than 6 inches (15 centimeters) in diameter. The flowers come in a wide range of colors, including white, pink, yellow, orange, red, and bicolor. The long, wide, arching, strap-like leaves often appear only after the plant is in bloom.

To flower an amaryllis a second time, feed it heavily during the growing season and supply as much light, even full sun, as possible. In autumn, or when the foliage begins to yellow on its own (whichever comes first), stop watering it to stimulate dormancy. When new growth appears, usually after about two months, you know that it's ready to begin a new season.

Display: Floor, table

Requirements: Full sun to bright light, drench and let dry (during the growing season), moderate to average humidity, normal to cool temperatures, flowering plant fertilizer, soilless mix

Propagation: Division, seed

Care Rating: Easy

Caladium (Caladium × hortulanum)

The claim to fame of the caladium (see Figure 4-5) is its strikingly colored arrow-shaped foliage, often so heavily mottled in white, pink, red, or combinations of those colors that little green is left. Dry air easily damages the thin leaves, so delay watering a dormant caladium until a humid time of the year or grow it on a humidity tray (see Chapter 10). Remove the odd-looking flowers that this plant produces. They weaken the tuber while failing to improve the plant's appearance.

Store the dormant tuber, pot and all, in a cupboard at room temperature. When new sprouts appear, often four to six months after the plant goes dormant, resume watering. Repot every two years, either to divide the numerous new tubers or to place the increasingly large plant into a bigger pot. Plant the tubers about 1 to 2 inches (2.5 to 5 centimeters) deep with the sprouts facing upward if you want large leaves; for a pot with additional but smaller leaves, plant the tubers upside down.

Display: Floor, table

Requirements: Bright to medium light, keep moderately moist (during the growing season), high to moderate humidity, warm to normal temperatures, all-purpose fertilizer, soilless mix

Propagation: Division

Care Rating: Fairly demanding

Figure 7-5:
Caladium
*(Caladium ×
hortulanum).*

Cyclamen (Cyclamen persicum)

This popular florist's plant grows from a large *corm* (bulb-like organ) half-buried in the potting mix. It produces a rosette of heart-shaped leaves with green and silver marbling above and reddish-purple coloring below on long, pink petioles. The curious butterfly-shaped flowers seem to grow upside down. They come in white, pink, red, purple, and bicolors. To achieve the longest possible bloom, buy cyclamens in flower or bud in early winter. This cool season plant remains in bloom until warm weather interrupts its dormancy. Water carefully, because any moisture that accumulates in the hollow at the top of the corm can cause rot. Consequently, many people prefer to take no chances and always water from below (see Chapter 9).

Reblooming the cyclamen is by no means easy. When flowering dies off in the spring and its foliage yellows, let it dry out and store it in a cool spot all summer. In autumn, as temperatures drop, it begins to resprout and you can resume watering. Floppy leaves and flowers are a sign of excessively high temperatures.

Display: Table

Requirements: Bright to medium light, keep moderately moist (during the growing season), high to moderate humidity, cool to cold temperatures, all-purpose fertilizer, soilless mix

Propagation: Seed

Care Rating: Demanding

Florist's gloxinia (Sinningia speciosa)

A large plant, it forms a rosette of downy, deep-green, oval leaves topped off by numerous, velvety, bell-shaped flowers in purple, red, pink, white, and bicolors. You can buy it in bloom (it is a popular florist plant) or as a dry tuber. When you pot this plant, leave the top of the tuber slightly exposed. (The pink sprouts indicate which side should be facing up.) Growing florist's gloxinia from seed is also surprisingly easy. Unlike the other bulbs described in this chapter, it usually zooms straight into dormancy after it finishes blooming, so stop watering it as soon as its last flower fades. When new sprouts appear, usually two to five months later, begin watering again.

Display: Table

Requirements: Bright light, keep moderately moist (during the growing season), high to moderate humidity, warm to normal temperatures, flowering plant fertilizer, soilless mix

Propagation: Leaf cuttings, stem cuttings, seed

Care Rating: Fairly demanding

Growing Indoor Bonsai

The term *bonsai* refers not to a type of plant, but to a type of *culture*. Bonsai (see Figure 7-6) is both the style of planting used to produce dwarfed plants and the plants grown in that manner. The art of bonsai consists of meticulously pruning and training plants to convey the impression of great age. The popular belief that all bonsais are very old is a misconception. Many collectible bonsais are only a few years old — they just *look* ancient.

Bonsai is a Japanese word that essentially translates to "potted plant." Most Asian countries have traditional planting methods much like bonsai (in Southern China, for example, such plants are called *penjing*), although the growing techniques may differ.

Does the idea of growing a bonsai appeal to you? Think about it before you invest in one. Bonsais need almost constant care. Their tiny pots have little room for water reserves and require your checking in on them daily.

Figure 7-6:
Bonsais
may look
ancient, but
many are
just a few
years old.

Don't assume that all bonsais are indoor plants. Many people make this mistake, which is understandable, because most of us here in the western hemisphere see bonsais on sale in stores or on display in public gardens and plant shows, but almost always indoors. The fact is, Asian people who raise bonsais traditionally keep them outdoors all year long, and bring them indoors only for short periods of time (such as when a guest of importance pays a visit). Indoor bonsai is a Western development that's based, of course, on traditional Eastern horticulture techniques.

The key difference between outdoor and indoor bonsai is that most outdoor bonsai cannot survive for long indoors. If you intend to grow a bonsai indoors most of the year, be sure to get an indoor one.

Basic bonsai techniques

Bonsai is as much a form of art as it is a branch of horticulture. The result is a true living sculpture. You can proceed in one of two basic ways: You can train young plants or seedlings to look like mature plants or you can gradually, usually over a period of years, prune down and train established shrubs to fit into a small pot. Bonsai involves root pruning, branch pruning, wiring, and many other specific techniques.

Explaining how to raise and train indoor bonsais goes far beyond the scope of this book. However, the following quick tips can help start you off on the right foot to growing bonsais:

- ✔ Even if you intend to specialize in bonsais one day, start out by growing regular indoor plants in regular pots. After you learn how to grow foliage and flowering plants, your chances of succeeding with bonsai are much greater.

- ✔ For indoor bonsai, pick only plants that can take tropical or subtropical conditions year round.

- ✔ Choose naturally small-leafed and small-flowered plants so that the bonsai appears to be more in proportion to the size of the pot.

- ✔ Before working on bonsai, take a bonsai course (many nurseries, garden clubs, and teaching institutions offer them) or read a book on the subject.

- ✔ Each indoor plant that you can use for bonsai has specific needs, so choose a plant that you know you can provide the right conditions rather than one that simply catches your eye.

- ✔ Start with an inexpensive but already formed bonsai adapted to indoor conditions and learn how to keep it alive and how to prune it before buying that costly bonsai of your dreams.

- ✔ Bonsai starter plants (basically rooted cuttings of good indoor bonsai species) are an inexpensive way to begin, but remember that training a young plant can take many years. If you're impatient, consider getting a well-developed bonsai and just work at keeping it alive.

- ✔ Never leave home, even for two or three days, without ensuring that someone knowledgeable about bonsai takes good care of your plants. Professional bonsai sitters are available in some cities. (For more information on caring for plants while you're absent, see Chapter 21.)

Sadly, the *vast majority* of bonsai plants die within only a few months, even those purchased by people who sincerely want to invest the effort necessary to grow them. Those you simply buy on a whim often die in less than a week. You can't become a bonsai master overnight. Watch, learn, and be patient. When you come to understand these tiny plants' needs, the art of bonsai isn't nearly as impossible it at first seemed.

No time for bonsais? Try a succulent instead

If you the like the look of bonsais, but the constant care that they require involves more time and effort than you have to spare, consider getting a "succulent bonsai." Many succulents, such as the jade plant have curiously thickened stems that make them look quite bonsai-like in pots, yet can get by on much less care. They are *not* true bonsais, but can supply that bonsai look without all the effort.

Good candidates for indoor bonsai

The following plants can all be adapted to indoor bonsai. They are not all run-of-the-mill houseplants, though, and you may have to do some looking before you find some of them (see Appendix B for some good sources). A number of the following plants are featured in the previous three chapters of this book.

- African boxwood *(Myrsine africana)*
- Azalea *(Rhododendron simsii)*
- Bougainvillea *(Bougainvillea glabra)*
- Calamondin orange *(× Citrofortunella microcarpa)*
- Coffee *(Coffea arabica)*
- Columnea *(Columnea)*
- Coral berry *(Ardisia crenata)*
- Crape myrtlette *(Lagerstroemia indica)*
- Creeping fig *(Ficus pumila)*
- Dwarf pomegranate *(Punica granatum nana)*
- Dwarf schefflera *(Schefflera arboricola)*
- English ivy *(Hedera helix)*
- False heather *(Cuphea hyssopifolia)*
- Flame-of-the-woods *(Ixora coccinea)*
- Flowering maple *(Abutilon × hybridum)*
- Fuchsia *(Fuchsia)*
- Fukien tea *(Ehretia macrophylla)*
- Hibiscus *(Hibiscus rosa-sinensis)*
- Jade plant *(Crassula argentea)*
- Japanese pittosporum *(Pittosporum tobira)*
- Japanese yew *(Podocarpus macrophyllus maki)*
- Kingsville box *(Buxus microphylla* 'Compacta')
- Laurel *(Laurus nobilis)*
- Ming aralia *(Polyscias fruticosa)*
- Miniature holly *(Malphighia coccigera)*
- Monterey cypress *(Cupressus macrocarpa)*

- Myrtle *(Myrtus communis)*
- Natal plum *(Carissa macrocarpa)*
- Norfolk Island pine *(Araucaria heterophylla)*
- Orange jessamine *(Murraya paniculata)*
- Poor man's tea *(Sageretia thea)*
- Rosemary *(Rosmarinus officinalis)*
- Schefflera *(Schefflera actinophylla)*
- Spiny black olive *(Bucia spinosa)*
- Tree of a thousand stars *(Serissa foetida)*
- Weeping fig *(Ficus benjamina)*

Part III
Growing Essentials

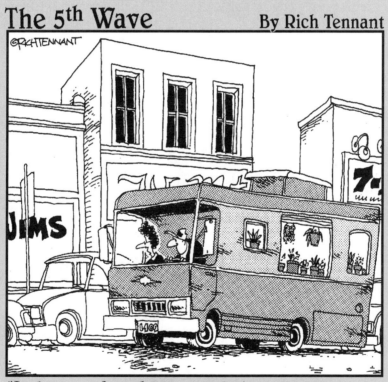

The 5th Wave   By Rich Tennant

@RICHTENNANT

JIMS

"Look for angle parking — my plants won't survive this much southern exposure."

In this part . . .

Unlike houseplants, outdoor plants have Mother Nature to supply nearly all of their basic requirements — fresh air, rain, sunlight, seasonal temperatures, natural fertilizer, and matchmaking from the birds and the bees (you know, pollination). Plants grown indoors, however, depend entirely on *you* for their essential needs.

In this part of the book, you discover the best way to provide your plants with light, water, humidity, fertilizer, temperature control, and potting mixes (no, you can't say potting "dirt" anymore after you read these chapters).

Chapter 8

Lighting Up Your Plant's Life

- -

In This Chapter

▶ Analyzing the amount of light your home receives

▶ Understanding how daylight hours affect plant growth

▶ Acclimating plants to changing lighting conditions

▶ Recognizing the symptoms of too much or too little light

▶ Using artificial light to stimulate growth

- -

*T*he number-one factor affecting plant growth in most homes is light. That's because plants depend on light for their survival. They derive all their energy from light, just as humans get all their energy from food. Give a plant good light and it usually thrives, even if some of the other growing factors aren't exactly up to par. Deny a houseplant its required amount of light, and eventually it's curtains for your energy-starved foliage, no matter how many humidifiers, hygrometers, fertilizer sticks, and automatic watering gizmos you use.

In this chapter, I show you how to determine the quality of sunlight entering your home, and how you can make some minor adjustments to get the most out of the light you do get. I also explain how "photoperiods" affect the amount of light your plants receive, and show you how a plant behaves if it's getting too much or not enough light. Finally, you can always decide yourself how much light a plant gets by plugging in a grow light or two, a subject I cover at the close of the chapter.

Let There Be Light: Room Orientation and Sunlight

In the world of indoor gardening, the term *orientation* refers to the direction a window faces. Whether a window is on the north, south, east, or west side of your home affects the intensity of light coming through the window, especially if the window is unobstructed by trees or overhangs. Light intensity determines how far away from a window you can situate a plant and still give it enough light to stimulate growth.

The illustration in Figure 8-1 shows you the approximate maximum distance natural light will fall depending on the orientation of the window. Few windows face exactly north, south, east, or west; nevertheless, the figure gives you a good idea of relative light intensity according to the direction of your windows.

Depending on how the building you're living in is situated, your windows will provide a southern exposure, eastern exposure (the two best orientations for growing plants), western exposure, or northern exposure (great TV show, lousy orientation for plants). Almost all plants like southern, eastern, and western exposures; fewer like northern ones.

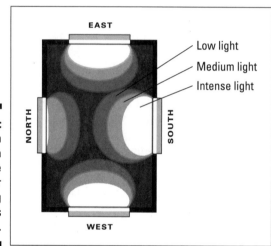

Figure 8-1: Orientation plays a major role in your determining a room's light levels.

Southern exposure

Windows that face south get the most sun. They let in *bright light* (good, intense light without direct sun) early in the morning, full sunlight throughout the middle of the day, and bright light once again in the evening. (By the way, in the southern hemisphere, a southerly orientation gets the same intensity of light as a northerly orientation in the northern hemisphere.)

South-facing windows give you the greatest number of options for situating your plants in a room. Sun-loving plants absolutely thrive when placed directly in front of windows facing south, while plants that require less light can be placed well inside the room and still flourish. In the short days of winter, all your plants would do well to be near a south-facing window. South windows do have one major drawback, however — they can let in too much heat. (I talk about temperature control in Chapter 12.)

Eastern exposure

East-facing windows receive full sun for a short period in the morning, then bright light all day. The morning sun is cool, so you never have to worry about overheating plants that are in proximity to a window with an eastern exposure.

You can grow just about any plant right in front of an east-facing window, although some sun-loving plants may prefer a bit more direct sun. Light levels drop off rapidly as you move away from an east window, so plants don't grow as well in the middle of the room as they would in a room with a southern exposure, especially in areas where the days are very short during the winter.

Western exposure

It would stand to reason that a window with a western exposure would be just as desirable for optimum plant-growing conditions as an east-facing window — after all, they receive an equivalent amount of bright light and direct sun. The difference is that a west-facing window's direct sun comes in the afternoon, not in the morning. Afternoon sunlight can make a room very hot, which can upset the balance between the amount of light a plant likes versus the amount of heat it can tolerate (at least during the summer).

Light levels drop off rapidly as you move inside and away from a west window, just as they do for an east window, so growing plants well inside a room with a west-facing window isn't as easy as growing them far back into a south window room, especially in areas where daylight hours are few during the winter.

Northern exposure

Growing healthy houseplants is difficult anywhere in a room with a northern exposure unless you put them right in front of the windowpane. Light levels directly in front of a north-facing window are medium in intensity, but drop off very quickly as you move away from the window and into the room. (In the southern hemisphere, a northern exposure is the most desirable orientation for growing houseplants.)

You're Standing in My Light: Other Factors Affecting Light Intensity

Other factors besides orientation affect light levels in a room. They include natural and man-made obstacles blocking light coming into the room, the size and position of a window, the color of a room, and even how clean you keep your windows.

Obstacles

Any obstacle to direct light reduces the amount of light plants get. Nearby walls, trees, or shrubs, curtains, overhanging roofs, and so on, can block or filter light rays entering a room, sometimes reducing light levels to almost nil.

Consider an overhanging roof (see Figure 8-2). It can provide some benefits or cause problems. In a southern exposure, it can reduce the extremely hot rays of the midday sun, something most plants appreciate, while still letting strong indirect light penetrate the room. An exaggerated roof overhang on an eastern, western, or northern exposure, on the other hand, can further reduce the already limited light levels.

No plant really needs the hot sun at midday. An overhanging roof cuts off the sun's rays at noon but lets them enter the room in the mornings and afternoons when the sun is lower in the sky. *Deciduous* trees and shrubs, which lose their leaves in autumn, can likewise filter the intense summer sun, yet let full sun in all winter, giving you good light year-round.

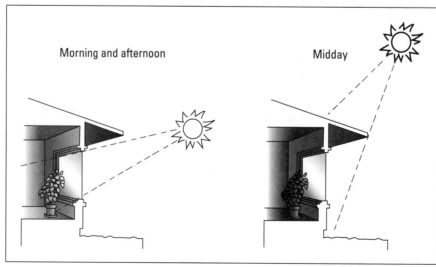

Figure 8-2: An overhanging roof can reduce the intense rays of the midday sun while still allowing weaker sunlight to enter a room.

Morning and afternoon

Midday

Window size

Window size greatly affects the amount of sunlight that enters a room. A small window facing due south doesn't let in nearly as much light as a large one facing due north. You can prove it yourself by using the shadow test in two rooms of your home facing the same direction but with two different-sized windows (see "Skip the Expensive Light Meters — Try the Shadow Test" later in this chapter). The bigger the window, the more light that gets in.

Many small windows can let in just as much light as one large one. Generally speaking, the more glass in a wall, the brighter the room, regardless of the room's orientation.

Window position

The position of a window is another light-limiting or light-enhancing factor. Any kind of window that extends out beyond the walls of a building lets in more light than a flat window. *Bump-outs* can include bay windows (see Figure 8-3), window greenhouses, sunrooms, or glassed-in porches. They provide more light because they allow rays to enter a room from the sides as well as from the front of the window.

Light pouring in from directly above through light wells or skylight windows is more intense than light entering a room through a conventional window. Likewise, although the windows in most rooms all face the same direction, rooms that have windows on two (or more) sides get more intense light than rooms with windows on only one side, regardless of orientation.

Figure 8-3:
A bay window increases light by allowing it to penetrate the room from multiple angles.

The condition of the glass

The condition of the window glass can also affect the amount of light that enters a room. Dirty windows can reduce light levels considerably, so keep your windows spotless in winter when you need more light. And, as far as your plants are concerned, it's okay if your windows are a little dirty during those all-too-hot summer months. Tinted and reflective glass also tend to reduce light — a good thing if the room faces south, but generally bad news otherwise.

Wall color

The color of your home's outside walls also affects light levels. (You remember your science class basics — pale colors reflect light; dark colors absorb it.) Depending on the color that your house is painted, it can absorb or reflect a greater amount of sunlight. In addition, a dark-colored structure situated across from your window can reduce light penetration considerably (a typical situation in many urban apartment buildings and high-rises). White or pale walls that are opposite your window can increase the amount of light entering your home. Interior walls can also absorb or reflect light, depending on the color they're painted.

The distance from plant to window

How far away a plant is from a window greatly affects the intensity of light that the plant receives. Direct sun illuminates a large portion of a room, but indirect light drops off rapidly as it enters a room. That's why you can grow many types of plants a number of feet away from a south-facing window, but only shade-tolerant plants a distance away from a north-facing window.

The darkest places in most rooms are along the walls on either side of a window. Those spots generally get no direct light, and whatever indirect light reaches them is by reflection, which amounts to almost no light at all except in the palest of rooms.

Skip the Expensive Light Meters — Try the Shadow Test

Inexpensive light meters are rarely accurate and give only vague readings. Quality light meters designed specifically for growing houseplants cost more than $100 — a healthy chunk of dough if you're growing only a handful of plants. You can use the light meter from a camera to calculate light levels in a room, but that involves using a complex mathematical formula. My recommendation: Use the shadow test. It's fast, easy, and is at least as accurate as the most expensive light meter.

On a bright day, lay a sheet of white paper where you intend to place a plant, then hold your hand about 1 foot (30 centimeters) above the paper. If you can see a clearly defined shadow, the spot receives bright light. If the shadow is fuzzy, but is nonetheless recognizable as a hand, the spot receives medium light. If you see only a faintly discernible shadow, that spot receives only low light and the choice of plants that can survive in that spot is limited. (See Figure 8-4.) Finally, if you don't see a shadow, you know that spot is basically equivalent to deep shade, and not a good place to keep plants other than on a strictly temporary basis.

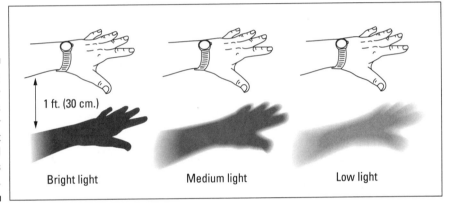

Figure 8-4:
The shadow test is cheaper than a light meter and almost as accurate.

1 ft. (30 cm.)

Bright light   Medium light   Low light

INSIDE DIRT

Extend "daylight" by just turning on a lamp

Moving plants to a brighter location during the autumn and winter can help considerably to get plants through their winter sunlight crisis but so can extending day length through artificial lighting. Although growing plants entirely under artificial light requires a specific type of lamp, no special kind of light is required in extending day length for plants already receiving natural light. Simply leaving an ordinary incandescent lamp burning from late afternoon until evening, or turning it on early in the morning (before dawn), gives light-impoverished plants a few more hours of light per day. The plants are already receiving most of the light they need from sunlight. The extra artificial light simply rounds off their day.

If you use artificial light to extend day length, the plants must be close enough to the lamp that they can benefit from its rays, yet not so close that the lamp actually heats them. To test for a proper distance, hold your hand under the lamp and move it gradually farther away until you can't feel any heat; then note the distance of your hand from the lamp. That's as close as you want to put any plant to that light. An extra four to six hours of "daytime" can help many plants survive the short days of winter.

Photoperiods and Their Effect on Houseplants

The word *photoperiod* is one technical term you should know. Many plants have an internal clock that allows them to respond to the amount of daylight they receive in ways other than their just growing bigger. A photoperiod is the minimum number of daylight hours a plant needs to perform to its potential. Photoperiods affect the production of flowers, so if you grow flowering plants you definitely want to read this section.

Fortunately, the extended daylight hours of summer don't seem to hurt plants. In fact, the growth rate of plants that lack intense light is improved by increased daylight hours. Cabbage plants in Alaska grow to enormous sizes not because of greater light intensity (sunlight weakens as you move closer to polar areas) but because they get nearly 24 hours of daylight. The fact that you can use longer days of weaker light to equal or even surpass a shorter period of more intense light is one of the reasons that so many plants grow well under artificial light.

On the other hand, the short days of winter can harm plants. Lack of light is the main factor limiting the growth of most houseplants, so any decrease in day length means less light, and the plant struggles to thrive and survive — even if it seems to be getting "full sun." Plants that grow vigorously right through spring and summer often weaken during the winter months, especially in regions where daylight lasts less than ten hours a day.

Day-neutral plants

Most flowering houseplants are *day-neutral,* meaning that they can bloom whether the days are short or long (they may, however, produce *more* flowers or bloom at an earlier age with long days, but that's simply because they can absorb more light energy during long days than during short ones).

Long-day plants

A few plants refuse to bloom, even under intense light, unless they get more than 12 hours of daylight every day. Called *long-day plants,* these plants include many garden annuals but relatively few houseplants (the exceptions being the calceolaria, cineraria, and hibiscus). These plants normally bloom during the summer months when days are naturally long, but you can encourage them to bloom during any season by artificially lengthening the "daylight" period to 14 hours or more.

Short-day plants

Short-day plants present a problem for many houseplant growers. These plants (Christmas cactus, chrysanthemums, kalanchoes, poinsettias, and many orchids and begonias) require *uninterrupted* nights more than 12 hours long before they can bloom. Their normal blooming season is autumn or winter, but they often fail to bloom indoors because their owners have the lights on at night, artificially extending the day length beyond 12 hours.

You can do any one several things to ensure that short-day plants will bloom indoors:

✔ If you have a room that you never use at night, use it to house the short-day plants during the autumn. Remove the light bulbs from any lamps in the room so that no one can turn the lights on accidentally during the night — even a short interruption of their 12-plus hours of darkness is often enough to cause them to interrupt the flowering process.

✔ If you live in a region where there's no danger of frost, leave the plants outside during the winter until they start to show color or produce buds, then bring them indoors.

✔ Place the plants under artificial lights, set a timer to keep the lights on no longer than ten hours a day, and then enclose the growing area with a box or some other opaque material to prevent any outside light from reaching in.

✔ One age-old technique is to simply put short-day plants in a closet or opaque box early each evening and then put them back in a brightly lit spot each morning until they start to show color. The catch is you have to repeat this action twice a day for up to three months, including weekends!

After you see flower buds, you no longer need to do anything special to meet a flowering plant's need for short days. You can just expose it to the same lighting conditions as your other plants.

Short days the easy way

Having trouble getting your short-day plants to bloom indoors because the lights you turn on at night throw them off their schedule? Set up a fluorescent light in a corner of the house where no one ever turns the lights on at night (a closet, perhaps) and set a timer to keep the lights burning no more than ten hours a day. Pull the plants from their closet home and show them off when they're in bloom!

Symptoms of Insufficient Light

How do you know when your plants are starved for light? They will tell you themselves. If you don't believe me, check out the following symptoms found in a houseplant suffering from light deprivation (also illustrated in Figure 8-5).

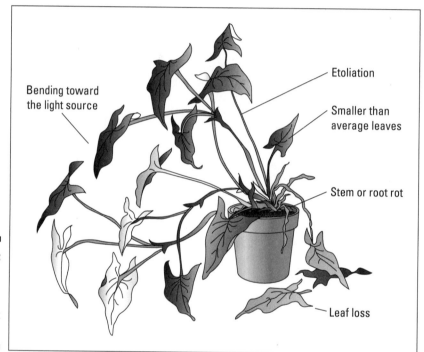

Bending toward the light source

Etoliation

Smaller than average leaves

Stem or root rot

Leaf loss

Figure 8-5: The most-common symptoms of light deprivation.

- ✔ **Weak, elongated, pale green growth:** In horticultural terms, this is called *etiolation,* the most easily recognized symptom of lack of light.

- ✔ **Abnormally small leaves:** You may find that the new leaves are smaller than the existing ones.

- ✔ **Bending toward the light:** All plants lean toward their light source over time, but if the leaning is exaggerated, the plant probably isn't getting enough light.

- ✔ **Lack of bloom or poor flowering:** Plants need more light to bloom than they do to simply grow. A mature, healthy, flowering plant that fails to bloom or blooms weakly or sporadically probably doesn't get enough light.

Taking a quarter-turn for even lighting

Indoor plants get their light mostly from a sideways direction, whereas outdoors plant catch their rays mostly from above. No wonder many houseplants have a tendency to lean sideways — they're leaning toward the light. A plant that continually leans in one direction eventually winds up flat on its side with its potting mix spread across your carpet. One solution to the leaning-plant problem is to install a skylight in your ceiling. Plants that receive light from above are naturally more symmetrical that plants that receive their light from conventional windows. For some of you, that window represents another mortgage payment, or if you're an apartment or condo dweller, it's just plain impossible. A cheaper solution is to simply to give your plants a quarter turn, always in the same direction, every time you water them. This technique is simple, cheap, and effective — and the plant grows evenly in all directions just as if you had a $2,000 hole in the roof.

✔ **No growth or abnormally slow growth:** Many foliage plants react to insufficient light by growing slowly, or ceasing to grow altogether. They simply live on their stored energy, sometimes for months, until they use it all up, and then they begin to show other symptoms of insufficient light.

✔ **Leaf loss:** Plants typically shed older leaves, but if you notice leaves falling off abundantly, you can suspect lack of light. Whereas many outdoor plants lose their leaves in the autumn, most houseplants (other than some flowering bulbs) do not.

✔ **Root rot or stem rot:** Plants that receive too little light can't absorb water properly and their potting mix remains excessively moist, leading to rot.

Sadly, the end result of a long-term lack of light is a dead plant.

If you have a very heavy plant, one that's difficult or impossible to rotate manually, just place it on a lazy Susan. If you can't find one at a garden shop or the plant section of your store, try the kitchen department where you can find lazy Susans designed for shelves and pantries. A large enough one should do fine.

Symptoms of Excess Light

Even low-light plants can tolerate far more light than they really need, so fewer houseplants suffer from excess light than from insufficient light. Cases of excess light usually turn up only in plants sitting on a south or west windowsill or in plants housed in a sunny greenhouse — where the sun beats down for long periods. Even then, it isn't likely to be a problem other than in late spring and summer. In temperate climates, nearly any plant can take full sun during the winter when light is naturally weaker.

Damage owing to excess light is actually due to overheating. With sunlight coming through a glass window and little air circulation, heat can build up tremendously, causing injury to even sun-loving, heat-tolerant plants such as cacti and other succulents. Temperatures right next to a sunny window can reach 140°F (60°C) or higher, which is more heat than most plants can tolerate.

Symptoms of excess light and heat include the following (which are illustrated in Figure 8-6):

✔ Wilting during the hottest hours of the day

✔ Foliage curled downward

✔ Brown spots or pale and translucent spots developing on the side of the plant exposed to the sun — referred to as *burning*

✔ Yellowing and thickening of new growth

✔ Excessively compact and stunted growth

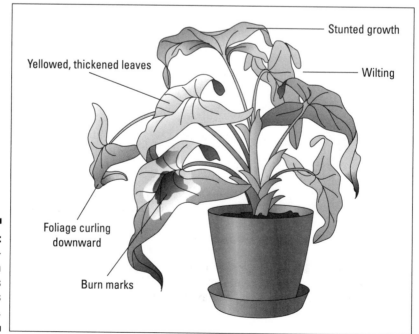

Figure 8-6:
The most-common symptoms of excess light.

Stunted growth

Yellowed, thickened leaves

Wilting

Foliage curling downward

Burn marks

If your plant shows symptoms of excess light, use any of the following methods to decrease light intensity.

✔ Move plants away from a window. The worst symptoms of excess light most often occur in plants that are almost touching a windowpane. Moving the plant just a foot (30 centimeters) away from the glass can help.

✔ Move the plant to a less brightly lit location, such as in front of an east-facing or north-facing window or to either side of a window.

✔ Pull sheer curtains between your plants and the window when the sun is at its brightest — around noon and during early afternoon.

✔ Plant outdoor trees or shrubs in order to shade your home's windows during the hottest hours of the day. Use deciduous plants in temperate climates. When they lose their leaves in the autumn, they let in more light just when plants need it. In tropical climates, evergreens make better choices because they filter the sun year-round.

✔ Put shade-loving plants behind other plants that *can* tolerate the high light levels in the room.

Acclimating Plants Gradually to Changes in Lighting

You can usually move plants from full sun or bright light to shade with little reaction other than some leaf loss. As the plant adapts to its new environment, it replaces any lost leaves. But, if you have plants that develop extensive (or fatal) leaf loss when you move them to low-light spots, you probably relocated them too suddenly. Instead, you should gradually move plants (especially weeping figs and crotons) to lower-light areas over a period of a few weeks (see Chapter 14 for more information).

Plants react dramatically when you move them suddenly from shade to bright sun. Plants grown in the shade produce thin leaves, which have little built-in sun protection. When exposed suddenly to sun, those thin leaves burn and develop brown or pale and translucent spots. Full-sun plants are equally vulnerable under such circumstances. Even a cactus burns under sudden exposure to sun after several months spent in shadier surroundings.

Make the shift to sunnier areas a gradual one. If you incrementally increase the light a plant receives over a period of a month, giving the plant a bit more light each day, you can avoid damaging it.

Simple Methods to Make the Most of the Light You Have

The easiest way to have success with growing plants is to make the best use of your home's natural lighting conditions and choose your plants accordingly. Low lighting can significantly limit your choice of plants, so try these few simple tips to increase the light levels in your home:

- ✔ Keep your windows clean in autumn and winter. Dirty windows, even those that look clean to you, can reduce the amount of available light.

- ✔ Move plants nearer to a window or other light source.

- ✔ Move plants to a different, brighter spot, such as in front of a south-facing window.

- ✔ Paint walls a pale color, preferably white, which will reflect light. Adding mirrors to a room also increases light reflection.

- ✔ Remove any obstacles blocking the light. Pruning back shrubs or thinning out trees located in front of a window can make a considerable difference in the amount of light available to plants. Open any curtains or blinds that block the light, at least during the daylight hours.

- ✔ Add artificial light. (See the section "Beyond Sunlight: Grow Lights to the Rescue" later in this chapter.)

Numerous other means of increasing light are at your disposal should you become a serious houseplant fanatic. They include installing larger or bumped-out windows, putting in skylights, adding a garden room or greenhouse, or moving to a brighter home.

Beyond Sunlight: Grow Lights to the Rescue

If your home doesn't get enough natural light to grow the wide variety of plants you desire, but you don't have the spare change or square footage to build a greenhouse, you can always employ those wonderful inventions — grow lights.

As I mention earlier in this chapter, you can use ordinary incandescent lamps to give your plants that bit of extra light that they need in the winter, but they can't be the only source of light. The light that incandescent lamps give off is rich in red rays, whereas plants need a nearly equal balance of red and blue rays in order to flourish. Even incandescent *plant* lights, supposedly color-corrected to a certain degree, do not have a good reputation among indoor gardeners.

Instead, you have two basic lighting choices: fluorescent lights or *high intensity discharge (HID)* lamps. Plants flourish equally well under both of these types of lighting — sometimes far better than they grow in any window. In fact, you don't really have to choose between HID lamps and fluorescent lights. Many indoor gardeners use both. Most houseplants thrive with 14- to 16-hour days under either HIDs or fluorescent lights.

One difference exists between the two types of lighting that you may want to keep in mind: Fluorescents are better for growing short plants and starting cuttings and seedlings; HID lamps are better for taller plants.

Installing lamps on a pulley allows you to lower or raise them to supply more or less light depending on how your plants react — lower the lamp if the plants stretch toward the light source; raise it if they bunch up.

Growing under fluorescent lights

Most indoor gardeners choose fluorescent lights. They're widely available, and inexpensive to buy, use, and replace. They also give off little heat, so ventilation is necessary only when you use 20 or more lamps in one place.

Fluorescent lights work best with low-growing and spreading plants, cuttings, and seedlings. You can use several tiers of lamps to grow many plants in a small amount of horizontal space. African violets, ferns, bonsais, and moth orchids, as well as dwarf versions of almost any plant, all make excellent choices.

Fluorescent lights don't work well with tall plants because the farther the leaves are from the lamp, the lower the light quality. A tall plant grown under florescents will show an abundance of growth at its tip, but little or none at its base.

The basic setup

The basic fluorescent grow-light setup consists of a dual-tube, 4-foot (120-centimeter) lamp suspended from the ceiling (via a cable or chain) over a table approximately 2 feet (60 centimeters) wide by 4 feet (120 centimeters) long (the surface space that one lamp can effectively illuminate).

You can set up fluorescent lights anywhere — in a basement, under a staircase, in a closet, under bookshelves, and so on. Many growers build or buy *light gardens,* which are two- or three-tiered plant stands with adjustable lamp heights.

If space is at a premium, you can get small, circular fluorescent lamps but they cost considerably more and provide somewhat lower light intensity. If you need stronger light intensities — for example, if you're growing cacti, succulents, and certain flowering plants — you can get four-tube or six-tube light fixtures.

Fluorescent tubes last about one or two years under standard indoor growing conditions. Most growers change them annually or when the ends of the tubes start to blacken.

Correct lamp-to-plant distances

To light foliage plants, position the lamp within 12 to 24 inches (30 to 60 centimeters) from the top of the plants. Flowering plants need more light, so place the lamp 6 to 12 inches (15 to 30 centimeters) away from the plants. You can adjust these distances according to your results. For example, plants that seem to stretch upward need stronger light, so move the lamp closer; yellowed leaves and slow growth indicate a need for less-intense light, so move the light source farther away.

Light is most intense at the center of the tubes. So, put your full-sun plants in the middle of the growing space and low-light plants at the ends or sides of the table.

Tube types

For foliage plants and many flowering plants, combine one cool white tube and one warm white tube (the standard types of fluorescent lights and also the least expensive). Some flowering plants, as well as arid land cacti and succulents, grow and bloom better under special horticultural tubes. If you think you that's what need, go for *full-spectrum tubes* (they're the most expensive) over the less-expensive *wide spectrum tubes*. The latter rarely seem to provide better results than the warm white/cool white combination, although their special phosphorescent coating does bring out the pizzazz in some plant colors.

Instead of growing plants under wide spectrum plant tubes, use them in places where you want to display your best plants. Plants virtually glow under this type of lighting.

Use a timer

Plants perform better when they receive regular periods of light at the same time each day, so be sure to use a timer to regulate artificial light. Most plants do well with 14- to 16-hour days, although some experts prefer to cultivate slow-growing seedlings, such as orchids and cacti, with 24-hour days because they can gain several months of extra growth per year.

Growing under high-intensity discharge lamps

High-intensity discharge (HID) lamps are becoming increasing popular and are beginning to replace fluorescent lamps for some uses. Two types of HIDs are available: *metal halide* and *high-pressure sodium* (*low-pressure sodium* is also available, but is used principally in greenhouse settings).

Metal halide versus high-pressure sodium models

Metal halide lamps are the best choice for overall growth. The light they emit (white with a faint greenish tinge) is more attractive for an indoor setting. They emit fewer red than blue rays, so some plants refuse to flower under them. These stubborn plants, however, belong to the minority. Most flowering houseplants bloom prolifically under metal halide lamps.

Many growers either move their plants from under metal halide lamps to sodium lamps to stimulate bloom or use both metal halide and sodium lamps in the same room. (Sodium lamps are often referred to as *flowering lamps.*) Sodium lamps have an intense orange light that's irritating to the eye; you really can't use these lamps anywhere other than in special grow rooms. That's why they're used most often in greenhouse environments.

Watt's the difference in light intensity?

Both types of HID lamps come in four different wattages: 1,000, 400, 250, and 150/175 watts. Many indoor gardeners believe they can get equal or better results with fluorescent lights than they can with the two lower-wattage HIDs.

Most houseplants do well under medium light, so suspending a 400-watt lamp 1 to 2 feet (30 to 60 centimeters) from the top of your plants, or suspending a 1,000-watt light 2 to 4 feet (60 to 120 centimeters) above your plants, usually generates good results. Place plants that prefer full sun 1 foot below a 400-watt lamp and 2 feet below a 1,000-watt lamp.

Each 400-watt lamp covers about 4 square feet (120 square centimeters) of growing area (less, if you grow plants needing high light intensities); each 1,000-watt lamp covers about 10 square feet (3 square meters).

You can normally run two (and sometimes even three) 400-watt lamps on a single 15-amp circuit (the standard in North America). That depends, however, on what other electrical devices share the same circuit because one circuit usually can handle no more than 1,500 watts. You can use only one 1,000-watt lamp per circuit and, furthermore, you cannot combine it with many other electrical devices. One of the great limitations of using HID lamps in homes built more than 30 years ago, when people used fewer electric devices, is finding circuits that aren't already overcrowded.

If you intend to use multiple HID lamps, you may need to add new circuits to your home (consult an electrical contractor).

A couple of structural details to keep in mind

When you go shopping for high-intensity lamps, you want to keep the following features in mind:

- ✔ HID lamps come with either integrated *ballasts* (the part that generates the most heat) or a separate *ballast box* that you can place a certain distance away from your plants. If you intend to use only one or two lamps, either type of ballast works well. If you intend to convert your entire basement into an indoor garden using a dozen lamps, the separate ballast box models are preferred because they give you more control over where the excess heat goes.

- ✔ Always buy an HID lamp with a *reflector;* otherwise, you lose 30 percent or more of the light. Standard horticultural lamps always include a reflector but industrial lamps (not particularly recommended for growing plants, anyway) often do not.

Replacement bulbs

HID lamps usually last about two to four years. Unlike fluorescent lights, which diminish slowly in intensity over time and therefore must be changed before they burn out, HID lamps maintain their intensity at relatively high levels throughout their life and require changing only when they finally do burn out.

Be careful when you buy replacement HID bulbs. You can use a 400-watt metal halide bulb only in a 400-watt metal halide lamp. The same goes for all other metal halide bulbs. Furthermore, some lamps are designed for horizontal use and others for vertical use, and *their* lamps aren't interchangeable, either.

To avoid errors when buying a replacement bulb, always give your dealer the brand name and model number of the lamp you're using.

Chapter 9

Water, Water Everywhere

. . . .

In This Chapter

▶ Determining when a plant gets too little or too much water

▶ Getting into a watering routine groove

▶ Discovering how the right-size saucer can make all the difference

▶ Watering from above or below your plants

▶ Getting rid of harmful chemicals from tap water

▶ Experimenting with hydroponic growing systems

. . . .

*N*o other houseplant-growing detail demands as much of your attention as watering. Adjustments in lighting and humidity levels are something you need to do only occasionally — usually when the seasons change, when you bring home new plants, or do a little rearranging. The potting medium (or soil as most people like to call it) is something you attend to once when you pot a plant, and then again only if serious problems arise and you need to get to the root of the matter.

Because watering requires your attention year-round, it's where most houseplant growers make the most mistakes. They either go nuts with the watering, thinking they're making their plants real happy, or they forget to water altogether. Then, the plant gets too much water, which can lead to rot, or too little water, which can stunt a plant or simply kill it. If you think that your watering habits may be doing your plants more harm than good, then this chapter was written for you.

Why You Can't Slack Off on the Watering Detail

It may seem that all a houseplant needs is a splash of water at the same time every week, but it's a little more involved than that (like I said earlier, this is the one area of houseplant care that requires a bit more effort than the rest). A number of factors influence a plant's need for water:

✔ Cloudy days during which plants *vegetate* (barely grow), and therefore need less moisture, can follow right on heels of sunny days that stimulate growth which uses up water, and vice versa.

✔ Plants sustain water loss and require greater amounts of moisture replenishment during the soaring temperatures of summer, and use water more efficiently and require less moisture during cooler weather.

✔ Still (or stagnant) air limits the amount of water lost to evaporation and *transpiration* (the passage of moisture through the plant's breathing pores, or *stomata*), which decreases a plant's need for water. But open a window on a windy day and your plants may need a thorough watering by nightfall.

You may be wondering what constitutes a "thorough watering." When you water thoroughly, pour in enough to ensure that the entire rootball is completely moist.

✔ Dry air in the winter can lead to excessive evaporation, which means you may have to water quite often even though the plant is barely growing.

✔ Finally, you can't trust a plant to need the same amount of water even when all other conditions remain stable because as it increases in size, its need for water increases.

Recognizing When a Plant Wants Water and When It Needs to Dry Out

Many inexperienced indoor gardeners pick up a deadly habit: Watering their plants whenever the potting mix appears dry. The problem is that potting mixes that look dry on top usually are still moist in the middle. Watering when you think the mix is almost dry, but really isn't, waterlogs the soil in the middle of the pot and at the bottom of the root ball. You can't keep a plant permanently soaking in water because waterlogged roots can't get the oxygen they need to breathe. When that happens, the plant may die from asphyxiation. On the other hand, you can't let a plant dry out to the point that the roots are dehydrated.

Now, you're probably wondering how you can tell if a plant's potting mix is moist, dry, or almost dry. That's what the following sections of this chapter are all about.

Sometimes the "eyes" have it

Potting mixes change color as they go from moist to dry. A moist mix appears dark brown, whereas a dry or nearly dry mix looks pale brown on the surface. One popular watering technique, therefore, involves simply watering those plants whose potting mix has turned pale. Judging by sight, however, isn't always reliable.

When the mix at the surface of a large pot appears dry, the mix may still be thoroughly moist at the base. When the mix at the surface of a small or shallow pot appears dry — especially one under four inches (ten centimeters) high — the entire rootball probably needs water. That's because when the medium in a small pot appears dry on the surface, it's usually pretty dry throughout the mix.

You don't need to do more than touch the surface of the mix for plants in pots smaller than four inches in height to determine if the plant needs water. But avoid repeatedly fingering the mix — jabbing the roots of small plants can do more harm than good.

Let your fingers do the testing

The easiest way to determine if a plant needs water is to stick your finger in the pot. Insert your index finger into the potting mix up to the first or second knuckle. If the mix feels moist, don't water. If it feels dry, water away.

You can use this method for plants in medium-sized pots up to 8 to 10 inches (20 to 25 centimeters) in height because it will give you a fairly good indication of the moisture level throughout the pot.

 Although plants in small pots can be harmed through repeated stabbing of their potting media, plants in deeper and wider pots tend to have root systems that grow deeper in the pot. Nevertheless, make sure you insert your finger near the outer rim of the pot, and not near the plant's base.

The weight-and-see "lift test"

You can determine if a plant needs water by simply lifting the pot. The soil mix of a recently watered plant weighs considerably more than that of a nearly dry one. Plants in plastic containers that are planted in standard potting mixes weigh roughly half their normal weight when the potting mix is nearly dry. (This is a rough estimate, however, and depends on the type of plant, the soil used, and the pot material.) Even plants grown in terracotta pots with a heavy soil mixture are noticeably lighter when the potting medium is dry.

To use it with any degree of accuracy, the "lift test" watering method requires some practice. Pick up your plants every now and again between waterings to get a feel for the weight difference between moist and dry potting mixes. After a while, you'll be able to distinguish between a lighter-weight pot that needs water and a heavier one that doesn't.

Using probes, meters, and other gadgets

Determining the watering needs of plants growing in deep pots — those 12 inches (30 centimeters) or more in height — has always been the bane of indoor gardeners. Testing the moisture level in the upper section of the mix is simple enough — a carefully directed jab of the finger does the job — but getting a good idea of the condition of the growing mix at the bottom of the pot is a bit more difficult. Plants grown in deep pots are in constant danger of overwatering. (See Figure 9-1.)

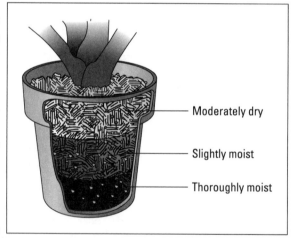

Figure 9-1: On the surface, plants in large pots may appear to need water, but the real story is buried down below.

Moderately dry

Slightly moist

Thoroughly moist

Knowing when plants in deep pots need water requires some technological assistance. Stick to using a probe or a water meter to test the wetness of the potting mix. It's the safest means of determining whether a plant in a large pot needs water.

Stick probes

Insert a wooden chopstick or pencil into the soil, stopping two inches (five centimeters) from the bottom of the pot, then pull out the stick and examine it. If you see moisture on the probe, you probably don't need to water the plant for at least a few days. If the probe comes up dry, water the plant thoroughly.

Standard moisture meters

Moisture meters are mechanical devices that measure the amount of water at root level (see Figure 9-2). They look somewhat like a meat thermometer except that their prongs are up to a foot (30 cm long) long. Expect to pay about $10 for a good one. To use a moisture meter, insert the metal prongs two-thirds of the way into the growing medium. The meter then points to "dry," "wet," or somewhere in between. Always wait until the meter reads dry before you water. If it reads "slightly moist" or "wet", test again in a few days.

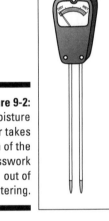

Figure 9-2:
A moisture meter takes much of the guesswork out of watering.

Be aware that moisture meters begin to give inaccurate readings when they wear out. Therefore, you should replace the meter once a year. Even new meters can give inaccurate readings if the potting mix contains abnormally high levels of mineral salts, which can happen if you have very hard water or if several years have gone by since the last time you repotted the plant. An obviously inaccurate moisture meter reading may be telling you your plant needs fresh potting mix.

Musical moisture meters

Now you've heard everything: Musical moisture meters indicate when a plant needs water by chiming or emitting some other musical sound. They're built somewhat like a standard moisture meter with a probe at one end, but instead of a dial at the other end they feature a sound transmitter. The two types of moisture meters cost about the same — $10 to $15.

These devices are great for people who habitually forget to water — but imagine the ruckus if every plant in your house were equipped with one? Buy just one musical moisture meter per room and keep it permanently inserted in the pot of a plant that always seems to dry out faster than the others. When the device chimes out, it's probably time to check every plant using a more traditional testing method, such as inserting a finger into the mix or lifting the plant.

Establishing a Watering Routine

Ideally, you should give a plant just enough water to make the soil moist. Allow all of the soil in the pot to become almost dry and then water again until the soil is moist. This prevents the roots from drowning and ensures that the plant gets enough water *and* oxygen. Fortunately, maintaining such a cycle is fairly easy to do — I give you some pointers in the following sections of this chapter.

Tepid water — an even mix of hot and cold running water — is recommended for watering all houseplants. Applying cold water to heat-loving tropical plants can actually cause root damage and leaf spotting. If you have access to only cold water, leave the water out for an hour or two at room temperature before pouring it on your plants.

Watering on demand

The watering method I recommend requires that you check on your plants regularly and water them only what they need it. I call this is the *watering on demand* system and it inevitably generates the best results. Part of the watering on demand process involves the *drench-and-let-dry* method — water plants thoroughly, then let them almost dry out before watering them again.

Almost dry isn't the same as *dry.* Ferns and other thin-leaved plants never like their potting mix to go anywhere beyond the almost-dry stage. As soon as their mix becomes dry to the touch, water them without delay. Cacti and other succulents, as well as many other thick-leaved plants, don't mind if their soil dries out. Those plants can go a few days with dry soil, or even go weeks without watering if they are in a dormant state.

Check each plant every three to four days using one or more of the methods described in the section "Recognizing When a Plant Wants Water and When It Needs to Dry Out" earlier in this chapter, and water only those plants that need it.

If you use the watering on demand routine, you'll probably discover that you tend to water the following plants more often than others:

- ✔ Plants growing in clay pots
- ✔ Plants with large or thin leaves
- ✔ Plants with thin stems
- ✔ Plants in full growth
- ✔ Underpotted plants

You can also expect to water *more* often if any of the following environmental conditions exist:

- ✔ High temperatures
- ✔ Strong sunlight or other bright light
- ✔ Dry air
- ✔ Air movement, such as a breeze coming through a window

You'll probably find that you water the following plants less often than your other plants:

- ✔ Plants in plastic pots
- ✔ Plants with thick, waxy, or hairy leaves, or with no leaves at all
- ✔ Plants with thick stems, such as you see on succulents
- ✔ Weak or sick plants
- ✔ Resting or dormant plants
- ✔ Overpotted or freshly repotted plants

You can also expect to water *less* often if any of the following environmental conditions exist:

- ✔ Low temperatures
- ✔ Cloudy days or dim light
- ✔ Humid air
- ✔ Little or no air movement

Once-a-week watering

Watering on demand may be the best way to keep most houseplants happy, but as a matter of convenience (or to counter any forgetfulness) many people simply water all their plants according to a regular schedule, typically once a week. *Once-a-week watering* can actually work quite well — for *some* plants, under *some* circumstances. The problem is that every plant's watering needs vary over time, depending on a number of factors. A plant that seems to be perfectly adapted to once-a-week watering may suddenly up and die if environmental conditions cause it to need more or less water than usual.

Once-a-week watering works best with indoor plants such as cactus, succulents, and a few thick-leafed foliage plants that can take just about any watering gaffes. The once-a-week schedule approach is less likely to appeal to flowering plants, which tend to be more particular about their care.

Of course, there's nothing wrong with growing only tough plants that can take unscientific watering methods, but if you want to grow a variety of plants that aren't ready to forgive you if you abandon your weekly routine, try the method I describe in the next section.

If you find that your watering routine tends to slip your mind, tape up a reminder on the inside of your front door so you're sure to see it, or stick a note under a refrigerator magnet reminding you to "Water the plants in the living room on Sunday." I use my computer's agenda program. It beeps when it's time to water — and if I just don't have time right then and there, I can tell it to beep me every 15 minutes until I get up and tend to the watering.

Modified once-a-week watering

The modified method combines the convenience of once-a-week watering with some additional commonsense practices. Modified once-a-week watering works for most plants; those plants that can't live with this type of watering schedule are few and far between.

For example, if you notice that the potting mix of one of your plants is still moist when you come around for the weekly watering, don't water it. On the other hand, if a plant seems more parched than any of the others when watering day rolls around, water it thoroughly and leave a bit of water in its saucer. If it continues to be the thirstiest plant week after week, plant it in a larger pot. The added potting mix surrounding its roots supplies greater water reserves that the plant's roots can dip into between waterings.

If you find that weekly watering simply doesn't suffice during the summer months when plants grow rapidly and transpiration and evaporation are at a maximum, step up the watering to twice a week until the weather cools off.

Do you tend to forget to water your plants? Put them in plastic pots. Plastic allows little moisture to escape, so the potting mix dries out much more slowly that it would in a clay pot. Or, do you tend to overwater your plants? Put them in clay pots. The porous clay material allows for moisture to escape through the entire surface of the pot, so the potting mix dries out more quickly than it would in a plastic pot.

Gizmos to Aid in Watering

You don't need much in the way of tools when it comes to watering your plants, as long as you have a container for pouring out the water and some trays for catching the excess. Or, you can get fancy and opt for a pot that waters itself.

The proper saucer for the pot

If a plant is in a pot with drainage holes, slip a saucer under it the minute you bring it home. A number of waterproof containers make for serviceable plant pot saucers — a ceramic bowl, an aluminum pie plate, a margarine container, or even a teacup saucer.

Avoid clay saucers that haven't been painted with waterproof coating because they will leave a stain from water seepage. (You can paint or shellac a plain clay saucer.) Beware, too, of metal trays; some may leave rust stains.

Some plants are sold in pots with built-in saucers that are so small they leave no room for water overflow, except out and over the sides of the saucer. Rather than risk spills, houseplant owners chronically underwater their plants until they have dead specimens on their hands. For the plants' sake, a saucer should be at least as wide as the brim of the pot and, preferably, a bit wider, as shown in Figure 9-3. If you water from below, you need an even wider saucer (see the section "Watering from below" later in this chapter).

Perhaps the best saucers are the transparent plastic ones now readily available in most garden centers and plant stores. (Unfortunately, most of them are a little flimsy and start to yellow and crack after a year of use.) Nevertheless, they remove much of the guesswork from watering — you can clearly see when water had drained out of the pot, a signal to stop watering, and exactly how much water the pot is sitting in.

Some saucers are lined with ridges (refer to Figure 9-3) that lift the pot up above the drain-off. If you accidentally overwater, you may not need to drain the saucer because the pot sits above the wetness instead of just soaking in it.

Here's a test for sizing up saucers: If a plant's potting mix becomes moist on the surface the first time you water without leaving a pool of runoff at its base, you've found the right size saucer. Plants that always end up soaking in excess water require a smaller saucer. By matching a pot to the right-size saucer, you can water each plant the same way — by filling its saucer to the brim. Watering plants from below then becomes a snap.

Watering cans, bottles, and wands

As your plant hobby grows, a watering can becomes an essential item. Either plastic or metal is fine as long as the can has a half-gallon to gallon capacity (two to four liters). Smaller ones won't hold enough water; larger ones may be too heavy to lift, especially when you need to reach a hanging plant.

Cans that have a sprinkling head at the tip (which gardeners call a *rose*) are designed for outdoor gardening and splash water everywhere. Buy a watering can equipped with a spout or a removable rose.

It you have trouble reaching your hanging plants with a watering can, invest in a waterer specially designed for hanging plants, like the one in shown Figure 9-4. They usually consist of a plastic squeeze bottle with a long nozzle that's hooked at the tip. They aren't built to last, but they're so inexpensive that you can afford to replace them now and again.

If you have lots of plants and are beginning to find the repeat trips to the faucet a bit tedious, consider using a hose specifically designed for indoor watering. This type of hose attaches to any indoor faucet and is equipped with a *watering wand* like that on a hanging plant waterer plus a water flow regulator. Some watering wands also have a fertilizer chamber so that you can fertilize as you water.

To use an indoor hose, just adjust the water until it is at the right temperature (tepid) and off you go!

Figure 9-4:
Hanging
plant
waterers
are
inexpensive
and handy
for watering
hard-to-
reach
plants.

Self-watering pots

Some plant containers are designed to be self-watering. Pots such as these are equipped with a *capillary wick* and built-in water reservoir that the plant can dip into as the need arises, as shown in Figure 9-5. As the soil dries out, the wick continuously pulls water up from the reservoir into the mix, keeping it lightly moist — yet never soaking wet — at all times. This type of pot can provide moisture for up to four or five weeks.

To use a self-watering pot, fill the reservoir to the top with tepid water and then wait until the reservoir is empty before watering again. It might be weeks before you need to repeat the procedure. Some models have a transparent window that lets you check the reservoir's status at a glance. If your model doesn't, dip a finger through the watering hole. If you feel moisture, you don't have to water.

Pick Your Technique: Pouring from Above or Soaking from Below

Most houseplant growers water their plants from above, that is, they pour the water directly onto the plant's soil. In-the-know houseplant growers also use a second technique — they water from below. Both techniques work equally well, so the choice is up to you.

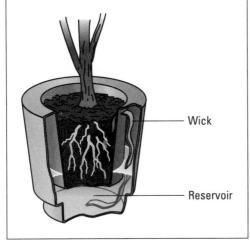

Figure 9-5:
This pot is
designed to
make
watering
less of a
chore.

Wick

Reservoir

Watering from above

Watering from above (see Figure 9-6) is the most "natural" way to water, because outdoor plants get most of their moisture from the skies in the form of precipitation. To water from above, lift the foliage or move it to one side, pour water directly over the area of the root system, and flood the potting mix until a trickle of water appears from the drainage holes at the bottom.

The main disadvantage of watering from above is that certain plants have delicate leaves, stems, or tubers that you can damage by overexposing them to water. You can either water from below (see the next section) or water from above, but water the potting mix, not the leaves. Just move the leaves out of the way as you water.

Watering from below

Watering from below relies on *capillary action,* that is, the movement of water from the wettest parts of the potting mix to the driest parts. When you let a nearly dry plant sit in a saucer of water, the moisture gets sucked up through the mix and into the plant's roots.

To water from below, simply fill the saucer with water. If the water quickly disappears (I've seen plants soak up water from their saucers almost as fast as I can pour it in), add some more. You know you've added just the right amount of water if an hour later the potting mix feels moist to the touch at the surface but the pot isn't sitting in a saucer full of water. If the soil feels dry, water the plant again. After the plant is done soaking in water, empty the excess from the saucer.

Figure 9-6:
Watering
from above
most
closely
imitates the
way plants
get water in
nature.

Plants that you water from below require leaching more often than plants that you water from above. You also may need to repot them more often because they tend to accumulate excess mineral salts more quickly (see "Leaching out minerals" later in this section).

Taking the Plunge: Watering Bone Dry Plants

When potting mixes go beyond the usual "slightly dry" to a nearly crispy "desert dry" a curious phenomenon occurs — the potting mix repels water. Any water you pour on a really dry plant does little more than moisten the soil's surface. That's because extremely dry potting mixes pull away from the sides of a pot, leaving a gap between the pot and the root ball, as shown in Figure 9-7. When you water these ultra-dry plants from above, the water runs off the top of the mix, down the gap between the pot and the root ball, and out of the pot and into the saucer.

When a plant reaches a state of extreme dryness from either neglect or long-term dormancy, watering from the top is almost pointless. The plant needs a real soaking so that it can recover. Fill a sink or bucket with tepid water and plunge the pot into it, using a weight (a rock or brick) placed carefully near the edge of the pot to keep the plant from floating around. Then, add a few drops (no more than that) of liquid dishwashing detergent to the water to help the water counteract the soil's repellent action.

Figure 9-7:
When soil is
excessively
dry, water
drains out
of the pot
without
moistening
the root
ball.

After about an hour, remove the plant and let any excess water drain through the pot. If the plant is still alive (not all plants recover from severe drought), it should soon plump up noticeably. Even after the root ball expands to its original size, an open space may remain between it and the edge of the pot. Fill in the gap with potting mix so that the moisture can soak *into* the root ball instead of flowing *around* it.

Plants in hanging pots lose water more rapidly to evaporation and transpiration than other plants. Plus, they usually come with those puny snap-on saucers that aren't up to the task of holding water for a pot of that size. The best watering method to use with hanging plants is to just plunge the plants into a sink or bucket instead of trying to water them where they hang.

Vegetables and Minerals: Dealing with the Potentially Harmful Stuff in Water

Any water that's fit for human consumption is fine for plants. You can also use rainwater, melted snow, water left over from cooking vegetables, well water, water from a dehumidifier, and spring water for watering houseplants. Just avoid any water source you know is contaminated with chemical toxins (herbicides, obviously, are particularly lethal to plants).

Draw the line at *gray water* — recycled wastewater taken from kitchen and laundry room drains. Sometimes considered acceptable for outdoor gardens, the soap and detergent it contains quickly gums up potting mixes — and sometimes contains toxic substances!

If you go
easy on the
watering and
provide them with
lots of light, cacti and
other succulents are among
the easiest plants to grow.
You can fill your home with loads
of other great houseplant varieties. Just
flip through the following pages and you'll
find dozens of indoor gardening favorites.

Arrowhead plant: *Syngonium podophyllum* Chapter 4

Banana-leaf fig: *Ficus maclellandii* Chapter 4

Boston fern: *Nephrolepis exaltata* 'Bostoniensis' Chapter 4

Caladium: *Caladium × hortulanum* Chapter 7

Calamondin orange: × *Citrofortunella microcarpa* Chapter 5

Cast iron plant: *Aspidistra elatior* Chapter 4

Cereus: *Cereus peruvianus* Chapter 6

China doll: *Radermachera sinica* Chapter 4

Chinese evergreen: *Aglaonema* 'Silver Queen' Chapter 4

Chinese fan palm: *Livistona chinensis* Chapter 4

Chrysanthemum: *Dendranthema × grandiflorum* Chapter 5

Columnea: *Columnea* Chapter 5

Corn plant: *Dracaena fragrans* Chapter 4

Croton: *Codiaeum variegatum pictum* Chapter 4

Dipladenia: *Mandevilla* Chapter 5

Dumbcane: *Dieffenbachia* Chapter 4

Dwarf schefflera: *Schefflera arboricola* Chapter 4

English ivy: *Hedera helix* Chapter 4

False aralia: *Dizygotheca elegantissima* Chapter 4

Flaming sword: *Vriesea splendens* Chapter 7

Grape ivy: *Cissus rhombifolia* Chapter 4

Guzmania: *Guzmania lingulata* Chapter 7

Hibiscus: *Hibiscus rosa-sinensis* Chapter 5

Lady Jane anthurium: *Anthurium* × *andreacola* 'Lady Jane' Chapter 5

Lipstick plant: *Aeschynanthus lobbianus* Chapter 5

Madagascar dragon tree: *Dracaena marginata* Chapter 4

Ming aralia: *Polyscias fruticosa* Chapter 4

Norfolk Island pine: *Araucaria heterophylla* Chapter 4

Oleander: *Nerium oleander* Chapter 5

Parlor palm: *Chamaedorea elegans* 'Bella' Chapter 4

Peace lily: *Spathiphyllum wallisii* Chapter 5

Poinsettia: *Euphorbia pulcherrima* Chapter 5

Pony tail palm: *Beaucarnea recurvata* Chapter 6

Pothos: *Epipremnum aureum* Chapter 4

Rubber plant: *Ficus elastica* Chapter 4

Schefflera: *Schefflera actinophylla* Chapter 4

Silver vase: *Aechmea fasciata* Chapter 7

Snake plant: *Sansevieria trifasciata* Chapter 6

Spider plant: *Chlorophytum comosum* Chapter 4

Spineless yucca: *Yucca elephantipes* Chapter 6

Swiss cheese plant: *Monstera deliciosa* Chapter 4

Tree philodendron: *Philodendron bipinnatifidum* Chapter 4

Warneckei dracaena: *Dracaena deremensis* 'Warneckei' Chapter 4

Wax plant: *Hoya carnosa* Chapter 5

Weeping fig: *Ficus benjamina* Chapter 4

You can group houseplants to not only great decorative effect, but also to create "microclimates" that provide plants with a healthy dose of humidity. For the ultimate in plant environments, you can install your plants in a solarium or greenhouse.

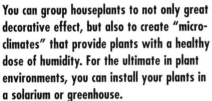

Houseplant terrariums come in all shapes and sizes, besides the familiar fish-tank shape. This garden in a bottle thrives in its own little micro-environment.

A pot with no drainage? No way

Take a pass on any houseplant pot that doesn't have drainage holes. If you pour excess water into a pot that lacks drainage holes, the plant's roots get waterlogged and become oxygen deprived, which leads to root death and eventually, rot. If you just have an attractive pot you want to put on display but it lacks a drainage hole, use it as a *cachepot* to hold a smaller pot with a drainage hole into which the plant is potted. If you have a plant in a container lacking a drainage hole, adding less water and rewatering again if necessary is infinitely easier than trying to remove excess water. If you think you've hopelessly waterlogged a plant, you can take some steps to mop up the excess:

✔ Tip the plant all the way on its side for 15 minutes to allow the water to drain out.

✔ Suck up the excess water by using a turkey baster, sticking the tip an inch or so (2 to 4 cm) into the soil.

✔ Cover the top of the potting mix with a dry rag to soak up the excess moisture. Replace it with a new one when the rag becomes saturated.

If the plant starts to lose leaves or to wilt, repot it immediately into a container that does have proper drainage.

Despite a persistent myth to the contrary, you don't have to let water sit for 24 hours to allow chlorine to evaporate. The parts-per-million of chlorine in treated water simply isn't significant enough to do any damage to a plant. Fluoridated water, on the other hand, can injure some plants, especially dracaenas, spider plants, and bulbs, causing leaf tips to burn (turn brown) at any concentration greater than 1 part per million. If you have doubts about your local water supply, check with your local water department and if they confirm a high rate of fluoride in the local drinking water, consider using another water source — at least for ailing plants.

Some areas, especially those in arid climates, have very hard or highly alkaline tap water. The minerals present in water can leave behind deposits that can threaten a plant's health. More than 1 part per million of boron, for example, can cause leaf margins to burn on some plants. Fortunately, there is something you can do about getting rid of harmful minerals. Just read on.

Leaching out minerals

Leaching involves watering plants to the point that excess water drains from their root balls. The drainage water is then discarded. The easiest way to leach a plant is to place it in a sink or bathtub, give it plenty of water, and allow the excess to go down the drain. Or, you can put your plants outdoors under a gentle summer rain for a thorough leaching as nature intended.

Although ordinary tap water does an excellent job of leaching out mineral salts, you can make it work more effectively by adding acid in the form of white vinegar. Add one teaspoon of vinegar per quart of water (five milliliters per liter) and pour it on. A one-quart mixture poured slowly is enough to do a small pot. Double or triple the quantity for larger pots.

You should leach your plants every three months under normal conditions. If your water is hard, you fertilize heavily, you always water from below, or your plants haven't been repotted in years, leach monthly.

Living with hard water

Hard water can harm plants, but if you *leach* regularly and repot a bit more often than usual (up to two or three times a year), hard water rarely poses a major problem. Hard water filtered or run through a *demineralizer* or *reverse osmosis system* (filtering systems that you may have in your home if you live in an area with extremely hard water) generally doesn't hurt your plants.

If you use a water softener to treat hard water, take your houseplant water from the pipe *before* it runs through the softener or use water from some other source, such as rainwater. Artificially softened water is toxic to plants!

Getting rid of mineral salts

Mineral salts are present in soil, water, and fertilizer, but pose no threat in small quantities. Over time, however, mineral salts tend to build up in the potting mix, eventually forming a crusty deposit on pots, on the surface of the potting mix, and at the base of plant stems.

Besides being unattractive, excess minerals salts are toxic, causing damage to stems, leaves, and especially roots. The salts can cause root tips to burn and eventually die back. If enough roots are damaged, the plant can no longer absorb the moisture it needs to survive.

One way to control mineral salt buildup is to regularly repot your plants into fresh mix. Thoroughly clean your pots and saucers to remove mineral deposits before reusing them. You can also control mineral salt build-up through leaching.

Water in Spades: The Secrets of Hydroponic Indoor Gardening

Hydroponics is a method of growing plants without soil of any kind. It involves bathing a plant's roots (continually or intermittently) in water that contains all the nutrients necessary for it to survive. Another term for hydroponic gardening is *soilless cultivation* because the only solid materials you use to grow a plant are its container and the *substrate* or *aggregate*, which is a material used to simply anchor the plant in an upright position.

The fact that plants can grow with their roots continually immersed in water seems to contradict the primary rule of proper plant watering — that soil must dry out a bit between waterings to ensure an adequate flow of oxygen to the plant's roots. The trick is, roots produced in a hydroponic system receive both loads of moisture and ample oxygen, so both needs are met at the same time.

Two types of hydroponic systems are most commonly used: passive and active. The following sections of this chapter examine both.

The passive hydroponics system setup

Also called *hydroculture,* passive hydroponic systems employ devices that look somewhat like self-watering pots (see the section on "Self-watering pots" earlier in this chapter). Figure 9-8 shows the setup in a typical hydroculture pot.

Passive hydroponics helps reduce the work and mess involved in raising houseplants. You rarely need to water more than once every two weeks and may never have to repot again because plants in hydroculture develop very few roots and, therefore, never become overcrowded. Even a large plant can spend its entire life in a small hydroponics pot. Soil insects, such as fungus gnats and soil mealybugs, are totally absent. And, passive hyproponics virtually eliminates your chances of losing plants to drought or overwatering.

Individual hydroculture containers with an appropriate amount of substrate start at about $10 for small pots and up to $50 or more for larger ones. You can find them in garden centers or in specialty stores, or you can order them by mail (see Appendix B for sources).

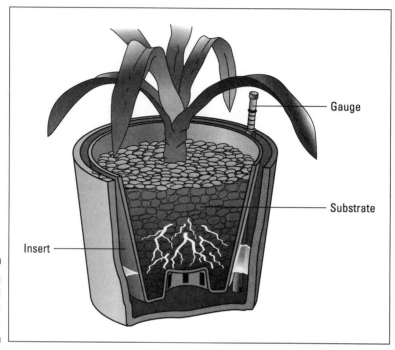

Figure 9-8:
A typical
hydroculture
setup.

Plants are potted up into a hydroculture *substrate* — an inert, granular material such as gravel, perlite, vermiculite, or clay pellets. The plant is potted into a special container called an *insert*. The substrate is poured around the plant's roots, and then the insert is set into a cachepot (or outer pot) that acts as a water reservoir.

A floating indicator gauge poking up from the insert indicates the level of nutrient solution, although some outer containers feature a clear window so you can see the nutrient solution level yourself. When the gauge or window reveals that the solution is used up, you fill the outer container to the halfway point.

Submerging the roots at each watering can lead to rot. Fill the water container to the brim only on those rare occasions when you'll be away from home for a few weeks and cannot water as often or at all.

Use water alone to top off the reservoir if the container already has nutrient granules or a nutrient disk (usually good for six months). Otherwise, use water with liquid or soluble hydroponic nutrients added according to the dilution ratio recommended on the nutrients package. Wait until the gauge or window indicates that the reservoir is empty before watering again.

Remove the insert every two or three months and pour tepid water through it to leach away any accumulated mineral salts.

While passive hydroponics is a fascinating alternative to growing a plant in potting soil, you should keep in mind the following caveats about this otherwise simple system:

✔ No actual soil (or any other organic matter) must ever enter into the system. Although some people claim you can move adult plants from potting soil to hydroculture systems just by rinsing off their root systems, that almost never works because at least some tiny amount of soil always remains. Start a new plant by rooting cuttings *in water;* then transfer them to the hydroculture system when roots begin to appear. (See Chapter 16 for how to successfully root cuttings in water.)

✔ When you first pot a cutting into a hydroculture system, add only water for the first 30 days so that it can adjust to its new environment. After the first month, add nutrients either with every watering or every six months.

✔ With no soil to buffer the effects of minerals and acids, top-quality water is vital whenever you use any form of hydroponics. If you know that you have naturally hard water, use a hydroponic nutrient designed specifically for hard water or buy distilled water.

✔ Don't expect miraculous results. Despite what some manufacturers claim, plants in hydroculture grow no more slowly or quickly given what the other growing conditions (light, humidity, temperature, and such) will permit. And, don't imagine that plants in hydroculture somehow can miraculously thrive in dry air or under poor light — like any other plant, they can't.

The active hydroponics setup

Active hydroponics (a system in which water is pumped over the roots) can result in much faster growth rates than *passive hydroponics* (in which the water simply sits there). Although popular among people who grow fast-maturing plants — such as vegetables, herbs, and annuals — active hydroponics offers few advantages over any other indoor gardening system when it comes to the naturally slow-growing flowering and foliage plants typically grown indoors.

The dozens of various active hydroponics systems vary in some way, but they all operate around the same basic setup:

✔ They mix water with soluble nutrients and store the mixture in a reservoir.

✔ Every three to five times a day (the frequency varies according to the type of substrate, how fast the substrate dries out, the growth rate, and the evaporation rate), an electrical charge is sent to a pump which then pulls the nutrient solution from the reservoir and pours it over the substrate where the plants' roots are growing.

✔ The nutrient solution drains back into the reservoir, leaving the roots freshly watered and fertilized.

The result of this operation is that roots get loads of water, fertilizer, and air all at the same time, which is why certain plants grow so quickly in active hydroponics systems.

Various media are used in active hydroponics including *rockwool* (a spongy substance created by spinning molten rock at a high speed to the consistency of cotton candy), clay pellets, vermiculite, and soilless mixes. Various kinds of containers are used to hold the roots, from tubs and trays to bags of rockwool or soilless mix with holes punched into them. Various types of water circulation methods are also common. In *trickle irrigation,* for example, a pump operates 24 hours a day, generating a slow trickle of water that drips continually over the plants' roots. Some systems, such as the *nutrient film technique* and *aeroponics,* employ no substrate at all — stakes hold up the plants and their roots grow right in the air.

Light is the growth factor most often lacking indoors, so most hydroponics users grow their plants under HID lamps or in a greenhouse where plants can get maximum light levels. Active hyproponics also augments humidity, owing to evaporation from the large water reservoirs (which also benefits nearby nonhydroponic plants) and some growers even add special carbon dioxide generators to their grow rooms or greenhouses for even faster growth. As with any other growing system, wet or dry, active hydroponics can stimulate faster growth only when you provide top-notch growing conditions.

Expect to pay about $100 for a small active hydroponics system (which will accommodate several plants) that includes a grow tray, reservoir, pump, timer, and some tubing. More elaborate ones can cost $250 or more. You usually can only get them at specialty stores (see Appendix B to locate a mail-order source).

Chapter 10

Something in the Air: Humidity and Circulation

Many houseplant enthusiasts take pains to make sure their plants get just the right amount of water, sunlight, fertilizer, and grooming, but overlook the quality of air their plants breathe. You can think of air quality as the Great Invisible Houseplant Growing Factor — you can't see it and you may not always feel it, but overly dry or stagnant air has helped to kill more plants than I care to count.

The biggest air quality factor is relative humidity, followed by air circulation. In this chapter, I explain how air quality affects houseplant growing conditions, how to control the air quality in your home, and which plants don't seem to mind the dry winter air found in just about every home.

It Ain't the Peat, It's the Humidity

Indoor growing conditions are pretty much the same throughout the world, so what's true for an indoor gardener in Toledo (Ohio or Spain) applies just as well to one in Tokyo, with one possible exception — *atmospheric humidity,* that is, how moist or dry the air is. In some climates, the air is dry year-round, both outside and inside. In other climates, outdoor air and indoor air are always humid. In many climates, indoor air tends to be humid during the summer but very dry during the winter when central heating drains the air of moisture.

Relative humidity refers to the relative amount of water vapor that the air contains. It is measured on a percentage scale from 0 (extremely dry air) to 100 (saturated air). The capacity of air to hold water varies according to the temperature, hence the term *relative*. Air that has a relative humidity of 100 percent at 32°F (0°C) may have a relative humidity of 30 percent at average indoor room temperatures. In fact, the relative humidity in many homes drops below 15 percent during the winter months, which makes the air drier than that in many deserts!

Understanding how various plants deal with dry air

Plants do their darndest to compensate for a lack of humidity in the air. They *transpire* (give off moisture) heavily under normal conditions, losing water to the air through their *stomata* (breathing pores). They transpire even more heavily in dry air, which accounts for much of the damage you see in plants grown in overly dry conditions — leaves curling under, brown or deformed leaves and leaf tips, flower buds turning brown without opening, and other signs of exteme dryness. Damaged tissues lose water more rapidly than the plant's roots can absorb it, which compounds the problem.

Most plants that come from arid climates, such as cacti and other succulents, are well adapted to dry air. They possess few stomata, which limits the amount of water they lose to the air. Many such plants keep their stomata closed during the day when the sun is hottest (and when water loss is greatest). In a way, they're "holding their breath" until nightfall.

In short, if you grow only native desert dwellers — arid land cacti and such — you don't need to worry about increasing the air humidity in your home. Likewise, dry air rarely bothers plants that have thick, leathery, waxy, or hairy leaves. These leaf surfaces reduce air movement in and around the stomata, cutting transpiration. Plants that have no leaves but respire through green stems (many epiphytic cacti, for example, have no leaves and "breathe" through their stems) are likewise immune to dry air.

Some thick-leafed plants produce papery thin flowers that may suffer severe damage in dry air. Many orchids, for example, have succulent leaves that suffer little damage in dry air, but have flower buds that don't open, fall off, or simply never form.

Plants with very thin leaves may not survive more than a few days in an arid environment. In many climates, these plants thrive during the summer months, then wilt and dry up as soon as you turn on your furnace.

Identifying plants that don't mind dry air

No plant really likes dry air (with 40 percent humidity or less), but the following plants are the best at tolerating it.

- Baby rubber plant *(Peperomia obtusifolia)*
- Bird of paradise *(Strelitzia regina)*
- Bunny ears *(Opuntia microdasys)*
- Cast iron plant *(Aspidistra elatior)*
- Century plant *(Agave americana)*
- Cereus *(Cereus peruvianus)*
- Clivia *(Clivia miniata)*
- Crown of thorns *(Euphorbia milii)*
- Donkey's tail *(Sedum morganianum)*
- Earth star *(Cryptanthus bivittatus)*
- Echeveria *(Echeveria elegans)*
- Golden ball cactus *(Echinocactus grusonii)*
- Heartleaf philodendron *(Philodendron scandens oxycardium)*
- Holiday cactus *(Schlumbergera × buckleyi)*
- Jade plant *(Crassula argentea)*
- Living stone *(Lithops)*
- Madagascar palm *(Pachypodium lamerii)*
- Medicine plant *(Aloe barbadensis)*
- Mistletoe cactus *(Rhipsalis baccifera)*
- Old man cactus *(Cephalocereus senilis)*
- Orchid cactus *(× Epicactus)*
- Pony tail palm *(Beaucarnea recurvata)*
- Pothos *(Epipremnum aureum)*
- Red ball cactus *(Gymnocalycium mihanovichii friedrichii* 'Rubra')*
- Rose-scented geranium *(Pelargonium graveolens)*
- Silver vase *(Aechmea fasciata)*
- Snake plant *(Sansevieria trifasciata)*
- Snowball cactus *(Mammillaria bocasana)*
- Spineless yucca *(Yucca elephantipes)*

> ✔ Wax plant (*Hoya carnosa*)
> ✔ Zonal geranium (*Pelargonium × hortorum*)

Defining ideal humidity

Even plants that are native to arid regions, such as succulents, prefer a relative humidity level of at least 40 percent. For most other houseplants, a relative humidity of 60 percent is desirable for continued growth and flowering. A humidity level of 70 percent and above is even better, but hard to maintain in most environments, and can generate unwanted side effects, such as condensation on glass surfaces and mildewed walls.

Fortunately, 60 percent humidity is also an optimum level for human beings and pets. Ample humidity helps prevent colds and other viral infections, and can help prevent dry skin. It also keeps your wood furniture from cracking and splintering. Paintings and antiques also remain in better condition when you keep the relative humidity at 60 percent or higher.

Determining your home's relative humidity

You can safely assume that the air in most homes in temperate climates is overly dry during the winter months when homes are heated. In arid areas, such as the southwestern United States or western Australia, indoor air is dry throughout the entire year. Air-conditioning also dries out air and in hot climates can turn what normally would be humid air into excessively dry air.

In climates where indoor and outdoor temperatures are nearly equal and rainfall is steady year-round, such as in some areas of the southern United States, dry air usually isn't a problem. Unless you have the air-conditioning on most of the time, if you live in one of these climates you don't need to worry about a lack of air humidity.

Using a hygrometer

If you want absolute precision in measuring the humidity levels in your home, you need a *hygrometer* (also called a *humidistat* or a *humidity meter*), a device sold in most hardware stores that measures relative humidity. Hygrometers are accurate but expensive. A good one costs from $50 to $150 or more.

If you invest in a hygrometer, you may find yourself checking it frequently right after you first buy it and then never again after the novelty wears off. After you determine your home's relative humidity at different times of the year, that about does it. Pretty much the same conditions repeat themselves year after year. Therefore, I suggest skipping a hygrometer altogether and using the drinking glass test, which I describe next.

Using the cheap but effective "drinking glass test"

Want to get an idea of your home's humidity without investing in a hygrometer? Try the so-called drinking glass test.

Put a drinking glass in the freezer for five minutes, then bring it into the room you want to test.

- ✔ **Does it frost up a lot?** If so, you have a very humid room.
- ✔ **Does it frost up just a little bit?** The room has average humidity.
- ✔ **Does it not frost up at all?** The room has dry air.

Locating the humid spots in your home

You can grow healthy houseplants in an environment with average indoor humidity levels without having to improve the humidity count throughout your entire home. One solution is to grow only plants that can tolerate dry air, or you can grow your plants in areas of your home that are normally more humid than the rest of the house.

The following spots typically have higher than average humidity and are ideal for plants that insist upon a decent amount of moisture in the air:

- ✔ Basement
- ✔ Laundry room, bathroom, and kitchen
- ✔ Floors
- ✔ On top of a pebble tray (see the section "Building a cheap yet effective humidity tray" later in the chapter)
- ✔ Where a number of plants are grouped together
- ✔ Rooms with a humidifier

Spotting symptoms that your plant is suffering from dry air

Dry air is a far more common problem in most homes than overly humid air. (If you're one of the few people with a home suffering from too much humidity, see "A cure for the opposite problem: Reducing humidity levels" later in this chapter.) If your plants exhibit any of the following symptoms (also shown in Figure 10-1), a lack of atmospheric humidity is the likely cause:

✔ Leaves curl under, develop brown patches, or become misshapen

✔ Leaves dry up and fall off prematurely

✔ Leaf tips dry out

✔ The soil dries out within three or four days after watering

✔ Flower buds form but dry up without opening (also known as *blasting*)

✔ Flowers wither prematurely

✔ Growth is sluggish even though all the other environmental factors seem close to ideal

Employing methods to increase humidity levels

You and your plants don't have to suffer with dry air conditions. A number of options are available to increase the relative humidity of any room where you want to grow houseplants. For the best possible humidity for your plants, use all three of the methods I describe in the following sections — try grouping your plants together, putting them on a pebble tray, and running a humidifier at all times.

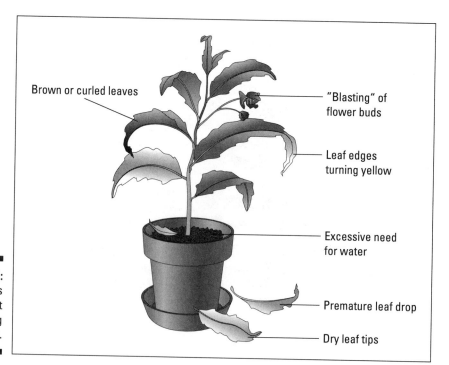

Figure 10-1:
Symptoms of a plant suffering from dry air.

Brown or curled leaves

"Blasting" of flower buds

Leaf edges turning yellow

Excessive need for water

Premature leaf drop

Dry leaf tips

Grouping your plants together

One way to easily and efficiently increase the relative humidity around your plants is to simply group them together. (See Figure 10-2.) Clustering your plants during the drier periods of the year is sometimes all you need to help your plants combat dry air.

By grouping plants together, you create a local *microclimate* in which air currents are limited and where the plants collectively contribute to increasing the relative humidity surrounding them through transpiration. The more plants in the crowd, the more each plant profits from the presence of the others.

Situate plants that need high humidity (usually those with thin leaves or those in bud or bloom) at the center of your plant grouping where the humidity is highest.

If you live in a dry climate, consider integrating groups of plants into your room decor to provide increased humidity all year long. In climates where low humidity is a problem only when you're heating your home, you can pool your plants in the winter and then break up the groupings and spread the plants around your house once again during the spring and summer.

Figure 10-2: The simple act of grouping together plants of any kind boosts the humidity level.

Building a cheap yet effective humidity tray

Another inexpensive and effective method you can use to surround your plants with increased humidity is stationing them on a *humidity tray* or *pebble tray* (see Figure 10-3). The moist pebbles or gravel that lines the tray actually helps boost the humidity levels. Plus, clustering the plants contributes even more moisture, making for a very humid microclimate that houseplants just adore.

Just about any waterproof container can serve as a pebble tray as long as it's high enough to support an inch or so (3 centimeters) of gravel. Although you can use a container as small as a flowerpot saucer, you're better off using a pebble tray that can hold several pots at once to get the maximum benefit out of the setup. The 2-foot-long (60 centimeter) plant trays commonly used under grow lights are good choices. Other choices for humidity trays include cake pans, plastic serving trays, and large casserole dishes.

To make the tray, fill the tray or saucer with 1 or 2 inches (2.5 to 5 centimeters) of pebbles, gravel, marbles, clay pellets, or any other similar material that doesn't rot or rust. Pour water into the tray until just the bottom half of the layer of pebbles is submerged. Water moves upward from the immersed pebbles to the dry, exposed ones via capillary action and then evaporates, creating a humid microclimate.

Figure 10-3:
A humidity tray emits humidity from stones that are kept constantly moist, yet the plants are never left soaking in water.

Waterproof tray lined with stones or pebbles

Place the pots either directly on the pebbles or put them in individual saucers first, which helps prevent soil-borne insects from traveling from pot to pot. Add water to the pebble tray when you water your plants, making sure the upper layer of pebbles is always exposed to air so that your plants are never allowed to soak in water.

Letting a machine do it: Running a humidifier

Running a humidifier is the quickest way to increase relative humidity throughout your home. Many models are available, from one-room units to humidifiers that hold several gallons of water and can treat several rooms at a time. Many models turn themselves off automatically if the humidity reaches rain forest levels, but that's rarely a problem in most homes. Your home may even have a humidifier integrated into its heating system. If so, find out how to adjust it to increase the relative humidity to at least 60 percent.

Humidifiers range from under $40 for a simple table-top model that you have to refill daily to $250 or more for models that feature large water reservoirs and sophisticated humidity controls.

Some ionizing humidifers have the nasty habit of leaving powdery dust residues from minerals in the water on nearby plants and furniture. Either avoid them or use only distilled water when running them. And make sure you keep your humidifier clean; otherwise, dangerous bacteria can build up. Special additives are available that you can add to your humidifier's reservoir to prevent bacteria buildup, but you should also clean your humidifier regularly, at least once every two months.

If you have an old-fashioned wall radiator (one with pipes or coils through which hot water circulates), you can easily create a cheap and simple humidifier — just set a shallow tray of water on top of it. The heat from the radiator causes the water in the tray to evaporate, increasing the humidity in the room.

Moving the more-delicate plants to a terrarium

Some plants have such delicate leaves or flowers that grouping them on a pebble tray and running a room humidifier round-the-clock still doesn't provide sufficient humidity. An open terrarium usually maintains a relative humidity of 80 percent, and conditions in a closed terrarium often approach the *saturation point* (100 percent relative humidity). You couldn't ask for more wetness in the air than that! (See Chapter 18 for more information on terrariums.)

Not enough light? Try boosting the humidity

Do you have a favorite plant that you'd like to grow in your home, but you just don't get the light it needs? Try increasing your home's relative humidity. Upping the humidity level from 30 percent to 70 percent greatly contributes to a plant's ability to change sunlight into energy. In fact, some plants can thrive with as little as 40 percent of the light they usually require if the humidity level is boosted.

When all else fails, just bag it

Some delicate plants are simply too large to fit into the average-size terrarium, but I do have one more trick up my sleeve. Keep the plant sealed inside a clear plastic bag for the duration of the cold-weather season (or whenever the air is dry). The humidity level inside a sealed plastic bag stays close to 100 percent. If water droplets form on the bag, indicating excess humidity, just open the bag for an hour or so to let some moisture evaporate.

If you recycle clear plastic dry-cleaning bags, they cost nothing and are large enough to cover almost any houseplant other than the tallest indoor tree. Don't worry that your plants can't breathe inside the bag. Thin plastic has microscopic holes that allow air to circulate. Besides, plants use and emit both carbon dioxide and oxygen, so they more or less produce their own air.

One danger exists with using plastic bags — any plant part touching the plastic may end up continually soaking in water, which can lead to rot. Use wooden, metal, or plastic stakes inserted into the pot to hold the plastic bag away from the plant.

A cure for the opposite problem: Reducing humidity levels

Excess air humidity is a rare problem except maybe in a terrarium, but if your home is plagued by condensation on your walls and windows, mildew buildup, or musty odors, the air is too darn humid. Although plants grow and bloom like never before, they likewise are prone to mildew and other diseases under such conditions.

Most indoor gardeners who have a problem with excess humidity are real plant lovers who have 200, 300, or more plants in their homes. Each plant gives off water through transpiration and evaporation, so moisture levels can get pretty high when you have a jungle's worth of plants. Your plants are not likely to complain about excess humidity (as far as most plants are

Misting: A momentary blast of moisture

Spraying houseplants with tepid water is a very popular and also very inefficient way to increase relative humidity. Many people spray their plants daily to increase air humidity, but it doesn't do much to help the plants. Theoretically, water sprayed onto and through foliage using a hand-held plant mister increases the humidity in the air and helps plants to grow. The spray lands on the leaves and surrounding surfaces and then evaporates, creating an immediate increase in relative humidity. However, the surrounding air carries that moisture away almost immediately. The positive effect of misting houseplants by hand is estimated to last a grand total of almost five minutes. However, it isn't a complete waste of time to mist your plants. Although it won't increase humidity levels, it does help to clean the leaves of dusty or sticky plants.

concerned, the higher the humidity, the better), but your family may, so you need to know how to control the excess humidity.

Increasing the air circulation by occasionally opening your windows helps considerably, as does running a fan in any humid enclosed room or venting it to the outdoors. You can also use a dehumidifier — just make sure to empty it regularly. You can find dehumidifiers in the $150 to $250 price range. The price depends mainly on size of the reservoir. Don't forget to empty your dehumidifier's reservoir before it fills to overflowing.

Unusually high humidity in a home often indicates an excessive use of vapor barriers (impermeable plastic layers) used in the home's construction, which also results in a reduction in air circulation, a common problem with many so-called "energy efficient" homes. If you have this problem, you may want to call in a contractor to find a permanent solution. Homes built before the 1970s rarely suffer from problems with excess humidity.

A Breezy Topic: Air Circulation

Air circulation, while not among the most critical houseplant growing factors, nevertheless figures into your ability to successfully grow just about any plant you choose. Air movement is important to a plant because it needs fresh air to replace the waste gases given off by leaves. But, truth be told, plants "breathe" so slowly that even the slightest air movement will do the trick.

Although indoor air circulation is negligible in most homes, as far as houseplants go there's usually enough of it to get by. Temperatures generally drop at night, so you automatically get a certain amount of air movement from the hot air rising and cool air sinking during the shift in temperature. Likewise, air currents develop when a window lets in heat from the sun, when you walk around the house, take a shower, turn on the oven, open the refrigerator, open and close doors, and of course, turn on a fan or air conditioner.

Some indoor gardeners install huge banks of fluorescent lights or high-intensity discharge lamps in cramped spaces that they've turned into *grow rooms*. These spots have notoriously poor air circulation. Movement of air around hanging plants near the ceiling can also stagnate to a dangerously low level.

If your plants seem to grow more slowly than normal or you're had a rash of plant diseases and you suspect stagnant air may be the culprit, consider running a small fan in the room. You don't need to direct the fan right at the plants (which can the dry leaves, causing further damage). Just making sure that it generates some additional air movement throughout the room.

Plants that insist upon ample air circulation

Only a few plants have special air circulation demands — and most of them are *epiphytes*. (Sometimes called *air plants, epiphytes* or *epiphytic plants* grow in the wild on trees and branches, not on the ground with their roots in the soil.)

Only epiphytes that grow at the very top of the tree canopy, such as certain bromeliads (especially those that have thick, grayish leaves) and many orchids, ever seem to suffer from a lack of air circulation in the home. These plants are said to require *buoyant air* — in other words, abundant air movement. Epiphytes that have thin leaves (a sign that they grow lower down on their host trees) don't seem to have special air circulation needs.

It may be difficult to spot when "upper-canopy" epiphytes aren't getting enough air circulation. They may not seem to grow as fast or be as healthy as they should. Run a small fan nearby to improve the air circulation and just watch their growth pick up.

Plants that tolerate stagnant air

Most plants do fine with only minimal air circulation, the proof being that so many plants thrive in terrariums where air circulation is almost nonexistent (see Chapter 18 for a list of such plants). Generally speaking, most small *terrestrial plants* (plants that grow on the ground rather than on trees) do great even in nearly stagnant air or closed containers, whereas epiphytes and desert plants generally fail to thrive — epiphytes because they need constant air circulation, and desert plants because they tend to rot in the intense humidity.

Chapter 11

Do Not Feed the Plants:
The Rules of Fertilizing

Forget the term *plant food.* What you apply to plants is *fertilizer,* the equivalent of mineral supplements for plants. And, at the risk of irking those indoor gardeners who think they have healthy and happy plants because they lay the fertilizer on thick, I have some news for them. The fact is, you can grow perfectly healthy houseplants without ever fertilizing them *at all.*

Plants get most of the minerals they need from the air, water, and whatever goodies are in the potting mix. As for what plants *eat* (outside of that giant Venus flytrap in "The Little Shop of Horrors"), they get their nourishment from light, not from so-called plant food.

In this chapter, I alert you to the signs of an overfertilized or underfertilized plant. Then I tell you about the various kinds of fertilizers and how to use them for the best results.

First — The Signs of Fertilizer Overkill

You can actually weaken or kill houseplants by overfertilizing them. In fact, far more indoor plants suffer from excess fertilization than from a lack of fertilization. An underfertilized plant simply grows more slowly and flowers a little bit less than it would if properly fertilized. The leaves and flowers of an underfertilized plant also tend to be somewhat smaller than normal. Otherwise, the plant usually remains surprisingly healthy for anyone who believes in the virtues of mega-fertilization.

An overfertilized plant may grow slowly or fail to flower correctly. Or, it may grow to be oversized yet limp — and still fail to flower. Such plants often suffer attacks by insects that can sense the plant's weakened state before we indoor gardeners do.

Because you usually apply fertilizer to the potting mix, the roots are the first part of a plant to suffer from excess fertilization. Roots respond to overfertilization by dying off. If a plant lacks sufficient roots to absorb the water it needs, its leaves turn yellow, or even wilt and die. You also may notice the leaf tips of an overfertilized plant turning brown, just as they do when the air is too dry. Severely overfertilized plants simply stop growing and die — either slowly over time or rapidly by rotting at their base.

Fertilizing Fundamentals

Now that I've frightened you half to death about the myriad dangers of overfertilization, I should tell you about the safe way to fertilize. The secret lies in (didn't you just know this was coming?) *moderation*.

Rule Number One: Less is more

The number-one rule for fertilizing plants bears repeating: When it comes to fertilizing your plants, less is more. Go ahead and fertilize your plants, but *never* give them as much fertilizer as the manufacturer's label suggests. Fertilizer companies want to encourage you to use as much fertilizer as possible (you use it up quicker, you buy more often). The dosage on the label usually represents the largest amount of the fertilizer that a healthy plant growing under ideal conditions can tolerate without feeling ill effects.

Under less than ideal growing conditions (like those in the average house or apartment), plants won't absorb large amounts of fertilizer. If a plant lacks light and humidity, it doesn't synthesize the fertilizer as quickly because it isn't operating at peak performance. Therefore, fertilizer builds up in the potting mix unused.

Of course, you can *leach* the plant regularly (see Chapter 9 for information on how and when to leach out mineral salts) to minimize the harmful effects of fertilizer buildup. But why pour your fertilizer money down the drain (literally) by giving your plants more fertilizer than they can handle?

Unless you're certain that you are providing your plants with absolutely perfect growing conditions, never apply more than *half* the recommended dose of fertilizer.

Rule Number Two: Never fertilize a weak plant

A plant that's in bad shape, such as one suffering from insects or disease, recovering from a bad shock (such as a spill to the floor), or struggling with root damage, simply can't utilize fertilizer properly. Wait until you see healthy new leaves appear or note other obvious signs of recovery before you fertilize the plant again. I repeat, *never* fertilize a weak plant.

Rule Number Three: Some plants don't live by the rules

Some plants *do* require more fertilizer than others. Flowering plants and plants grown for fruit require more light, more water, and more humidity than other plants. If you boost the amount of growing essentials (and you have to if you want them to perform), it stands to reason that they require more fertilizer as well.

Just don't go overboard: It's easier to add a little more fertilizer if necessary than to remove excess fertilizer from a plant that you've pretty much poisoned by overfertilizing.

When's the Best Time to Fertilize?

Wait for a month or so before fertilizing newly purchased or freshly repotted plants. Not only does their mix usually already contain fertilizer, but the last thing they need as they acclimate to their new pot or home is an extra dose of fertilizer. (*Remember:* Never fertilize a weak plant. Plants adapting to a new environment qualify as weakened.)

Fertilize plants only during their active growth phases. Most plants grow most strongly from spring through summer and need the most fertilizer at that time. Begin reducing the fertilization rate in the autumn (an excellent time to apply a bit of tomato fertilizer, which is rich in potassium, to help the plant through the dark days of winter). You may want to apply fertilizer at half the recommended rate in spring and summer, then cut back to a quarter of the rate in autumn.

Most plants grow slowly, if at all, in winter. Give them either no fertilizer during this time of year, or only a weak dosage. Never fertilize a plant that is completely dormant.

Plants grown under artificial lights — except the few that go entirely dormant — often continue to grow vigorously throughout the year. Fertilize them in the autumn and winter just as you would in the spring or summer.

Reading the Label: The Elements of Fertilizing

Packaged fertilizers typically list the percentages of the three *primary nutrients* that plants require: nitrogen, phosphorus, and potassium, in that order. Plants need more of these three elements than any others. Each of the primary nutrients plays a specific role, which I cover in the following sections of this chapter.

Wondering what those numbers mean on fertilizer package labels? They refer to the proportion of primary nutients in the fertilizer. If you see, for example, "9-10-5" on a label, that fertilizer contains 9 parts nitrogen, 10 parts phosphorus, and 5 parts potassium.

Nitrogen

Nitrogen is vital to the production of *chlorophyll,* the green pigment that not only gives foliage its green color, but also allows plants to absorb light, their sole source of energy. Fertilizers rich in nitrogen help produce healthy new leaves and stems.

On the down side, too much nitrogen can promote overly abundant new growth that is highly susceptible to insects and disease. Savvy houseplant growers kmow to avoid using fertilizers that are too rich in nitrogen. Rather than nitrogen-rich *foliage plant* formulas (for example, a formula with 30-19-15 or 25-10-10 on the label), many indoor gardeners are turning to the so-called *all-purpose* or *balanced* fertilizers (ones with 15-15-15 or 10-10-10 on the label), which generally encourage somewhat slower but healthier growth than do foliage plant formulas.

Phosphorus

Phosphorus is especially useful in the development of flowers and fruit. You can apply phosphorus-rich fertilizers (those listed with a number such as 19-30-15 on the label) to plants just before they flower and to plants in full bloom.

Phosphorus does not stimulate flowering — only good growing conditions can do that. However, a fertilizer rich in phosphorus can help make flowers grow larger and last longer. It also encourages better coloration. In fact, phosphorus-rich fertilizers are often sold as *flowering plant* fertilizers.

Potassium

Potassium is especially useful in helping plants to store up reserves for future use and build up resistance to insects and diseases. A good time to use potassium-rich fertilizers is when plants just finish blooming because they help the plants regenerate for the next flowering.

Plants that have well-defined periods of rest or dormancy — such as bulbs, cacti, and succulents — also appreciate extra doses of potassium to help them store up reserves for the hard times ahead. Some cactus fertilizers are rich in potassium, but many indoor growers actually use cheaper and more widely available *tomato fertilizers* as a rich potassium source.

Some minor players

Most fertilizers also contain minute quantities of elements other than nitrogen, phosphorus, and potassium. Plants need three of the minor elements (calcium, magnesium, and sulfur) in fairly large quantities, but most potting mixes and municipal water provide these elements in sufficient amounts. You rarely need to add these elements, although most complete fertilizers do include them.

Plants also need several *trace elements* (elements required in extremely small quantities). These elements are also called *micronutrients*. The most common trace elements added to fertilizer include iron, manganese, copper, boron, molybdenum, chlorine, zinc, and nickel.

Most of the trace elements are already present in many potting mixes. When they aren't (artificial soil mixes, discussed in Chapter 13, are usually totally lacking in trace elements), you can add them by using a *complete* fertilizer, one specifically designed to include all plant nutrients, including trace elements.

Using a complete fertilizer occasionally, say only once or twice a year, can help ward off hard-to-spot trace mineral deficiencies. The most obvious signs of mineral deficiencies are stunted growth, deformed leaves, and leaves with unusual red, purple, or yellow splotches.

You may see the word *chelated* on fertilizer labels. It indicates a product that has been specially treated to make it more readily useable by a plant and its plant tissues. Chelated fertilizers generally cost more than other fertilizers, but they generate more immediate results if you have an ailing plant.

Specialized Fertilizer Formulas

If you've ever visited a plant store or nursery, you've probably seen fertilizer formulas for just about everything that grows indoors: foliage plants, flowering plants, cacti, orchids, African violets, and more. Usually, you can get by with using just the basic fertilizers — those sold as *all-purpose fertilizer* or *flowering plant fertilizer*.

Sometimes, however, specialized formulas do have their advantages. You don't need to buy an African violet fertilizer if you grow just one African violet or an orchid fertilizer if you have only a couple orchids, but if you grow dozens of plants of the same type, purchasing a specialized fertilizer can prove worthwhile.

Alternating between formulas

A favorite fertilizing program for many houseplant growers is to simply alternate between an all-purpose (or balanced) fertilizer and a flowering plant formula each time they apply fertilizer. If you use *soluble fertilizer* (see "Soluble powders and crystals" later in this chapter), you can apply balanced fertilizer one month, flowering plant fertilizer the next, balanced fertilizer again the following month, and so forth.

If you have plants that like to store up energy for future use, such as flowering bulbs or cacti, add a high-potassium fertilizer to the all-purpose fertilizer/flowering plant fertilizer cycle. Simply fertilize once with an all-purpose fertilizer, once with a flowering plant fertilizer, and once with a tomato (high-potassium) fertilizer, then start a new three-month cycle.

If you alternate between two or three different fertilizers, try to make one of them a complete fertilizer (one that contains all the trace elements). Then, you can rest assured that your plants are getting all the nutrients they need.

Acid formulas

Acid fertilizer (also know as *acid-reaction fertilizer*) can benefit members of a small but rather specialized group of plants that prefer acidic growing mixes. (For a list of those plants, see Chapter 13.) Acid fertilizers not only help keep the potting mix on the acidic side but often also contain an extra dose of chelated iron. Acid fertilizer is sold under the names *rhododendron*, *azalea*, or *evergreen fertilizer.*

Dispensing Fertilizer

Fertilizers come in an almost endless variety of formulas, and an equally endless variety of ways to dispense it — including powders, liquids, pellets, tablets, and even sticks and spikes.

Never apply fertilizer to plants when their potting mix is totally dry, especially not at the concentration recommended on the label. Doing so can burn the roots and damage the plant. If the mix is at least slightly moist, go ahead and fertilize, but if the mix is completely dry, use plain water for a day or so before you apply any fertilizer.

Ready-to-use liquids

Although they're the easiest to dispense, ready-to-use fertilizers are expensive when compared with other forms of fertilizer. That's because a bottle of ready-to-use fertilizer contains more water than fertilizer, yet costs almost as much as the concentrated fertilizers. A ready-to-use liquid fertilizer contains no more than $1/50$ th of the actual fertilizer that an equally priced concentrated soluble formula contains, and therefore costs about 50 times more!

Concentrated liquids

Concentrated liquids do contain some water, but they still qualify as an economical choice. Dilute concentrated liquids according to the instructions on the label, or dilute them even more by adding more water or less product. Using two to four times as much water as the label recommends gives you a safe-to-use fertilizer that doesn't burn your plants or cause damage to their leaves and foliage. Apply this type of fertilizer whenever you water.

Soluble powders and crystals

As with concentrated liquids, you can dilute powders and crystals in water and then apply them when you water your plants. This type of fertilizer costs less than just about any other on the market depending on the specific formulation. You can dilute them to whatever concentration you prefer — just add less fertilizer or more water.

The easiest way to apply soluable fertilizers is to mix them with the water in your watering can and pour them onto the plant.

Most commercial soluble fertilizers are designed to be applied once a month, or you can use the constant fertilizing method, which I explain in the section, "Constant fertilization" later in this chapter.

Slow-release pellets, powders, and granules

You mix slow-release pellets, powders, and granules into the top layer of the potting mix. Just apply the amount recommended (or even less) for the size of pot you have and work it in with a fork. Depending on the brand, slow-release fertilizers remain effective for three to six months — and sometimes for a full year. Many indoor gardeners find them very handy, but they do have certain drawbacks, including the following:

✔ Although slow-release fertilizer mediums are supposed to release the fertilizer over a period of several months, the rate of release actually depends on the specific growing conditions. If the pellets release faster than indicated, your plants may be suffering from a lack of fertilizer toward the end of each fertilizing cycle. Worse yet, you may end up adding more fertilizer to a plant that already has plenty, which can be damaging to a plant.

✔ Meeting the various fertilizing needs of many plants over time also presents a challenge. A typical flowering plant, for example, prefers a balanced fertilizer when it's young and a phosphorus-rich fertilizer (or at least a fertilizer less rich in nitrogen) after its buds form. That's easy enough to do when the fertilizer is used up rapidly, but not so easy to do when the fertilizer remains effective for three to six months.

Whenever you use slow-release pellets, powders, or granules, make a note on your calendar to remind you when you need to apply them again. As with any fertilizer, always apply less than the recommended dosage and never more.

Slow-release spikes, tablets, and sticks

Insert concentrated fertilizer spikes, tablets, and sticks into the potting mix all the way down to the base of the plant (see Figure 11-1). Some come with special applicators so that you can be sure of inserting them deep enough. But you don't need to spend extra money on gizmos to insert the fertilizer properly — you can do it just as easily by using a finger or pencil.

Figure 11-1:
Insert fertilizer spikes into the potting mix down to the base of the plant.

Slow-release fertilizers, spikes, and tablets remain effective for several months (always read the label to see exactly how long). As with pellets, powders, and granules, the problem is figuring out just when you need to replace them.

One problem with spikes, sticks, and tablets is that they tend to dispense concentrated amounts of fertilizer in one small area of the pot. At repotting time, you may find that the plant's roots have died back in a perfect circle all around the fertilizing product as a result of the fertilizer concentration in that spot being too strong. The harm isn't permanent (the plant probably has plenty of healthy roots elsewhere), but seeing it for the first time can be alarming.

Foliar fertilizers

You can apply most soluble fertilizers as a *foliar spray*. Just dilute the fertilizer with water, but use no more than *one quarter* of the recommended concentration (higher concentrations can burn leaves). Spray the mixture on your plants until you have thoroughly coated their surfaces (any excess simply drips into the potting mix, where the roots can absorb it). Some fertilizers leave a powdery residue on leaves. If you find that yours does, rinse it off — and next time look for a formula specifically recommended for foliar spraying.

Most plants readily absorb fertilizer through their leaves. If a plant seems a bit yellowed and you suspect it may lack nutrients, foliar fertilizing can green it up — often within days!

Many bromeliads, such as the *Tillandsia*, have root systems that act strictly as anchors and can't absorb water or fertilizer (see Chapter 7). Using foliar sprays on the plants' leaves or plunging the plants into a diluted fertilizer solution are the only two ways to effectively fertilize them. Use fish emulsion or liquid seaweed fertilizers on these plants because other fertilizers contain colorants that can stain the leaves.

Constant fertilization

If you tend to forget to fertilize your plants, the *constant fertilization* method may be for you. It requires adding fertilizer with each watering. The secret to this method is to dilute the fertilizer so much that you actually end up adding no more fertilizer than you would if you used any other method. Just dilute the fertilizer to $^1/_8$ th of the recommended monthly dosage. During autumn and winter, you can dilute it even more — to $^1/_{16}$ th of the usual dose.

The main advantage of constant fertilization is that applying fertilizer becomes a habit. Adding a pinch or so of fertilizer to the watering can become part of your normal routine, but the plant isn't in danger of overfertilization because of the weak fertilizer solution. You can continue constant fertilization even during the autumn and winter — $^1/_{16}$ of a normal dose of fertilizer isn't enough to harm plants that are dormant or resting, yet is just enough to boost the nourishment of those plants still growing strongly.

Another advantage of constant fertilization is that it provides for even growth. Fertilizing a plant abundantly once a month is a bit like gorging yourself at dinner parties and eating nothing in between. You're either stuffed and bloated, or weak and famished.

Plants react to one-a-month fertilizations by growing in spurts shortly after you apply the fertilizer, then slowing down or stopping two or three weeks later, resulting in leaves of unequal size and flowers blooming sporadically. Plants that get the "constant fertilization" treatment always have some minerals at hand, and therefore tend to grow more consistently and sustain longer-lasting blooms. Most people who win top prizes in plant shows use constant fertilization to grow their plants.

Chapter 12

The Heat Is On: Temperature and Growing Cycles

. . . .

In This Chapter
▶ Seeking out the hotter and colder spots in your home
▶ Finding out which plants like it hot and which prefer to chill off
▶ Discovering the growth, rest, and and sleep cycles in plants
▶ Deciding whether to let your plants grow year-round, or force them to rest

. . . .

*I*f you feel comfortable with the air temperature in your home, probably so do the vast majority of your houseplants. The average houseplant can handle indoor temperatures ranging anywhere from 10 degrees higher or lower than a person's comfort range, which means the temperature in your home can be anywhere between 55°F to 85°C (13°F to 30°C) at any time of the year with none of your plants suffering in the least.

But some plants are more picky than others when it comes to the air temperature they require to thrive, flower, or even stay alive. In this chapter, I tell you how to go about investigating all the nooks and crannies around your house so you can take advantage of your home's natural temperature differences. I also list the plants that insist on warm temperatures, cool temperatures, or downright cold conditions to keep going. Temperature also figures into a plant's growth cycle. Among other factors, a change in temperature can cause a plant to go dormant, or just take it easy for a while.

Identifying the Hot Spots and Cold Corners in a Room

You can easily tell when a room is hot, cold, or anything in between just by standing in it. But how often do you sit on a windowsill overnight during the winter when temperatures drop to well below freezing outside and just inside it's no more than 32 degrees, or at noon on a hot summer's day where the temperature just inside the glass can skyrocket to 140 degrees or higher? In addition, think about your hanging plants that cook from warm air rising to the ceiling. Just what kinds of temperatures are they enduring?

Searching out microclimates with a minimum/maximum thermometer

You may on occasion receive a gift plant that likes temperatures on the cool side — almost all florist plants do — or you may inherit a plant that has special temperature needs. If you find yourself with a "special needs" plant, you can take advantage of your home's warmer or colder *microclimates* — individual mini-climates that naturally occur within the overall climate of your home (Chapter 2 of this book has more on the subject).

Temperatures vary quite a bit within the average home and a conventional indoor thermometer tells only part of the story — the temperature of the room at a particular point in time — but not variations in temperature over a period of time. Temperatures vary greatly within any enclosed space, and the most savvy indoor gardeners know just where the spots are in their homes that get hotter or colder depending on the seasons and the time of day. A device called a *minimum/maximum thermometer* comes in handy for this purpose. (See Figure 12-1.)

A minimum/maximum thermometer shows not only the current temperature, but also the highest and lowest temperatures over a period of time. To use one, just set both the high and low temperature scales at the current temperature by pushing a button . . . and wait. Next time you check, you'll be able to read not only the current temperature, but the highest and lowest temperature recorded from the time you reset the thermometer. Both mercury and digital minimum/maximum thermometers are available, and both are fine for determining microclimates.

Hang the thermometer anywhere you want to situate those plants you think may be persnickety about room temperature. Note the high and low temperatures recorded over a three- or four-day period. These readings provide a picture of that particular microclimate's average temperature range.

You can find minimum/maximum thermometers in the bigger garden centers or by mail order from indoor gardening tools suppliers (see Appendix B of this book for a list of sources).

Most houseplants prefer a slight temperature drop at night of 5°F to 10°F (2°C to 4°C). If you have a thermostat and central air-conditioning or heating, you can pick the nighttime temperature you want, or you can take advantage of your home's natural microclimates. Temperatures drop at night in many parts of your home without your doing a thing. Use a minimum/maximum thermometer to test nighttime temperature fluctuations in various places in your home. You might find it surprising just how much temperatures drop at night on a window ledge, for example.

Figure 12-1:
Minimum/
maximum
thermometer.

Typical cool spots

Flowering bulbs, florist plants, and other plants that prefer cooler-than-average temperatures usually do well in the following areas:

- ✔ Near a north-facing window in the northern hemisphere; a south-facing window in the southern hemisphere
- ✔ The basement
- ✔ Near any window in the winter (in temperate climates)
- ✔ Close to the floor
- ✔ In an unheated room
- ✔ Away from stoves, ovens, radiators, TVs, stereo systems, and anything else that produces heat
- ✔ In an air-conditioned room, particularly a bedroom
- ✔ Between a window and curtain in the winter
- ✔ In areas that have a regular flow of air

Typical hot spots

The following places are usually warmer than the rest of your home. They make ideal spots for plants that love heat — but can be a deathtrap for plants that like a little nip in the air.

 ✔ Near a north-facing window in the southern hemisphere; a south-facing window in the northern hemisphere

 ✔ In the attic

 ✔ Near any window in the summer (and year-round in warm climates)

 ✔ Any overheated room of your house in the winter or any room with no air-conditioning in the summer

 ✔ Near the ceiling

 ✔ In front of or just above a radiator

 ✔ Near stoves, ovens, and other heat-producing appliances

 ✔ Kitchens, bathrooms, and laundry rooms

 ✔ Places with little air movement

Some Like It Hot, and Some Like the Air-Conditioning on Full Blast

Ninety percent of all houseplants do just fine with the range of temperatures found in the average home. But some plants get the chills if the room temperature falls below 65°F (18°C).

The following plants fall into the heat-loving category:

 ✔ African violet *(Saintpaulia ionantha)*

 ✔ Aluminum plant *(Pilea cadierei)*

 ✔ Caladium *(Caladium × hortulanum)*

 ✔ Corn plant *(Dracaena fragrans)*

 ✔ Episcia *(Episcia cupreata)*

 ✔ False aralia *(Dizygotheca elegantissima)*

 ✔ Flaming sword *(Vriesea splendens)*

 ✔ Florist's gloxinia *(Sinningia speciosa)*

 ✔ Guzmania *(Guzmania lingulata)*

- Lady Jane anthurium *(Anthurium × andreacola* 'Lady Jane')
- Madagascar dragon tree *(Dracaena marginata)*
- Ming aralia *(Polyscias fruticosa)*
- Peace lily *(Spathiphyllum wallisii)*
- Pothos *(Epipremnum aureum)*
- Warneckei dracacena *(Dracaena deremensis* 'Warneckei')
- Wax plant *(Hoya carnosa)*
- Zebra plant *(Aphelandra squarrosa* 'Dania')

Other plants like a little chill in the air, something they may not get if you keep your home well-heated in the cold-weather months. To make the following plants happy, give them cool to cold conditions during the winter, from 50°F to 65°F (10°C to 18°C). If you can't offer temperatures that cold, most of these plants will still survive, but may not do their best.

- Azalea *(Rhododendron simsii)*
- Baby's tears *(Soleirolia soleirolii)*
- Bougainvillea *(Bougainvillea glabra)*
- Cattleya *(Cattleya)* — many but not all types
- Chrysanthemum *(Dendranthema)*
- Clivia *(Clivia miniata)*
- Fuchsia *(Fuchsia)*
- Gerbera *(Gerbera jamesonii)*
- Lady's slipper *(Paphiopedilum)*
- Living stone *(Lithops)*
- Oleander *(Nerium oleander)*
- Orchid cactus *(× Epicactus)*
- Orchids (several kinds)
- Strawberry begonia *(Saxifraga stolonifera)*

The following plants like temperatures that are more than just cool — meaning, temperatures below 50°F (10°C), something that not everyone can easily provide. Most of these will still grow at normal temperatures indoors, but many will bloom poorly or not at all if they are kept constantly warm.

- Cactus — many kinds including the Golden ball cactus *(Echinocactus grusonii)* and Old man cactus *(Cephalocereus senilis)*
- Cyclamen *(Cyclamen persicum)*

- Easter lily *(Lilium longiflorum)*
- Forced bulbs (crocus, narcissus, hyacinth, tulip, and such)
- Hortensia *(Hydrangea macrophylla)*
- Miniature rose *(Rosa)*
- Mother-of-thousands *(Tolmiea menziesii)*
- Pocketbook plant *(Calceolaria)*
- Primrose *(Primula)*
- Snowball cactus *(Mammillaria bocasana)*

A window, a radiator, and a couple of added gizmos = plant heaven

For some reason, radiators and windows always seem to go together, which is inconvenient for houseplants. Winter is when most plants need the brightest light possible — which is usually right in front of a window. Consequently, when the heat is on, the hot, dry air from the radiator parches the poor plants sitting on window ledges.

Fortunately, there's a simple solution: Install a shelf at the base of the window (see the figure in this sidebar). Not only does it give you more surface space on which to grow plants, but it also directs heat toward the center of the room (which is where you want it anyway).

Because warm air rising in front of the shelf can dry out your plants, equip the shelf with a humidity tray (see Chapter 10 for more information). Then, your plants will have bright light, great humidity, and nice, warm air — heaven on earth for houseplants.

A Time to Grow and a Time to Kick Back: Houseplant Cycles

Some plants do and some plants don't . . . go dormant, that is. Dormancy is one of the three basic ways (the others being rest and active growth) that plants react to changes in their surroundings. In their natural environment, plants follow the seasons, going dormant, resting, or simply slowing down during periods of drought, cold weather, or reduced daylight, and become more active when water, warmth, and light are abundant. The question is whether you need to encourage plants to rest when you grow them indoors.

In the following sections I describe the three basic growing states that plants are in at any given time, and how that affects the type of care you need to give your plants throughout the year.

Dormant periods

Dormancy is a temporary state of total inactivity. The plant stops growing and generally loses its leaves. Hardy plants that go dormant usually do so in winter, but in the wild, tropical or subtropical plants that go dormant usually do so during the dry season (just when that occurs varies according to the climate). Dormant plants require much less water than usual. In addition, they don't absorb any energy from the sun, and therefore don't need any light — in fact, you can keep fully dormant plants in total darkness.

Rest periods

A *rest period* is simply the part of a plant's life cycle when it puts out no new growth but does not go entirely dormant. A *resting plant,* for example, retains at least some of its leaves but produces no new ones and doesn't bloom. A rest period is part of the natural cycle of many tropical and subtropical plants, often corresponding to the dry season, although some skip their rest periods and grow year-round when kept indoors where there are no changing seasons.

Active growth periods

An *active growth period* is just what it sounds like — the plant puts out new leaves, increases in size, produces flowers, and so forth. All plants go through a period of active growth at least once a year and many, especially those that live in tropical or subtropical climates that are humid year-round, grow actively throughout the year.

Active growth does not mean that the plant grows at top speed. Even plants that grow year-round grow more quickly when light, water, humidity, nutrients, and so on, are administered in the proper amounts and less quickly when one or more of those elements is lacking. Whenever a plant puts out *any* growth at all, however slight, it counts as active growth.

If they snooze, do you lose (or save) the plant?

It used to be that houseplant enthusiasts went to great lengths to force all their plants into dormancy once a year because they thought a plant's natural sabbatical was vital to its survival. To this day, many books on the subject of houseplants insist that cutting back on water and fertilizer during the winter months is essential to give plants a needed rest.

The truth of the matter is that plants are opportunistic. If conditions are good, they continue to grow year-round, even if they go dormant or rest in their native environments. Even in nature, plants often skip their rest periods if the local dry season turns out to be rainier than usual, and plants that normally grow year-round often take a rest when growing conditions are poor. Nevertheless, you sometimes do need to encourage plants to go into a rest period, a subject I cover next.

Hardy plants

For some houseplants of temperate origin (notably, hardy bulbs such as crocus, hyacinths, narcissus, and tulips, or shrubs and perennials forced indoors), a dormant period at cold temperatures is an absolute must. Otherwise, not only do these plants not bloom, they usually die in short order.

Is leaf loss a sign of dormancy?

Loss of leaves is not necessarily a dormancy or that a plant is in a rest period. It all depends on the degree of loss. Most tropical and subtropical plants (that is, most houseplants), unlike hardy plants that need a period of cold weather every year to perform as they should, lose leaves throughout the year. Older leaves simply drop off as new ones appear.

Leaf loss that's more prolific than usual may be a response to poor growing conditions or a growth slowdown. Many plants, for example, react to the shorter days and declining growing conditions of autumn (weaker light, drier air, cooler outdoor temperatures) by losing more leaves than usual. If they also continue to produce new ones, they're still in a phase of active (albeit reduced) growth.

Cacti, succulents, and some orchids

Other plants, such as many cacti and succulents (as well as certain orchids), thrive indoors but do not bloom if you keep them in full growth year-round. Nature has taught them the best time to flower is when the rains return after a period of drought. They prefer to stick to nature's plan even when you give them great growing conditions year-round. If you want to see flowers, you have to supply these plants with a period of rest or dormancy.

When cacti, succulents, and orchids are young plants, you may actually want to keep them growing year-round so that they reach maturity faster. Keep them warm, brightly lit, and well-fertilized, and water them according to their needs until they reach flowering size. Only then do you need to give them an annual rest period.

Begin cutting back on the watering and fertilizer and begin exposing them to cooler temperatures, starting in the late autumn for cacti and succulents and after blooming for most orchids. Orchids usually only need a few weeks of rest and a slight drop in temperature before they will bloom; succulents and especially cacti, on the other hand, often bloom abundantly only when you keep them dry and cool all winter. Raise temperatures and begin normal watering and fertilizing after the rest period ends.

Supplying cool winter temperatures is easy enough if you have an unheated or barely heated room at your disposal, but many indoor gardeners may not have a spot in their homes where they can maintain the cool 68°F (20°C) days and 55°F (13°C) nights that many of these plants prefer.

A spot right near a cold window is just perfect, even if the temperature inside the room is considerably warmer. (To determine whether a particular windowsill is a good spot for your plant, use the minimum/maximum thermometer described earlier in this chapter.) For a list of other places in the home where temperatures may be cool enough to encourage full dormancy, see "Typical cool spots" earlier in this chapter.

You also may want to consider placing these plants outdoors in the autumn, bringing them back indoors only when frost threatens, or placing them in cold storage (a root cellar, for example) for several months. Make sure that the plant is thoroughly dry before storing it without light, otherwise rot can set in.

If you live in a tropical climate where temperatures remain warm both indoors and out all year long and want to grow plants that bloom readily, you may do better to choose plants other than desert cacti. (For more specific information on these plants and the conditions they need during their periods of rest or dormancy, see Chapter 6.)

Year-round growth and its effect on your plants

Most houseplants happily grow year-round if the conditions are right. Almost all foliage houseplants belong to this category, even plants such as the English ivy that normally go fully dormant in winter when in their natural environment.

Many flowering plants can either bloom year-round under the right conditions or can take their cues on when to bloom from factors such as the shortened daylight hours of winter or the extra daylight hours of summer, which can force many plants to bloom independently of any rest period.

Do you really want your plants to continue growing all year long? You're initial response may be "why not?" but first consider the results: Winter brings shorter days and weakened light. Plants that continue to grow rapidly under winter's feeble sunlight (especially in a room not all that brightly lit to begin with) soon show the growth patterns typical of plants not getting enough sun — they become weak-stemmed, etiolated (pale and less vigorous), and lean toward the direction of the light source.

Forcing a rest period

You can always prune off the weakened stems when the longer, brighter days of spring arrive, but that can stress the plant and doesn't always produce attractive results. Consider forcing it to rest during the winter instead by doing the following:

- ✔ Start in the autumn by cutting back on fertilizer or not fertilizing at all.
- ✔ Water the plant less often, letting the potting mix get a bit drier between waterings.
- ✔ If possible, put the plant in cooler surroundings.

  Even if you can't control the temperature, just reducing watering and fertilizer still helps considerably in preventing weak winter growth.

If you grow plants where light remains strong all year long — for example, under artificial lights — or, if you can move all your plants to a sunny window for the winter, you probably don't need to worry about slowing plant growth during the winter months. Maintain normal temperatures and keep fertilizing and watering them and they can grow perfectly well throughout the year.

Chapter 13

The Real Dirt on Mixes and Potting

. . . .

In This Chapter

▶ Discovering the ingredients in today's fortified potting soil

▶ Stirring up your own potting mix

▶ Picking the right mix for your pot

▶ Recognizing when a plant is pot-bound

▶ Trying your hand at potting techniques

▶ Topdressing the soil when you can't repot

. . . .

*I*t may be said that it was potting soil that ushered in the era of modern indoor gardening. Prior to the introduction of today's scientifically formulated potting mixes, houseplant enthusiasts were limited to growing whatever rugged foliage could survive in plain old dirt. Now you can find a wide variety of soils to suit a number of growing needs, which I tell you about in this chapter. You can also find out how to whip up your own potting soil mixes — just like the indoor gardening pioneers of yesteryear.

The second half of this chapter covers potting — the best times to pot, when to avoid repotting, when to "pot up" and "pot down," and techniques to make potting quick and safe for your plants, with a minimum of mess.

The Sands of Time: A History of Houseplant Potting Mixes

There's dirt and then there's potting soil, although at one time there wasn't much of a difference between the two. Until a few decades ago, most potting mixes available on the market consisted of nothing more than outdoor garden soil or garden soil mixed with sand. The problem with garden soil as a potting medium is that it hardens when you put it in a pot. Although it may remain loose and crumbly outdoors, thanks to activity of earthworms and other busy animals, garden soil straight out of the ground quickly turns into a rock-solid mass when you stuff it into a pot.

Garden soil/sand mixes were later *pasteurized* (heated until any harmful microorganisms were killed). Sometimes the larger rocks and stones were removed and maybe some fertilizer was added, but little else was done to potting media for another 20 years. Few houseplants were able to thrive because nearly all plants prefer loose soil that their roots can penetrate easily. Avid houseplant growers were forced to concoct their own potting soil mixtures if they wanted to keep their houseplants alive.

In the 1970s, the world of potted-plant horticulture changed dramatically with the introduction of artificial mixes, and by the mid-1980s, artificial mixes were beating out "dirt" as the potting mix of choice for growing indoor plants. Almost all potting mixes sold today are *soilless* or *artificial* mixes; they contain *no* actual soil. Soilless mixes are composed of a combination of organic materials (derived from once-living organisms) and inorganic materials (what most folks call "rocks").

Flour, Sugar, and Sphagnum Peat Moss

The basic element of most of today's soilless mixes is *sphagnum peat moss*, which is partially decomposed sphagnum moss harvested from peat bogs. Peat moss is a sterile product as far as houseplants go. It contains no harmful microorganisms — mostly because it's too acid for them.

Peat moss is *well-aerated* (contains ample air pockets), holds water and nutrients well, and improves the structure of natural soils. Now for the bad news. Peat moss is highly acid. Adding alkaline products to peat-based mixes is a necessity to counteract their natural acidity. Peat also contains virtually no nutrients, so you have to fertilize more often.

Peat substitutes

Where peat moss is rare or expensive, such as in the southern U.S., potting mix manufacturers frequently use substitutes. One such product is *coir,* a dark-colored, fibrous residue derived from coconut shells. Coir is especially abundant and therefore inexpensive in tropical climates. Fine bits of composted bark and decomposed sawdust also serve as a peat moss substitute in some mixes.

Other elements in the mix

Potting mix manufacturers typically add inorganic materials to peat that are specifically designed to give the soil a looser texture. Minus these additional materials, peat moss tends to become compacted. The two main inorganic materials used in potting mixes today are *perlite* and *vermiculite.*

✔ Perlite is a whitish, crunchy-textured product made of expanded (heated until it puffs up) volcanic rock.

✔ Vermiculite is a golden-colored product consisting of expanded mica.

Perlite is now more popular than vermiculite because vermiculite tends to become compacted over time (although more slowly than peat moss), whereas perlite holds its form indefinitely. If you don't repot often, mixes that contain more perlite than vermiculite tend to work better. Sometimes potting mix manufacturers add tiny pieces of *styrofoam* instead of perlite. Although styrofoam does an adequate job, it's less popular than perlite, mainly because it isn't as environmentally friendly.

Some mixes, especially those designed for succulents, contain *sand* rather than, or in addition to, perlite and vermiculite.

✔ Sand improves drainage — water simply drains right through sand, which is ideal for succulents that don't like waterlogged soil.

✔ Sand also adds weight which helps to steady the pot, but has no capacity to store minerals, so you have to fertilize sand-based mixes more carefully.

If you make your own sand-based mix, insist on *river sand*. Beach sand may contain harmful concentrations of salt if it's not washed first.

You're also likely to find all sorts of other ingredients in potting mixes, including

✔ Charcoal (to absorb toxic products that sometimes form as soil decomposes)

✔ Crushed or powdered limestone or dolomite limestone (to reduce acidity and supply calcium and magnesium)

✔ Crushed eggshells (to reduce acidity and add certain minerals to the mix)

Make sure that you aren't buying plain old dirt instead of real potting mix. Some manufacturers still toss dirt into a bag and call it potting soil. Take a look through the bag to see if you can find bits of perlite and vermiculite, make sure the mix is brown or reddish-brown in color (not the nearly black color of garden soil), and that it doesn't consist of very fine, dust-like particles. Unfortunately, few potting soil manufacturers bother to include a see-through panel in the bag so you can find out.

When in doubt, lift the bag. "Dirt" is heavy; artificial soil is measurably lighter. Better yet, if you're in a nursery or plant store where they know their products, ask a clerk to help you pick out a good brand. When you find one that gives you good results, stick with it.

Making Your Own Potting Mix

If I had written this book before the mid-1980s, I would have devoted a whole chapter to potting mix recipes. That's because few commercial mixes back then were good enough to use indoors without additional preparation. Many were little more than garden soil in a bag!

Today, the opposite is true: You rarely find a commercial potting mix *not* of top quality. However, steer clear of the ones that are heavy and very dark, both signs that they are soil-based rather than soilless, which means they can hardened up and choke off a plant's root sytem.

Want to try your hand at preparing your own mixes? The following are three recipes you can use to make your own houseplant potting mix.

Basic soilless mix

This recipe gives you a good all-purpose mix, much like what you obtain if you buy a bag of artificial growing mix. You can use it on just about all your houseplants, except orchids. On the other hand, if you add up the cost of the ingredients (available in any nursery or garden center), buying a commercial potting mix often is cheaper.

- 1 part blond peat moss (or substitute coir or composted fine bark)
- 1 part medium-grade perlite
- 1 part medium-grade vermiculite (substitute river sand if you use the mix to grow succulents)
- 1 tablespoon powdered dolomite limestone per quart of mix (15 milliliters/liter)

Extra-rich mix

If you like gardening with the rich humus found outdoors, this mix is for you. It doesn't require as much fertilizer as most artificial mixes and offers a bit of a boost for fast-growing and flowering plants. One of the ingredients, leaf mold, isn't nearly as widely available as it once was so you may have to phone ahead to find a nursery that still carries it.

- 1 part blond peat moss (or substitute coir or composted fine bark)
- 1 part leaf mold (decomposed forest litter)
- 1 part medium-grade perlite

✔ 1 part medium-grade vermiculite

✔ 1 tablespoon powdered dolomite limestone per quart of mix
(15 milliliters/liter)

The dirt-lover's retro mix

For those feeling nostalgic about the good ol' days when potting mix contained real dirt, this recipe gives you a heavier mix that's ideal for those top-heavy plants that just can't stand up on their own and larger plants that you don't want to have to repot more than every few years. It costs a bit less than the basic soilless mix.

✔ 1 part sterilized fibrous soil

✔ 1 part blond peat moss (or coir or composted fine bark)

✔ 1 part medium-grade perlite (substitute sand if you use the mix to grow succulents)

 Never use soil straight from the garden. If you insist on using garden soil, pasteurize it by moistening it well and baking it in the oven at 180°F (82°C) for one hour. But, I really don't recommend it because the stink is unbearable. If you must use real dirt, buy it in a bag marked "pasteurized."

Specialized Mixes

If you have a mixed bag of houseplants, you can grow almost any of them — including ferns, cacti, African violets, foliage plants, and so on — in a standard soilless mix. But, if you're specializing in growing a specific group of plants (for example, cacti, African violets, orchids, or others), you can also buy specialized mixes in garden centers and nurseries or create your own from the recipes I list in the previous sections of this chapter.

Cactus mix

Cacti and succulents are among the plants many people prefer to pot up in special mixes, but most do perfectly well in standard soilless mixes (try the recipe in the section "Basic soilless mix" earlier in this chapter). If you prefer a special cactus blend, start with the recipe for the basic soilless mix and substitute river sand for vermiculite.

Another cactus blend mixes one part river sand with two parts standard soilless mix. The sand facilitates water drainage, but its greatest benefit is the extra weight it adds that helps support top-heavy succulents. Of course, you can always just buy a specific cactus blend.

Orchid mix

Orchids (and, to a certain degree, bromeliads) are major exceptions to the rule that you can grow just about any plant in a standard soilless mix. Few orchids can grow in standard mixes, largely because most orchids are *epiphytes,* plants born to live on branches and tree trunks with their roots exposed to the air. Because their thick roots are built to absorb moisture from the surrounding air, they need a special orchid growing mix.

You can grow orchids in all sorts of well-aerated products, including medium-size bark fragments, sphagnum moss, pot shards, rock wool, and clay pellets, alone or mixed together depending on the recipe. The simplest approach is to buy a preblended orchid mix. You also can grow orchids on supports such as *osmunda fiber* or slabs of wood (see the discussion of slab culture in Chapter 7 for the details) using no potting mix at all.

Orchid mixes also make good potting mixes for bromeliads, although many bromeliads can adapt perfectly well to growing in soilless mix.

On a Scale of 1 to 14: Acid or Alkaline Mixes?

You could grow houseplants for the rest of your life without knowing how pH figures into the process and without adjusting a potting mix to a particular pH level. The symbol *pH* refers to hydrogen-ion concentrations, which is something you don't really need to know, but you do need to know that some plants grow well only in acid soil mixes, and some prefer alkaline mixes.

The level of acidity and alkalinity in a substance is measured in pH values. The *pH scale* ranges from 1 to 14. Any pH value from 1 to 6.9 is in the *acid* range, and values from 7.1 to 14 are in the *alkaline* range, with 7 being a *neutral* value.

The vast majority of houseplants prefer a slightly acid potting mix in the 6.0 to 6.9 range, so most commercial potting mixes are designed for a pH of about 6.5. The potting mix recipes listed earlier in this chapter provide a pH level in the "slightly acid" range. In fact, powdered dolomite limestone is included in two of the recipes simply to reduce the mix's acidity.

To *acidify* a mix, add powdered sulfur according to the instructions on the label. You also can prepare an acid potting mix by following the basic soilless or extra-rich mix recipes supplied earlier in this chapter but leave out the limestone or add $1/2$-part peat moss to any standard houseplant soilless mix.

Plants that remain for years in the same pot can experience a significant change in pH levels over time. The mix gradually becomes more alkaline if you have hard water, more acid if you have soft water. If the leaves of your plant turn yellowish — a sign of pH-stressed plants — repot the plant into a fresh mix. You almost always see a quick recovery.

A few houseplants prefer a more acid pH — from 5 to 6, for example — and some plants prefer a neutral or even slightly alkaline growing mix with a pH between 7 and 7.8. (Most of them will also grow in a mix with a pH of 6.5.)

Plants that prefer acid potting mixes

Some plants have such a strong preference for acid growing mixes that it's difficult to grow in an ordinary potting medium. They include the following:

- Azalea *(Rhododendron simsii)*
- Camellia *(Camellia japonica)*
- Calamondin orange × *(Citrofortunella mitis)*
- Gardenia *(Gardenia augusta)*
- Hortensia *(Hydrangea macrophylla)*
- Staghorn fern *(Platycerium bifurcatum)*
- Zebra plant *(Aphelandra squarrosa* 'Dania')

Plants that tolerate alkaline potting mixes

Although no common houseplant really qualifies as "alkaline-loving," the plants in the following list don't mind a mix that's on the alkaline side. They can all tolerate ordinary potting mixes (which are slightly acid by nature), but they do prefer that their mix contain some limestone. These are among the few plants that grow fairly well in areas where hard water turns any growing mix alkaline.

- Desert cacti *(many kinds)*
- Geranium *(Pelargonium)*
- Maidenhair fern *(Adiantum)*
- Purple passion plant *(Gynura aurantiaca* 'Purple Passion')
- Spider plant *(Chlorophytum comosum)*
- Swiss cheese plant *(Monstera deliciosa)*
- Succulents (many kinds)
- Wandering Jew *(Zebrina pendula)*

Getting Potted

Some plants can stay in the same pot for years if you *leach* them (rinse them with clear water) regularly and fertilize them occasionally. However, after a few months to a few years of growth, most plants run out of root space and start to slow down or stop growing altogether. Also, over time, any potting mix does tend to decompose, become compacted, or become contaminated with excess mineral salts that get harder and harder to leach out. At some point, you're going to have to repot.

The root of the matter: Pot-bound plants

To keep growing above ground, plants must also have room for their roots to grow underground. In fact, the two are closely linked: Anything that slows roots below ground also slows above-ground growth, and anything that keeps leaves and stems from growing at their normal rate also slows root growth.

A plant is *pot-bound,* or *underpotted,* when its pot is so full of roots that it has no more space left to grow. Many flowering plants actually bloom more abundantly when slightly pot-bound, but when the roots begin to circle all around the pot (something, unfortunately, that you can see only by unpotting the plant), get ready to repot.

You may have heard the term "root ball" and wondered if it's somehow related to rugby. *Root ball* is just the standard term for a mixed mass of roots and soil that clings together when you remove them from a pot. The term is a bit of a misnomer: Roots in pots rarely take on the shape of a round ball — in fact, they quickly take on the same exact shape as their container.

Sure signs you need to repot

It's better to repot plants before they suffer from overcrowded roots or deteriorating potting mix. Many indoor gardeners simply repot all plants annually as a matter of course; others wait until their plants show some signs of being pot-bound. Many experienced houseplant owners repot fast-growing plants more than once a year or whenever their expanding size seems to indicate a need for more root space.

In addition to annual maintenance repotting, keep an eye out for signs that you may need to repot plants sooner that once a year:

✔ **The roots extend through the drainage holes.** Unpot the plant and take a look. If only a few roots reach out of the hole and you detect no signs that either thick roots are circling around the inside of the container or that a mass of fine roots has invaded all the available space, you can put the plant back into its pot. If the roots do appear numerous and compressed, you need to repot.

- ✔ **A mass of circling roots is pushing the plant out of its pot.** You commonly see this in plants with thick *anchor roots,* such as dracaenas and spider plants. Anchor roots (or *tap roots*) are long, thick roots that sink deep into the ground. Their primary purpose is not to absorb air, water, and nutrients, but to anchor the plant into the ground.

- ✔ **Growth is slow or negligible.** This symptom is indicative of a problem during the plant's normal growing season.

- ✔ **The plant is top heavy and falls over on its own.**

- ✔ **The plant dries out within four or five days after a watering.** It needs more room for its roots. Repot it without delay into a larger pot.

- ✔ **The plant appears overly large for its pot.** This is a judgment call on your part. Generally, the diameter of the pot should be about a third of the plant's diameter or, if it grows more in height than in width, a third of its height. Young cuttings and seedlings may grow so quickly that you need to repot them three or four times during their first year.

- ✔ **The plant shows signs of rot.** Limp, yellowish growth and a tendency to tilt to one side are signs of possible rot. You also may notice a pungent scent at the plant's base. If so, remove most of the old potting mix as you repot and prune out any sick, dead, or dying roots or stems. Such a plant usually needs potting down (see the "Potting up or potting down?" section later in this chapter).

- ✔ **Mineral salt buildup appears on the pot or the stem.** If you see yellow, orange, or white crust just above the soil line, it's most likely salt buildup. Leaching can help remove salt buildup, as can topdressing (see the section "When You Can't Repot: Topdressing" later in this chapter). Eventually, however, you must repot the plant into a clean pot with fresh potting mix.

- ✔ **You haven't repotted the plant in well over a year.** You can, of course, keep a plant going for many years in the same pot by leaching and topdressing regularly, but these are stopgap measures. Few plants are truly happy unless you repot them at least once every 18 months.

Potting up or potting down?

Many indoor gardeners are under the impression that you should always *pot up* — that is, repot plants into containers larger than the ones they're already in. But the fact is, the only plants that you should put into larger pots are those that you want to keep getting bigger. (For more information on the variety of pots that are available, see Chapter 18.)

If the plant is already as big as you want it to get, repot it into the same pot or another pot that's the same size as the current container to keep the plant's growth under control. Most potting mixes deteriorate over time, so repotting is often a matter of changing the *soil,* not the pot.

Many flowering plants flower best when slightly pot-bound, so you also want to repot them into a pot of the same size unless they show signs of severe underpotting (see "Sure signs you need to repot," earlier in this chapter).

Sometimes you might even want to *pot down* — that is, repot the plant into a smaller pot.

- ✔ A plant suffering from rot or root damage recovers more readily when you transplant it to a smaller pot.
- ✔ Some owners like to pot shrubs down bit by bit over a number of years to make them fit into a tiny bonsai pot.

Recommended repotting seasons and cycles

The ideal repotting season for any plant is just as it begins a new growth cycle. Plants typically produce new roots early in a growth cycle, so it's an especially good time for the plant to reap the benefits of fresh, loose mix into which it can stretch. Most plants begin their annual growth cycle in late winter or spring.

Size really does matter

If you leave a plant in a pot that's too small, it grows slowly or not at all. Repotting a plant into pot that's much too large is equally unwise. If the new container is much bigger than the root ball, the roots inevitably fail to reach certain parts of the growing mix for months, and water tends to accumulate in those places. The constant moisture chases out the oxygen, which leads to stagnation and possibly root rot. The general rule for repotting, therefore, is to put the plant into a pot only one or two sizes larger than its previous container. If, for example, you need to repot an arrowhead plant that's growing in a 4-inch (10-centimeter) pot, replant it into a 5-inch or 6-inch (12-centimeter or 15-centimeter) pot.

You may also want to repot during other seasons, or less often or more often, depending on a number of factors:

- **Young plants in full growth:** You should repot these youngsters several times a year, regardless of the season.

- **Plants growing year-round:** These plants have no special potting season. This category also includes most plants grown under artificial lights.

- **Plants repotted following an accident:** If Rover knocks over your plant in mid-autumn, don't wait until spring to repot it!

- **Plants brought indoors after a summer outdoors:** These plants have often doubled or tripled in size. Repot them just before you bring them indoors.

- **Whenever repotting is most convenient for you:** If you don't have time to repot in spring, repot in summer, autumn, or even winter. Leave only completely dormant plants to rest.

Doing the deed: The steps to fool-proof repotting

Ready for a little repotting? It's not that difficult even if it's your first try at repotting a plant, and if you're an old hand at it, you may discover some helpful new techniques. Before you remove a plant from its pot, always make sure that you have enough potting mix on hand, and then follow these steps:

1. **A day or two before you plan to repot, give your plants a thorough watering because they're easier to repot when the growing mix is moist.**

2. **Pour some potting mix into a bucket or bowl and add an equivalent amount of warm water, then blend thoroughly.**

   Most soilless potting mixes are somewhat water repellent when dry, so it is important to stir them. Aim for a consistency a little drier than muffin batter. If the mix is too dry, add more water; too liquid, add a bit more medium. Adding a drop or two of liquid soap to the water also helps the mix to absorb moisture more readily.

   You can seal any leftover mix in a plastic bag or container and save it for your next potting session.

3. **To remove the plant from its old pot, slip your hand over the top of the pot, holding the plant's stem between your fingers, and turn the pot upside down, as shown in Figure 13-1.**

4. **Tap the rim of the pot firmly against a hard surface such as a table, then gently pull the pot upwards to remove the plant (again, see Figure 13-1).**

   If the plant refuses to budge, tap the pot against the hard surface a few more times and try again. It may take two pairs of hands (one pair pulling on the pot while the other pair holds the plant) to remove big plants from large pots. You also may have to run a knife blade around the inside of the pot's rim to remove the plant or first cut away roots extending from the drainage holes. If that doesn't work, you may actually have to break the pot to remove the plant.

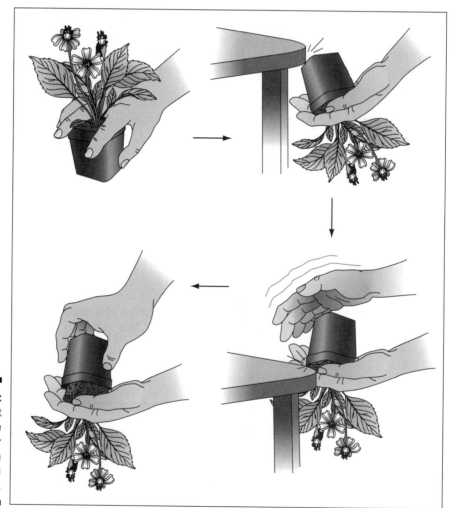

Figure 13-1: The correct technique for removing a plant from its pot.

5. **Examine the root ball.**

   If it's full of healthy roots that don't wrap around the inside of the pot and you've been repotting the plant regularly over the years, you can skip to the section "The quick repotting method" coming up and repot the plant using the steps that I list there. If the root ball is less healthy or if the plant has been in the same pot for more than 18 months, you must do some cleaning up before repotting it.

   If some of the roots appear dead, damaged, or rotten (or circle the inside of the pot, indicating probable underpotting), you need to prune them off.

6. **If thick roots totally encircle the plant, cut away a ¹/₂- to 1-inch (2- to 3-centimeter) slice of roots and soil with a sharp knife — not only all around the pot, but also from the bottom (see Figure 13-2).**

   Don't cut away healthy roots of plants that don't like being repotted, such as the clivia (see the section "When you Can't Repot: Topdressing" later in the chapter).

   If you intend to repot the plant into a pot of the same size or smaller, prune back even more harshly. You can remove up to one-third of the old roots (or one-third of the root ball) without harming the plant.

Figure 13-2:
If the root ball is entirely circled by thick roots, slice a portion of roots and soil from the sides and bottom.

7. **Remove about one-third of the old potting mix from the root ball, loosening it gently with your fingers, a stake, a pencil, or a chopstick inserted straight down into the roots.**

   It's no loss — the soil is most likely contaminated with mineral salts.

8. **Pour in a layer of the premoistened potting mix made in Step 2.**

   Use just enough so that the top of the roots are at the same level as the pot's rim projection.

9. **Set the plant in the pot, turning it to make sure it is completely centered, and begin adding soil.**

   Use your fingers or a chopstick to work the potting mix down among the roots. Press just hard enough to eliminate any large air pockets without compressing the soil.

10. **Add the potting medium until the roots are well covered, then even out the mix with your fingers or a spoon.**

11. **Water well, let drain, and you're done!**

Try to keep any newly repotted plant out of full sunlight for a week or so, then reintroduce it to its permanent home. You can begin fertilizing again in about one month.

One important note before you actually repot the plant: Don't waste the already limited space in an average pot with a layer of useless pot shards. Use a good potting mix from top to bottom. Studies show that so-called drainage layers don't actually help drainage at all. On the contrary, pots actually drain *better* when the potting mix is evenly packed in the pot.

The quick repotting method

If no root pruning is necessary and the soil seems to be in good shape, you can use the following fast and easy method when you repot. If the plant's root ball is intact, you can just form a mold of soil using the old pot and slip the plant into its new home. The complete steps follow:

1. **Remove the plant from its pot.**

2. **Pour enough moist potting soil into the base of the new pot to bring the plant up to the desired level.**

3. **Now slip the old pot into the new one and center it.**

4. **Pour in potting mix all around the old pot (see Figure 13-3), compress lightly with your fingers, then remove the old pot.**

   The old pot leaves a perfect mold of the plant's root ball.

5. **Slip the root ball into the mold and smooth the potting mix over. You're done!**

Figure 13-3:
The quick
and not-
too-dirty
easy
repotting
method.

Fast and easy repotting is especially useful when you have difficult-to-handle plants, such as those with spines or thick lower leaves that make traditional repotting difficult.

Handling a sticky situation: Repotting cacti

Not sure how to repot a spiny cactus or crown of thorns without stabbing a finger? First, prepare a root mold following the method outlined in the earlier section "The quick repotting method." Then, gently grip the plant's stem with a pair of tongs, or use a rolled up piece of newspaper, looping it around the stem and holding both ends of the newspaper tightly (see Figure 13-4). Then just remove the plant from its pot and drop the root ball into the mold.

When You Can't Repot: Topdressing

Generally speaking, you should repot at least once a year, preferably just as the growing season is about to begin, but you may have some plants that you don't want to repot immediately, perhaps because you like their present size and repotting them into fresh soil would only stimulate new growth. Or,

Figure 13-4:
Playing it
safe with
repotting
a cactus.

maybe they're among the group of plants that dislike being repotted. Or, perhaps they've simply become so large and heavy that repotting them is an impossible chore.

Instead of repotting unwieldy or delicate plants, try _topdressing_ them annually. Topdressing imvolves scraping off the top layer of growing mix with a fork, removing up to two inches (five centimeters) of soil, and replacing it with fresh mix. Combining topdressing with regular leaching helps prevent mineral salt buildup and gives plants some amount of fresh growing medium annually.

Most houseplants prefer regular repotting into larger pots, but a few do not. Many tropical bulbs (such as amaryllis) and a few other houseplants (such as clivias, birds-of-paradise, and hoyas) actually _do better_ when you _underpot_ them, that is, grow them in pots smaller than a plant of that size would generally require. Those plants that dislike repotting may actually take a year or two to recover and begin flowering again after you repot them. On the other hand, they can remain for a decade or more in the same pot and not suffer in the least if you topdress them regularly.

If you have a plant that is simply too heavy and unwieldy for you to repot on your own, you probably want to delay repotting the plant as long as possible, so topdress it annually for a few years. When you can no longer delay repotting (few plants can live more than ten years in the same pot without suffering), call in a friend or neighbor, or take the plant to your local nursery, florist, or garden center and have them repot it.

Part IV
Potted Plant Maintenance

The 5th Wave   By Rich Tennant

"I never minded the watering and cleaning, but lately we've begun hearing drums at night."

In this part . . .

Wouldn't it be nice if you could bring home any plant you desire from the store, pull it out of its wrapper, stick it on a windowsill or in the middle of a table, and never have to think about it again? There's a name for that kind of houseplant . . . it's called *artificial*. The fact is, for your plants to survive and look good, too, you have to take care of them on a routine basis.

This part of the book covers houseplant maintenance — from acclimatizing new plants to your home, to pruning and staking your plants to keep them under control, to combating pests, diseases, and other unwelcome houseplant invaders. And, in case you want to try your hand at multiplying your houseplant population, I included a chapter on propagating new plants from the ones you already have.

Chapter 14

Preparing Plants for the Domestic Life

*W*hether you buy your houseplants from a nursery or grocery, or bring them in from the garden or patio, you have to take some precautions to ensure that they adapt to their new indoor surroundings with a minimum of stress and disturbance.

In this chapter, I give you some pointers on how to get store-bought plants home safely, and once you get them there, how to acclimatize them to their new environment. I also tell you when and how to bring your plants in for the cold weather season, or for when you just want to bring some outdoor color indoors.

Home from the Store, Safe and Sound

If you're a typical houseplant grower, more than 90 percent of the plants that you grow in your home come from some sort of commercial outlet, such as a nursery, florist shop, supermarket, or outdoor market. Getting those plants home safely from the store is the first step in your having success with growing any plant.

Wrap it up, I'll take it

No matter where you buy your plants, always insist that the clerk wrap them carefully in a sheet of paper or plastic and place the plant inside a bag that can be tied or folded shut before you leave the store. Never walk out of a store or market with a houseplant exposed to the outdoor air. Houseplants are not outdoor plants that have always grown out in the open, and they certainly aren't acclimatized to outdoor conditions.

A tropical plant that has always grown under cover, or any plant that's lived its life in the confines of a greenhouse, can withstand only a few seconds of exposure to cold wind or hot sun. And even houseplants bought at outdoor markets likely have never been exposed to full sun, so insist on protection for them just like any other houseplant.

Nurseries, florists, and garden centers always wrap houseplants as a matter of course. You can usually trust them to do a great job of packing your plants before you leave the store. Sales clerks in department stores, hardware stores, supermarkets, and so on, on the other hand, may not think of treating plants as anything but dry goods. An orange sticker and register receipt tell store security that you paid for the plant, but they don't ward off pests or protect the plant from cold, heat, or sunburn!

Remember: Minimal protection for any plant in any season, even when the weather is nice, means bagging them, and sealing or stapling the bag.

Garden centers and other specialists generally use *plant sleeves,* which are tubular wrappers narrow at the base and wider at the top, designed specifically for plants. The clerk just slips the plants into the sleeve, folds the top down, staples the sleeve, and voilà!

Buying large plants from non-specialty shops (that is, somewhere other than a gardening center or nursery) presents a special problem because department stores rarely carry plant sleeves and may not have bags that are large enough for this purpose. Ask the salesperson to drop the plant into one bag and carefully slip another over the top — and then ask to staple the two bags together to hold them securely.

Getting ready for the ride home in any weather

Once your new plant pal is out of the store, you have to make sure it weathers the ride home with a minimum of disturbance. The following information provides some tips for both cold-weather and warm-weather rides.

In hot weather, temperatures can reach as high as 170°F (77°C) in a car parked in bright sun, enough heat to do in the toughest plant. If you're driving home, try to keep the plant out of the hot sun by placing it on the floor of the car. If your return trip includes another stop, park the car in the shade and leave the windows open a crack. Better yet, don't stop on the way home. Make your plant purchase the last one of the day.

You can buy plants in any season, but in cold climates you need to take some special precautions during the winter months:

- ✔ Insist on paper wrapping. It's a better insulator against cold than plastic.

- ✔ If it's really cold out (below freezing), ask the clerk to *double-bag* the plant by placing the plant first in a sealed paper bag and then in a larger plastic bag. Inflate the outer bag by blowing it up, then tie it shut to trap the warm air inside.

- ✔ In subfreezing weather, always heat the car before putting a plant inside. If you intend to set the plant on a cold floor or seat, put a layer of insulation between the pot and the cold surface. You also can ask the store for an extra paper bag and put that under the plant.

- ✔ Never let the foliage touch a cold window.

- ✔ Make sure that your plant purchase is the last stop for the day: Don't leave a plant sitting in a car that's getting colder by the minute.

- ✔ If you bring a plant home by foot or by bus when temperatures drop well below freezing, you run a big risk of killing it. You don't want to have the plant outdoors any more than five minutes, even well-wrapped. Why not splurge and take a taxi?

- ✔ Always take adequate care of large plants in any weather. If you can't fit the plant in the cab of your vehicle, arrange for delivery in a closed truck. An open pickup simply doesn't cut it, even for well-wrapped plants.

Plants that don't cotton to winter moves

You generally can buy houseplants in any season without worrying too much about their ability to adapt to your home. But, if you're considering a plant that has a reputation for reacting badly to change, such as the weeping fig or croton, or one that has thin leaves, such as the nerve plant, you may want to put off your purchase until spring or early summer. The superior light and higher humidity of spring and summer helps your plant to better adapt to its new conditions and gives it time to acclimatize perfectly before the short days and drier air of autumn and winter arrive.

Acclimatizing Plants to Their New Surroundings

Moving from a humid greenhouse to a dwelling built for humans can exact quite a toll on a tender houseplant. It says good-bye to a life of basking in warm sunshine and breathing moist humid air and says hello an environment where both adequate light and humidity are generally at a premium. Even if you buy your plant at a store that lacks climate control, don't assume that the plant's transition is made any easier. In all likelihood, that plant was residing in a humid greenhouse only a few short weeks before and probably is already in shock from its first move.

Plants that are moved too quickly from one environment to a vastly different one may begin to show yellowing leaves, lose foliage, drop flowers or fruit, suffer sudden attacks of insect infestation or disease, or simply droop unhappily, never quite looking their best. If the contrast between the old and new environment is very extreme, you may ending up saying R.I.P. to that plant you just bought.

Whenever possible, give any new arrival the Royal Treatment. Acclimatize it gradually to its new home by giving it the best possible conditions at first, and only slowly introduce it to its ultimate growing environment. Most plants adapt amazingly well to even substandard conditions, as long as you don't rush them.

Here are few tips on how to gradually get a plant accustomed to your living quarters:

✔ Give the plant the brightest possible light at first. Place the plant near a window or even in a room that's more brightly lit than the one it will eventually live in. However, avoid a full onslaught from the blazing sun or you risk giving the plant a case of sunburn. After two weeks, gradually move the plant way from the sunny spot until, about four to six weeks later, you have moved it to its destined place.

✔ Increase the relative humidity of the environment (if possible). You especially need to increase the humidity in your home when you buy a plant during the winter when heated indoor air is especially dry. You may want to put the plant in the laundry room at first — if your laundry room is well lit! — or set it on a *humidity tray* (I talk about humidity trays in Chapter 10).

You can also seal your plant inside a large plastic bag (you can use one from a dry cleaner) for the first few weeks, then gradually roll the bag down to expose more of the plant over a four-week period. To keep the bag from touching the moist leaves, prop it up with a couple pieces of wooden doweling (see Figure 14-1).

Figure 14-1:
To provide high humidity for a newly purchased plant, seal it inside a clear plastic bag propped up with a couple of sticks.

✔ Avoid fertilizing for the first month (at least). Your plant has enough to do just adjusting to the new conditions. Fertilizers designed to stimulate new growth can only hinder, not help, under these circumstances. Besides, in all likelihood, its potting mix already contains fertilizers left over from when it was in the greenhouse. If your plant continues to sulk after a month or so in its new home, delay fertilizing even longer until it starts producing new and healthy leaves. Remember one of the Golden Rules of Fertilizing: *Never fertilize a weak plant!*

✔ Put the plant in quarantine to prevent any insects or diseases that it may harbor from spreading to your other plants. (For more information on quarantining, see Chapter 17.)

Any plant prefers a period of acclimatization when you move it to a new home, but flowering plants that you purchase for temporary use (the so-called florist plants) pass away to plant heaven long before the four- to eight-week "royal treatment" ends. Just put these temporary guests wherever they look best and just enjoy them for the time being.

Bringing Garden Plants Indoors

Bringing outdoor garden plants indoors is a great way to increase the variety of plants in your home at little cost, but the thought of bringing an outdoor plant into the home scares many indoor gardeners silly. They are so afraid of bringing insects and diseases in with the plants that they don't even consider using this free source of houseplants. (See Chapter 1 for information on how to deal with pests that may hitch a ride on outdoor plants brought indoors.)

Besides the classic container plants, such as fuchsia and oleander (for others, see Chapter 1), that really do have two lives — a summer one outdoors and a winter one indoors — you can also bring any number of outdoor plants indoors.

If you live in a subtropical or tropical climate, such as parts of Florida, California, Texas, Louisiana, or anywhere else frost rarely occurs, the plant's size probably is your only limitation on what will work indoors. Just about everything you grow in your outdoor garden, from shrubs and trees to edibles, annuals, and perennials, you can also raise indoors.

That isn't quite so true in colder climates. Many hardy plants *need* a cool-to-cold winter in order to thrive and, therefore, are best left outdoors. Most hardy trees, shrubs, and perennials make poor houseplants. Two categories of plants, however, can adapt to being grown indoors permanently or brought indoors only for the winter — edible plants and annual flowers. To learn how to care for annuals indoors, see the next section, "Making true annuals into houseplants."

As for *edible plants,* you can grow most herbs and vegetables indoors — if you can supply *full sun.* Consider miniature vegetables and herbs; standard-size veggies often take up far too much space indoors for the results they produce. And, while some herbs (such as basil, bay, and parsley) make fairly decent-looking houseplants, other herbs and most vegetables look more like edibles than houseplants.

Making true annuals into houseplants

Some flowering annuals really *are* annuals: They grow from seed to bloom in less than one year and die after they produce seed. Thinking of them as permanent houseplants, therefore, is pointless — but you can bring them indoors in the autumn to extend their growing season.

You also can sow annual seeds indoors (see Chapter 16 for information on how to grow plants from seed) or buy young plants during outdoor planting season and then grow them indoors over the next six to ten months until they die their natural death.

Flowering annuals require strong indoor light, even full sun, so are best-suited to summer blooming. If you can provide enough light, however, you can start them in the autumn for blooming in winter or spring. Strong, direct light is vital, especially if you grow them from seed.

Among the dozens of true garden annuals that you can find in any seed catalog, garden center, or open-air market, the following are the ones you can successfully grow indoors:

- ✔ Aster *(Callistephus chinensis)*
- ✔ Baby blue eyes *(Nemophila menziesii)*
- ✔ Baby's breath *(Gypsophila elegans)*
- ✔ Balsam *(Impatiens balsamina)*
- ✔ Beefsteak plant *(Perilla frutescens)*
- ✔ Bidens *(Bidens ferulifolia)*
- ✔ Butterfly flower *(Schizanthus pinnata)*
- ✔ Cape daisy *(Venidium fatuosum)*
- ✔ Cape marigold *(Dimorphotheca sinuata)*
- ✔ Cardinal climber *(Ipomoea quamoclit)*
- ✔ Cockscomb *(Celosia argentea cristata)*
- ✔ Feathered amaranth *(Celosia argentea plumosa)*
- ✔ Flossflower *(Ageratum houstonianum)*
- ✔ Marigold *(Tagetes erecta* and *T. patula)*
- ✔ Moonflower *(Ipomoea bona-nox)*
- ✔ Morning glory *(Convolvulus tricolor, Ipomoea coccinea, I. purpurea)*
- ✔ Nemesia *(Nemesia strumosa)*
- ✔ Pot marigold *(Calendula officinalis)*
- ✔ Rose moss *(Portulaca grandiflora)*
- ✔ Swan River daisy *(Brachycome iberidiflora)*
- ✔ Sweet alyssum *(Lobularia maritima)*
- ✔ Wishbone flower *(Torenia fournieri)*

Be on the lookout for dwarf *cultivars* (cultivated varieties) to bring indoors. Many standard-size annuals *etiolate* (that is, they stretch) when you grow them under home conditions, which makes them less attractive. Dwarf plants naturally tend to remain compact.

Making tender perennials (posing as annuals) into houseplants

Many plants, including geraniums, impatiens, and bedding begonias, are widely accepted as annual flowers in temperate climates, when in fact they're actually perennials or shrubs when grown in subtropical and tropical areas. Unlike true annuals, you can bring these "imposters" indoors in the fall and keep them going throughout the winter until planting-out time the following summer. You can even grow them indoors permanently.

You can grow most *tender perennials* (perennials that can't support frost) from seed or you can purchase plants during outdoor planting season. As with true annuals, all of the following perennials grown as annuals require *very strong* light when they're indoors.

- African daisy *(Arctotis stoechadifolia)*
- Anagallis *(Anagallis monelli)*
- Bacopa *(Sutera cordata)*
- Bedding begonia *(Begonia × semperflorens-cultorum)*
- Blue marguerite *(Felicia amelloides)*
- Browallia *(Browallia speciosa)*
- Calibracoa *(Calibracoa)*
- Coleus *(Coleus × hybridus)*
- Cup-and-saucer vine *(Cobaea scandens)*
- Diascia *(Diascia)*
- Dusty miller *(Senecio maritimum* and *Chrysanthemum ptarmiciflorum)*
- Everlasting *(Helichrysum bracteatum)*
- Fan flower *(Scaevola aemula)*
- Flowering tobacco *(Nicotiana alata)*
- Fountain dracaena *(Cordyline australis* and *C. indivisa)*
- Fuchsia *(Fuchsia)*
- Garden verbena *(Verbena)*
- Gazania *(Gazania ringens)*
- Geranium *(Pelargonium hortorum* and *P. peltatum)*
- Heliotrope *(Heliotropium arborescens)*

✔ Impatiens *(Impatiens wallerana* and *I. × hawkeri)*

✔ Licorice plant *(Helichrysum petiolare)*

✔ Lobelia *(Lobelia erinus)*

✔ Madagascar periwinkle *(Catharanthus roseus)*

✔ Marguerite *(Argyranthemum frutescens,* also known as *Chrysanthemum frutescens)*

✔ Monkey flower *(Mimulus)*

✔ Morning glory *(Ipomoea nil* and *I. tricolor)*

✔ Osteospermum *(Osteospermum barberae)*

✔ Painted tongue *(Salpiglossis sinuata)*

✔ Petunia *(Petunia)*

✔ Polka-dot plant *(Hypoestes phyllostachya)*

✔ Potato vine *(Solanum jasminoides)*

✔ Scarlet sage *(Salvia splendens)*

✔ Transvaal daisy *(Gerbera jamesonii)*

✔ Winged pea *(Lotus berthelotii)*

From garden to jardiniere: Potting up outdoor plants

Plants already growing in containers such as hanging baskets, flower boxes, and so on are the easiest plants to bring indoors in the autumn. Just clean up the container, treat the plants for insects (see Chapter 1 for details), put them in quarantine (see Chapter 17), position them in a sunny spot, and enjoy!

Plants growing in the garden with their roots in the soil require a little more effort to acclimatize, be they annuals, perennials, or shrubs. Dig them up carefully toward the end of the growing season but sometime before autumn (late August is ideal in the northern hemisphere). Try to get out as much of the root system as possible.

Pot up your garden plants (that is, plant them into pots) using standard potting mix and pots just slightly larger than the root ball, then water the soil thoroughly. Leave the plants outdoors for a week or two to give them a chance to recuperate from the trauma of leaving the garden before moving them indoors. After that, just move annuals straight to a sunny spot of your house and move hardy plants to a cold storage area for *forcing* (see Chapter 7 for information on forcing plants).

If you grow *tender perennials* as annuals, you can bring them indoors in one of the following two ways:

- ✔ Bring them in using the procedure I just described, adding just one extra step. Cut each stem down to about two inches (five centimeters) from its base.

  Such a drastic step may seem harsh, but tender perennials often end up looking rundown by fall and don't appear their best unless you prune them severely. After a harsh pruning, they quickly sprout anew and soon become as attractive as ever.

- ✔ Take in cuttings instead of bringing the entire plant indoors. Cuttings produce compact plants that still have the vigor of youth.

  Snip off a few stem cuttings in late summer from the most vigorous and floriferous tender perennials in your garden and root them in a plastic bag (I tell you how to do that in Chapter 16). The cuttings should root and begin producing new leaves in just weeks. *Pinch* them a few times to stimulate dense growth, then let them bloom (see Chapter 15 for more on pinching plants). Most flower within a few weeks after the final pinching.

Putting off the inevitable

True annuals typically go into sudden decline after a few months indoors. Most of their leaves turn yellow and they begin to dry up. You can try to delay this reaction by pinching off faded flowers so that they don't go to seed, but after a while, just remind yourself that you can't fool Mother Nature indefinitely.

Most annuals are genetically designed to go through their whole life cycle in less than a year, and that's that. Simply toss them into the compost pile after they've seen their last days. Don't pinch off *all* of the faded flowers, though; you can at least recuperate some of the seeds and start them anew that way.

Tender perennials, on the other hand, can remain in growth — and even in bloom — for much longer and many, in fact, can remain indoors for years. Just pinch them from time to keep them from becoming too straggly, and remove their faded blooms as well.

Chapter 15

Cleaning, Pruning, and Staking

· ·

In This Chapter

▶ Maintenance Rule Number One: A cleaner plant is a healthier plant

▶ Maintenance Rule Number Two: Pruning makes for a lusher houseplant

▶ Maintenance Rule Number Three: Support weak plants by staking them

· ·

Are you one of those people who thinks it's a good idea to rub leaves with mayonnaise to make them shinier? Do you know how prevent tall and spindly growth in a plant you'd like to keep closer to the ground? Have you noticed that some plants prefer to just lie around all day? I'm talking about plants that are alive and technically healthy, but that aren't quite what you'd hoped for when you brought them home.

In this chapter, I address those seemingly picky little details about plant culture that make all the difference between a merely healthy houseplant and a truly beautiful specimen.

Keeping Your Plants Spic and Span

Trying to keep a home clean is a constant battle. Dust, grease, pet fur, cigarette smoke, food and drink spills — this stuff threatens to make a mess of your indoor environment, and not only that, every one of them can affect plant growth.

Any substance that accumulates on plant leaves creates a barrier between the leaves and their source of energy — sunlight. Not only do these by-products of daily indoor living get in the way of sunlight reaching your plants, they can also clog up a plant's breathing pores (the *stomata*), slowing down respiration and growth. Living plants, fortunately, are partly self-cleaning. They absorb some of the particles that otherwise become dust in your home. But they can't do this "vacuuming" all on their own. Most plants do require at least an occasional cleaning.

How often should you clean your plants?

How often you need to clean your plants depends on your growing conditions. In most homes, two or three times a year, or whenever the leaves start to look dusty, is sufficient. Plants that live in the kitchen, where cooking grease is a problem, require more frequent showers, such as every month. So do plants growing in urban areas or industrial centers that have greater amounts of air pollution.

Dusting is for furniture — give your plants a shower instead

The way most people clean off their plants is to give them a good dusting now and again. The fact of the matter is that dusting rarely does any good. Even the softest of dusters or brushes that aren't specifically designed for cleaning plants can scratch delicate leaf surfaces. A better way to clean dust off your plants is to give them a shower.

Outdoors in humid climates, nature does much of the plant cleaning by supplying regular rain showers. If you have a yard or sidewalk, put your plants outdoors on a warm, rainy day. They come back inside clean and rejuvenated! (If you're worried about soil splashing up onto the leaves and stems, cover the potting mix with a rag before you put the plant outside.)

Another way to clean your plants is to take them outside on a gray day (but never in the hot sun) and hose them down. Use soapy water if you like because it helps dislodge the grime — just be sure to rinse your plants with fresh water afterward. Soap residues (especially if the plant is washed often) sometimes clog up stomata (breathing pores).

During the cold weather months, or if you're an apartment dweller and hauling your plants into an elevator is more trouble that it's worth, just put your plants in the bathtub, turn on the shower, make sure the water is tepid, pull the curtains, and give them a bath that way. Let the plants dry for an hour or so before moving them back to their usual place to keep them from dripping all over your floors.

Some plants, such as African violets and cyclamens, dislike rain and showers. Clean their leaves individually with a soft rag dipped in soapy water, using hand soap or mild dish-washing detergent. To keep the leaf from snapping off, slip your hand underneath it, supporting it lightly, then softly brush from the base of the leaf to its tip. Rinse out the rag often to remove grime. Let the plant dry off for an hour or so before putting it back in the light.

Polishing 'em off with useless goo

Although sold in many nurseries, products designed to make leaves look shiny are actually bad for plants. These products provide a shiny "gloss" by coating the leaf with substances that block the plant's stomata, cutting off the plant's respiration, as well as partly blocking essential sunlight. Worse yet are homemade concoctions. Some people shine their plants' leaves with beer, milk, cooking oil, and even *mayonnaise*. Not only do these products block the stomata, but many of them make leaves greasy so that they more readily collect dust, further worsening the plant's state. The natural shine that results from removing grime with soapy water is all the luster that your plants need.

You may want to hand-clean plants that don't mind showers if they have stubborn stains, such as the whitish spots from pesticide often present on newly purchased plants that resist simple rinsing methods. You also can clean dusty plants by passing lightly over their leaves with a shaving brush. (Shaving brushes are the softest brushes of all and among the few that don't scratch leaves although they don't always remove grease and stubborn stains.) You can also buy fleece cleaning mitts designed specifically for grooming plants.

Trimming away the dead stuff

To keep plants looking their best, you need to regularly remove fading leaves and flowers and trim off brown leaf tips. Dying leaves also attract insects like a magnet (many insects are attracted to the yellow color of wilting leaves). Faded leaves and flowers are places where plant disease is more likely to develop. Rot, mildew, and gray mold often start in dead plant material, then spread to healthy stems and branches.

Many plants have the good sense to drop faded flowers and leaves, making cleanup a snap. Other plants are more stubborn, forcing you to pull off dead leaves or flowers or even cut them away. But, be careful not to break off healthy leaves and stems in the process.

Many plants' leaves die bit by bit, starting at the tip, especially those that have long and narrow leaves, such as spider plants and dracaenas. Instead of entirely removing an otherwise healthy leaf because its tip has died off, you can use scissors to cut away the dead part of the leaf and cut into the healthy part. So that is doesn't look like blunt surgery, you can trim it to a natural-looking point, as shown in Figure 15-1.

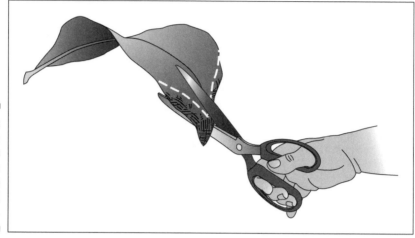

Figure 15-1:
You can
trim plants
with brown
leaf tips to
a natural
point.

Trimming is not a cure-all. A dying leaf will continue to die back over time. When you can no longer trim it without rendering it disproportional to the rest of the plant, or if the leaf has begun to fade and turn yellow, remove it entirely at the base.

The Hardest Cut of All — Pruning

First-time indoor gardeners, and even long-time hobbyists, often suffer from "prunophobia" — the fear of pruning. Yet, these same people have no qualms about mowing a lawn or trimming a hedge. In fact, nature prunes plants all the time. Strong winds, heavy rains, and hail, not to mention various and sundry animals, together work to gently trim plants into shape. Without weather and wild animals to trim back indoor plants, they are free to shoot straight up to the ceiling while producing the fewest branches possible.

You actually end up with a fuller plant

Part of being a responsible houseplant owner involves giving plants a shaping up every now and then. *Pruning* is the process of snipping, cutting, trimming, or pinching away part of a plant to make it not only more shapely, but also to spur growth.

Each time you prune out a shoot, you actually stimulate the plant to branch more abundantly and become fuller. That's because the loss of a stem tip stimulates dormant buds lower on the stem. Where the plant once had just one stem, it soon has two or three. And, if you trim those new stems, even more branches will form.

The three basic pruning techniques

Pruning involves more than just hacking away at a plant until you've trimmed it down to size. A variety of techniques can be used to prune plants. The three basic pruning techniques are pinching, pruning to shape, and cutting back, and each one serves a different purpose.

As for the right pruning tools, you can use outdoor pruning shears on houseplants, but most experienced indoor gardeners simply use tools they already have on hand around the house, such as scissors, sharp knife, or a razor blade. As a precaution, always dip your pruning tools in alcohol between cutting each plant in order to reduce the danger of transmitting diseases from one houseplant to another.

Pinching

Pinching is the most basic pruning technique and does the least damage. You usually can pinch plants without leaving a trace of your fingers having touched the plant. Pinching does, however, require thinking ahead. The harsher pruning techniques — pruning to shape and cutting back (which I talk about next) — correct errors already visible, but pinching is done in an effort to *prevent* errors from ever happening.

Pinching is exactly what it sounds like. You simply squeeze the soft tip of a stem between your thumbnail and your index finger until the tip comes off. You may need to use a pair of scissors or fingernail clippers to "pinch" the more stubborn plants. You can usually pinch out about $1/4$ to $1/2$ inch (5 to 10 millimeters) of young growth without leaving a notable scar. Pinch to just above a leaf or *leaf node* (the point where leaf joins stem).

The best time to start pinching plants is when they're young. Pinching cuttings (newly rooted pieces of plant), for example, results in denser growth and a fuller appearance.

Pruning to shape

Pruning to shape requires cutting off any excessively long branches that develop or slightly rounding off shrub-like houseplants to give them a more uniform shape. Just *prune* (chop off) a stem or branch to a point just above a growth bud or *node* (the point on a stem at which a leaf is attached or was attached), as shown in Figure 15-2. The replacement stem or stems grow out from this node. Cutting close to the node avoids unsightly stubs.

Always cut stems at least $1/2$ to 1 inch (1 to 3 centimeters) *shorter* than the length you really want. Don't worry: They quickly sprout new growth. If you cut them to exactly the desired length, you end up needing to prune again before you even have a chance to sit back and admire your handiwork.

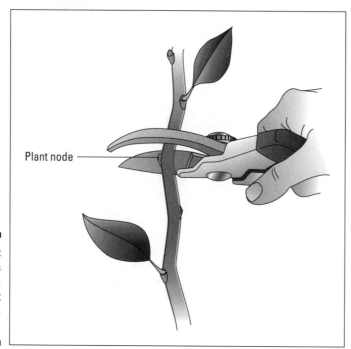

Plant node

Figure 15-2:
Always prune to a point just above a node.

Stopping up leaky pipes and avoiding toxic sap

Some houseplants, like euphorbias, oleanders, and figs, produce copious amounts of clear or milky white sap when you prune them, sometimes leading pruners to imagine that the plants are "bleeding to death." Don't panic: Just spray the plants with water, or dust the wound with powdered charcoal; either way, the sap quickly coagulates.

A word of warning: The milky sap from many plants, notably euphorbias and oleanders, is toxic. Some euphorbias, for example, contain poisons that can be deadly if you swallow them; others merely cause a burning sensation in the mouth, result in rashes, or can irritate your eyes. Be sure to keep your hands away from your eyes and mouth while pruning these plants, and wash your hands thoroughly afterward. Some people even wear gloves and goggles when they prune plants with copious sap.

Cutting back

Cutting back is the harshest form of pruning, but it's often necessary to shape up an ungainly plant that hasn't been pinched or pruned to a desirable shape earlier in its life. Again, cut back to just above a bud or a node to avoid being left with ugly stubs.

Never cut back more than one-third of the growth of a woody plant (such as an azalea or calomondin orange) in one session; cutting back any more than that can limit the ability of those kinds of plants to grow back. If you need to prune a plant more severely, do it in two steps — prune back once by one-third, and then repeat the action again a year later to avoid damage.

You can, however, prune fast-growing plants that have green or semi-woody stems (geraniums, columneas, begonias, or tender perennials) much more harshly than you can woody plants. If a green or semi-woody plant becomes straggly over time, you can rejuvenate it completely by cutting the entire plant back to within 2 inches (5 centimeters) from the surface of the potting mix. These plants quickly resprout and are as good as new in only two or three months. If you see dead branches or stems at any time of the year, prune them out at their base.

When to prune

You can perform pinching and light pruning at any time of the year, and you should make a point of pinching and pruning when a new growing season begins — usually in late winter or early spring. You should *confine* heavy pruning, on the other hand, to the beginning of the growing season.

Off with their heads: Chopping trees down to size

Many "indoor trees," such as dumbcanes and dracaenas, eventually become tall and lanky, lose their lower leaves, and threaten to poke a hole in your ceiling. You can chop these plants back to ground level if you like because they readily sprout from the base. You also can save the tops of pruned indoor trees by air layering them or by taking a cutting. (See Chapter 16 for more information on both of these procedures.) Avoid cutting back plants that produce a single rosette, such as African violets, even if they do look ungainly over time. If you chop off the head of an African violet, it produces a bevy of new rosettes, and the plant loses its original symmetry. If such a plant begins to show a naked "trunk" after a few years, unpot it, and prune back its roots (see Chapter 13 for more on that), chopping off an inch or so (2 to 3 centimeters) at the base. Then drop it back into the pot, placing the reduced-size root ball directly on the bottom of the pot. This technique lowers the plant in its pot and then you only need to cover the bare stem with fresh potting mix. The freshly buried stem soon roots into the surrounding growing mix.

The beginning of the growing season is also the ideal time to remove the weak and *etiolated* growths (ones with excessively spaced leaves and thin stems) that often sprout under the low light of winter. Cut them off and let new stems sprout under the brighter sunlight you get during the growing season. The result is healthier, more compact plants.

Don't prune flowering houseplants just before their main blooming season or you may accidentally remove all or many of the blooms! The safest time to prune any flowering plant is immediately after the last flower fades.

If a plant gets too big for its available space, break the rule about not pruning until the last flower fades and prune it back in the autumn. Pruning at the beginning of the growing season stimulates abundant and rapid new growth. Those plants will soon grow bigger than ever. Pruning flowering plants during the off-season slows down regrowth, which cuts back your pruning needs in future years.

Pruning everbloomers

Some plants, like flowering maples and geraniums, just refuse to stop producing new flower buds, which makes pruning these plants a touchy matter. No matter when you prune, you're suppressing some bloom. If you don't prune, however, those plants can become unsightly or overgrown.

The secret to pruning plants without robbing them of all their bloom is to prune gradually. Try following these steps:

1. **Remove one stem every two months — choose the longest one and cut it back, buds and all, almost to its base.**

   The other branches continue to bloom while the cut-back stem begins to sprout anew.

2. **Two months later, cut back another branch.**

3. **Repeat Step 1 in another two months.**

   Continue in this way throughout the year and by year's end your shrub will sport a healthy mixture of mature, blooming branches and young, strong ones ready to take over and bloom in their turn.

Pruning those oddball plants

Many popular houseplants that feature variegated foliage or crested, contorted stems also occasionally produce normal growth. Pinch or prune these sections out, because normal branches grow more strongly than mutated ones. They may end up taking over unless you eliminate them quickly.

Letting your plants go to seed

Many flowering plants do not produce seeds indoors, given the absence of insects needed for pollination. The plants' flowers simply fade after blooming and either fall off or hang on lifelessly until you remove them. Some houseplants are self-pollinating and start to produce seed pods after they bloom. Unless the fruit is attractive or you're into collecting seeds, cut off the seed pods whenever they begin to form. Producing seeds is not desirable in most houseplants because it uses up considerable amounts of energy, often enough to slow down growth or to stop the plant from blooming.

Several types of houseplants are grown expressly for their attractive fruit, including the Christmas pepper (*Capsicum annuum*), Jerusalem cherry (*Solanum pseudocapsicum*), and Calomondin orange (× *Citrofortunella microcarpa*). Not only do you want to let these plants produce seed, you may even consider pollinating them by hand if you can't put them outside for the bees to do the job. To do so, just go from flower to flower with a cotton swap or artist's brush, sticking the utensil into the center of each flower and shaking lightly. By doing so, you pick up pollen and transfer it to other flowers.

Solid Support: The Art of Staking

In a perfect indoor gardening world, you wouldn't need to support a non-climbing plant. Their branches would be thick and solid, perfectly capable of holding the plant up, even when it's loaded down with leaves, flowers, and fruit. In reality, though, houseplants are prone to weak growth. Their stems often stretch for the light source, and the relatively long distance between each leaf node means that they're less rigid than plants growing outdoors.

Indoor plants are sheltered from strong winds, which are instrumental in strengthening plant stems outdoors. As winds push a young plant first one way and then the other, the plant's stems toughen up. Indoor plants rarely feel any wind (air conditioners and fans don't count), and consequently never develop strong stems.

Try pruning first before staking

Pruning and pinching are alternatives to staking. If you prune a plant carefully, removing weak and excessively long stems, or pinch regularly to prevent weak growth from ever occurring, the plant likely won't require staking. When a stem starts to bend over, decide whether the plant would be more attractive without that weak branch and, if so, prune it off rather than stake it.

Staking, by its very nature, tends to make a plant even weaker. After you attach a plant to a stake, it moves even less freely, which leads to even weaker new growth. Consider staking a temporary measure. Make it your goal to prune a plant back to encourage thick, strong, and healthy stems.

Out-of-sight staking

When you must stake a plant, try to make the stake as unobtrusive as possible because there's nothing pretty about a plant wearing a splint. Try the following suggestions:

- ✔ Insert stakes near the center of the plant, hidden among the leaves and branches.

- ✔ Consider using the plant itself as a support. You can do this by attaching a weak branch to a stronger neighbor.

- ✔ If you need to stake several branches, use individual stakes for each branch. A web of strings and ties wrapped around a single stake and tied to several branches adds up to one messy eyesore.

- ✔ Avoid brightly colored stakes. Dead branches, green-tinted bamboo, olive-green plant stakes, and so on, work like camouflage. Or, wrap a colored stake in green florist tape.

- ✔ Avoid highly visible fasteners. Green twist ties, green or natural-colored raffia, garden twine, and soft plastic plant ties in off-green shades make good choices.

- ✔ Try to re-create the plant's natural growth pattern when you attach the branches to stakes. Avoid bunching stems together or cramming flower heads up against each other.

Be sure to firmly anchor the stake in the pot. Push it far down into the potting mix, and to the base of the pot, if necessary.

The ties that bind

Avoid fastening ties too tightly; they can cut into the plant and injure it. You can get special plant ties covered in soft plastic or foam to help prevent injury to the plant. Also avoid using ties that can easily cut plant tissue. Transparent fishing line, for example, although unobtrusive, is so thin and sharp that it tends to wound tender stems.

Move plant ties every six months so that they don't have time to start digging in. And, always leave a little space between the tie and the plant for future growth.

A weighty solution to a top-heavy problem

Sometimes plants don't need staking as much as they just need some extra weight at their base. Many plants (cacti especially) become top-heavy as they grow. You can partially offset this problem by planting them in larger pots, but guard against overpotting. Too much potting mix around a limited root system can lead to rot. Consider repotting into the same-size pot, but using a heavier *mix* (sand-based mixes are excellent for that purpose) and a heavier pot (for example, clay weighs more than plastic).

Another way to handle top-heavy plants is to *double-pot*. Fill the base of a larger pot with heavy stones or gravel, insert the top-heavy plant's pot into it, and then fill the empty space around it with more gravel.

The Sky's the Limit: Support for Climbing Plants

Many people grow climbing plants upside down, letting their branches trail and using them as hanging plants. There's nothing wrong with that, but you may prefer watching the plant act naturally and reach for the sky. Over millions of years of evolution, climbing plants have developed various means of making sure that they can climb. Climbing plants are categorized by their climbing techniques (see Figure 15-3):

- *Leaners,* such as bougainvillea, produce long branches that lean on other plants. Some leaners (climbing rose, for example) add hooks (thorns) to their arsenal so they are less likely to slip free.

- *Rooters* (English ivy, philodendrons, pothos, Swiss cheese plant, creeping fig) produce aerial roots that stick solidly to their supports.

- *Twiners,* such as morning glories and hoyas, have stems that grow in spirals, then wrap around any narrow object they encounter.

- *Clingers,* such as grape ivy, have special organs called *tendrils* that wrap around branches and stems. Some clingers even have adhesive disks allowing them to climb up rocks and trunks.

Trying to attach a climbing plant to a bamboo pole or other plant stake can be an exercise in frustration. Unlike shrubby plants, whose woody stems do most of the support work, climbers make no effort to hold themselves up. As they become taller and heavier, the ties that support them tend to slide back down the stake, leaving the plant lying limply on the floor.

Figure 15-3:
The four
basic types
of climbing
plants and
their
techniques
in action.

Although some plant stakes today have specially designed ties that don't slip downward, a climbing plant stretching up a narrow stake isn't always the most attractive presentation. The following sections tell you about some ways that you can get your climbing plants to grow upward, in style.

Bark supports

In the wild, many climbing plants naturally climb up tree trunks using aerial roots or adhesive disks. Indoors, they cling just as readily to bark. A slat of wood with the bark still attached makes an excellent support.

Beware: Most climbers quickly overpower the 3-foot (90-centimeter) bark slats often sold in nurseries. You can always attach a new piece of bark to the top of the first one, but a single slat of wood is more solid than two pieces nailed together. Just remember to choose a piece tall enough for your needs.

You also can use a *moss support* — a stake or piece of plastic pipe wrapped in sphagnum moss and held together with fishing line. Ready-made moss stakes are available and give top marks to any store-bought model that allows you to add new segments as the plants grow. You can also make your own by just wrapping a stake in sphagnum moss and fishing line (see Figure 15-4).

Figure 15-4:
It's easy to make your own moss support.

Trellises

When you think of climbing plants, the image of a trellis almost always comes to mind. Trellises are a common sight in outdoor gardens, but no rule says you can't use them indoors as well.

Small plastic trellises for indoor use are widely available. Just sink the trellis's base into the potting soil and weave the plant's stems around the rungs of the trellis for instant support. If you have a tall climber, most indoor plant trellises are usually too small. Instead, bring outdoor trellises indoors. An endless array of models is available in both wood and plastic.

The weight of a climbing plant on a trellis can tip over the average-sized pot, so consider planting two or three climbing plants in a large tub and inserting the trellis in the middle of the tub. You usually need to weave the stems of most climbing plants through the trellis yourself, although some do climb on their own.

Wall supports

I'm sure you've seen outdoor ivy-covered walls, but did you know that you can also train plants to permanently grow up a wall inside your home? Simply attach a trellis to a wall and train plants to grow onto it. For a really striking effect, attach a trellis to both sides of a window and allow the climbing plants to cover the glass. Or, try another technique that's just as effective and costs next to nothing — stretch twine from the floor to the ceiling, nail it into place at both ends, and train climbing plants to grow up the length of the twine. Do this in front of a window for a fast and easy living curtain!

Obviously, any plants attached to immovable supports become permanent "indoor landscape features." Before you attach them to their supports, plant them in larger-than-usual pots because you can't easily repot these guys. And forget about the regular "quarter turn" to give a plant even light (see Chapter 8). These plants will never move again.

In the case of *force majeur,* such as your moving to a new home, your best course of action is to chop your indoor wall-climbers down to their base and allow them to resprout in their new home rather than to try to move them with their supports.

Chapter 16

Multiplication and Division: Propagating Houseplants

- -

In This Chapter

▶ Growing houseplants from seed and spores

▶ Cultivating houseplants from cuttings and offsets

▶ Taking cuttings to multiply your plant supply

▶ Reproducing new plants by layering bits of another plant

- -

Dolly the Sheep has nothing on plants — they've been doing the cloning thing for millions of years. A single branch or leaf breaks off and falls to the ground, and the next thing you know it's taken root and sprouted new leaves, producing a plant absolutely identical to the original. Plants are also able to produce seed at prolific rates: A seed capsule can contain anywhere from a single seed to 5,000-plus seeds.

All and all, plants have amazing reproductive capabilities, and if you know how to take advantage of those capabilities, you can fill your house with many plants where you once just had a few. In this chapter, I tell you about inexpensive and easy techniques for propagating houseplants by using both seeds and vegetative reproduction (dividing, grafting, and such).

The Benefits of Houseplant Farming

A number of good reasons exists for propagating (that is, multiplying) houseplants in your home, other than their obvious decorative value:

✔ **To replace aging plants:** Some of the faster-growing houseplants only look good for a year or so unless you keep pruning them back severely. Even then, those plants won't be as vigorous as a young plant just started from scratch.

✔ **To make your home a healthier place to live:** Given the extraordinary power of plants to clean and humidify the air we breathe, the more greenery the merrier.

✔ **To exchange plants with other indoor gardeners:** You can exchange young plants with neighbors, friends, or family. Some gardening clubs also sponsor plant exchanges.

✔ **To avoid throwing out leftovers:** The dog knocks a plant over and you're left with a loose branch, another plant grows too tall and you have to chop some of it off, or another overcrowds its pot so you have to divide it. Rather than toss out those spare plant parts, you can make good use of them and plant them into a pot of their own.

✔ **To use as gifts:** Have you ever met someone who doesn't like plants? They're the perfect hostess gift and wonderful things to bring along when you visit a friend in the hospital. And mentioning offhandedly that you grew it yourself earns you some respect, and sometimes even awe.

Sex and the Single Houseplant: Growing Plants from Seed

Unlike animals, plants have *two* means of reproduction — sexual reproduction and asexual, or *vegetative,* reproduction. In the following sections of this chapter, I examine sexual plant reproduction, which involves growing from seeds. Later in the chapter, I explore vegetative reproduction, which involves propagating new plants from bits of existing plants.

Some pollen here, a little stigma there, and you end up with seeds

Except for a few sterile individuals (hey, Mother Nature was at the spa that day), all plants — even foliage plants — are capable of sexual reproduction. Let me tell you about the birds and the bees. They flutter from flower to flower, looking for nectar, and while doing so pick up some *pollen,* which they carry to other plants. When the pollen (the male half of the relationship) from one plant touches the *stigma* (the female half) of another plant, pollination occurs and seeds begin to grow.

Some plants count on the wind for pollination. They have extremely lightweight pollen that the slightest breeze can carry away to some available flower a distance off. Other plants self-pollinate: They drop pollen on their own stigma and reproduce without needing any outside help. Those plants can produce seeds all on their own, without having to hook up with other plants.

Pollinating plants and harvesting seeds yourself

Plants descended from wind-pollinated or animal-pollinated flowers usually fail to produce seeds indoors because their pollinating "agent" simply isn't present. Nevertheless, you can get plants to produce *fruit* (the fleshy part surrounding the seeds) and seeds in either of two ways:

- ✔ Put them outdoors during their flowering period so that the wind or animals can take care of the job.
- ✔ Pollinate the plants yourself.

Pollinating a flowering houseplant by hand is a snap. Just take a cotton swab or a small paintbrush, insert it into the flower and wiggle it about, and then move on to another flower and do the same. You don't even have to know an *anther* (the male organ producing pollen) from a stigma. In most cases, flowers produce pollen, a whitish or yellowish powder, so abundantly that it sticks to everything that touches it, including not only the paintbrush or cotton swab, but also to any other flower's stigma.

If your pollination efforts are successful, the flower's base swells and turns into a seed capsule or fruit; otherwise, the whole flower dries up and falls off as it ages. Either way, be patient. It usually takes from several weeks (with impatiens, for example) to as long as a year (with some orchids) for the seeds to ripen, depending on the type of plant.

Most seed capsules simply turn brown when ripe, a sign for you to clip them off before they open on their own and allow the seeds to fall out. Just hold something underneath the seed capsule to catch it (a business-size envelope works) and cut it at its base. If the capsule doesn't open on its own inside the envelope after a few days (most do), just squeeze it between your index finger and your thumb until it splits apart or cut it open across the middle when you're ready to sow seeds. It's best to sow houseplant seeds when they're fresh, but you can store some for up to a year or more. Just seal them in paper envelopes and place them in a cool, dry place.

Fruits are more interesting than seed capsules because they usually change color as they ripen — from green to yellow, orange, red, purple, or blue. You don't have to harvest the fruit right away; you can leave it on the plant as long as it looks attractive. When they start to turn brown or drop off, open them up and remove the seeds from the fruit's pulp. The Calamondin orange is an example of a houseplant whose fruit is particularly attractive.

Starting plants from seed

Although growing houseplants from seed is tempting, think twice before trying it. You can get much faster results if you multiply the plant via vegetative means, such as with cuttings or offsets.

On the other hand, all great houseplant cultivars owe their origins to someone transporting pollen from one promising plant to another, so if you want to experiment, don't hesitate to try making your own crosses. Who knows? You might come up with something really special!

You can sow seeds indoors at any time of the year, especially if you grow them under artificial light, but many plants grow especially well under the lengthening days of spring. You can use either store-bought seeds or harvest your own from the plants you have. In Chapters 4 through 7, I note which houseplants are commonly propagated from seed.

Many outdoor gardeners who grow vegetables or annuals from seed sow the seeds in large planting trays designed for that purpose, but you won't need anything that elaborate if you're growing houseplants from seed. To grow a couple of plants from seeds, you just need the following supplies:

✔ Some clean plastic pots $2^1/_2$ or 3 inches (6.5 to 7.5 centimeters) in diameter — use one pot for each plant you want to produce to avoid the rather difficult and risky process of transplanting young seedlings.

✔ Potting mix — freshly opened bags are best because they're less likely to carry airborne diseases.

✔ A mixing bowl, warm water, spoon, and spray bottle

✔ A pencil or chopstick and labels for the plant names

✔ Plastic sandwich bags and twist ties

After you gather the necessary materials, just follow these basic steps:

1. **If your plant produces large seeds with hard coatings (if you can't make a dent in the seed with your fingernail, you know it's hard), soak the seeds in warm water overnight to soften their tough exterior.**

   To keep the water warm, pour it into a wide-mouthed thermos and drop the seeds in. Small seeds need no special pretreatment.

2. **Pour some potting mix into a bowl, add warm water until the mix is moist but not wet, and blend.**

   Pour a small amount of the potting mix into the bowl, moisten very slightly and rub it gently in your hands. If it holds its shape on release, it contains the right amount of moisture. If the soil is glistening, it is too wet and you need to add more potting mix.

3. **Spoon the moistened mix into a pot to about $^1/_2$ inch (1 centimeter) from the top and press down lightly with the back of the spoon just enough to smooth out the mix.**

4. **Using a pencil or chopstick, drill a shallow hole in the center of the pot to a depth of three times the seed's diameter.**

5. **Drop three seeds in the hole and cover with mix.**

By planting three seeds per pot instead of just one, you avoid disappointment; usually at least one will germinate.

Do not bury any tiny, dust-like seeds. Sprinkle them lightly over the growing mix and mist lightly to make sure they stick to the top of the mix.

6. **Write the date and the plant's name on a label and insert it into the mix.**

7. **Place the pot inside a plastic sandwich bag and seal it tightly.**

8. **Place the pot in a warm spot that gets bright light but no direct midday or afternoon sun.**

An east or north window ledge is good, as are spots under fluorescent lights.

When green growths appear in the potting mix (most seeds produce two "seed leaves" or *cotyledons*), open the plastic bag slightly to increase air circulation and remove the bag bit by bit over the course of a week, first opening it a crack, then gradually pulling it down until the seedling is entirely exposed to the surrounding air. Examine the plant carefully, lightly touching the soil daily to make sure it never dries out entirely, and water just enough to keep the mix slightly moist. The plant soon produces normal leaves (seed leaves are often very different from the plant's usual leaf).

Often, more than one plant germinates from the three seeds dropped into the hole. If that happens, a week or so after germination, simply cut off the weakest plants, keeping only the one that seems the largest and most vigorous. When a plant develops six or seven true leaves (they look like miniature versions of the adult leaf), you can safely begin treating it like an adult plant, as far as watering, lighting, and so on.

Don't be surprised if certain plants don't exactly follow the pattern of two seed leaves followed by multiple adult leaves. Cacti, for example, produce the usual two seed leaves, but after that, instead of more leaves, only a thick and often spiny stem. Start treating cacti like adult plants when their seed leaves dry up, which can take more than a year for these slow-growing succulents.

Plants you can grow from seed

Most popular houseplants are far easier to propagate from cuttings, but the following ones grow so quickly from seed that they're well worth trying.

✔ Asparagus fern (*Asparagus densiflorus* 'Sprengeri')

✔ Coleus (*Coleus × hybrida*)

✔ Florist's gloxinia (*Sinningia speciosa*)

✔ Flowering maple (*Abutilon × hybridum*)

✔ Impatiens (*Impatiens wallerana*)

✔ Polka-dot plant (*Hypoestes phyllostachya*)

✔ Zonal geranium (*Pelargonium × hortorum*)

Growing ferns from spores

Ferns don't produce seeds but their *spore cases*, usually located on the backs of their leaves, produce abundant dust-like *spores*. Growing ferns from spores is a slow and delicate process. Try your hand at growing plants from seeds first, and when you feel ready for a real challenge, take a stab at growing some ferns from spores.

Look for spore cases on the backs of the fern fronds (they're green or brown bumps). Find a frond that has brown spore cases, cut it off, and seal it in a paper envelope. After a week or so, the envelope should be filled with tiny, brown spores that are visible only because of their numbers.

Prepare a pot of moist soil (see the section "Starting plants from seed" in this chapter), and lightly sprinkle the spores on the potting mix. Mist the soil lightly with warm tap water and seal the pot in a sandwich bag. Place the pot in a warm, well-lit spot — but not under direct sun.

After a few months, the pot fills with curious, moss-like or algae-like growths, called *prothallus* — the beginning of the sexual stage of the fern's life cycle. Although you can't see it, fertilization occurs under the prothallus's protective covering and a small fern develops at the tip of the prothallus (see the figure in this sidebar). It usually takes at least a full year to grow even a small fern from the spores. After the young fern produces three or four fronds, open the bag gradually to acclimate the fern to the outside air; then pot it up on its own.

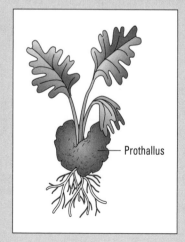

Prothallus

Vegetative Propagation

Although plants reproduce sexually (via seeds) in nature, vegetative propagation (that is, asexual propagation) is the fastest and easiest way to reproduce plants indoors.

You definitely want to opt for vegetative reproduction in some cases:

- ✔ With plants that take years to grow to a usable size.
- ✔ To ensure that the new plant is identical to the mother plant.

   When you grow plants from seed, you also have to expect the new plants to differ at least a little from their parents.

You can propagate nearly every type of houseplant through some form of asexual reproduction, which includes techniques such as dividing, grafting, and layering, as well as through the plant's ability to produce plantlets and offshoots.

 You can use any of the vegetative methods throughout the year, but you're more likely to have success if you propagate when the plant is just coming out of a dormant period or during late winter to early summer when the days are growing longer.

Multiplication by division

Division is a low-stress propagation method (for the plant, especially) because each plant starts off its new life as an independent being with its own share of roots. Many plants grow in *clumps* (clusters of multiple plants, each with its own root system) that can be divided, including the nerve plant, the peacock plant, and most begonias. Sympodial orchids (see Chapter 7) also divide well.

You can divide any plant that grows in clumps into two or three smaller clumps. Just unpot the plant, untangle the foliage, with one hand grasp all but the one clump you want to remove, and with the other hand gently pull on the single clump until it breaks free from the rest of the plant.

Division sounds simple in theory, but pulling it off requires patience and some effort because the roots are often severely tangled. Before dividing the root system, do the following:

1. **Rinse off some of the potting mix to get a better look at how the plant is divided.**

2. **With a clean, sharp knife, slice between the clump you want to divide off and the rest of the plant.**

When you work with plants that have exceptionally tough roots, such as the asparagus fern, you may even need to use a saw or an ax to divide the plant in two.

3. **Give each divided section its fair share of the roots, as shown in Figure 16-1.**

4. **Repot the new clump into fresh potting mix, using a pot about three times the diameter of the new plant, then water thoroughly.**

5. **Put the freshly repotted plant in moderate light for a week or so.**

After that, you can treat the plant section an established plant.

Figure 16-1:
When you divide a plant, make sure each section gets a share of the roots.

If you want more new plants, you can separate additional clumps from the mother plant. Or, you can even break the entire mother plant into smaller individual clumps from the start. If one new plant is all you want, you can simply repot the mother plant back into its original container.

If the plant wilts heavily after division, slip it into a clear plastic bag to improve the humidity it receives until new roots can grow out.

Multiplication through offsets

Offsets, or *pups,* are simply small replicas of the mother plant that occasionally appear, sometimes directly from the mother plant's base, and sometimes from the end of secondary stems that grow a short distance from the mother plant. If you're thinking, "Hey, that sounds like an umbilical cord setup," you're on the right track. Bromeliads, bulbs, and many succulents produce offsets.

You generally remove offsets while plants are in full growth, with bulbs being the one exception. The best time to remove a bulb's offsets is at annual repotting time, just when the plant is starting to come out of its yearly dormancy.

You remove offsets using the same techniques involved in multiplication by division (see the previous section of this chapter). The process, however, is more traumatic for the young plant because its root system is not yet fully established. Therefore, use the following steps:

1. **Wait until the offset reaches about one-third the size of the mother plant, then unpot the mother.**

2. **Clear away some soil from the mother plant's base to determine where to cut.**

3. **With a sharp knife, carefully sever the lifeline between the mother and baby, and then pot up the offset on its own.**

   Your goal is to separate the offset without damaging the mother plant, so cut just at the point where the baby's stem meets the mother's.

If the pup already has a fairly decent root system, it may not require any special treatment other than less light than usual for a week or so. If it has few or no roots, treat it like a cutting (see the section "Tip cuttings" later in this chapter).

Multiplication by grafting

Grafting involves joining two different plants together. The plant rooted in the soil is called the *rootstock*; the one inserted onto the top of rootstock is called the *scion*. Grafting requires your having compatible plants of the same family and it's a rather complicated process for anyone but an expert, so I don't go into much depth on the subject.

Among indoor plants, cacti are the ones most often grafted. For example, the albino cactus, which has no *chlorophyll* (the green pigment that gives plants their normal coloration), can survive only when grafted onto another cactus. The red ball cactus (*Gymnocalycium mihanovichii friedrichii* 'Rubra') is an example of an albino cactus. With no green pigment, it can survive only when grafted onto a green cactus.

You can graft other kinds of plants. For example, you can graft English ivy onto a schefflera, because the two are closely related — but the result is more curious-looking than beautiful.

Propagation through plantlets

Plantlets are miniature replicas of the mother plant that appear in unusual places, such as on leaves, stems, flower stalks, and *stolons* (long, creeping stems). In nature, most plantlets will eventually touch the ground (where they can root into the soil to form an independent plant) or drop off the mother plant completely when disturbed by winds or an animal (and thereby soon root on their own). In culture, houseplant owners typically cut them off and treat them like cuttings (see "Tip cuttings" later in this chapter).

The following are a few of the most popular plants that produce plantlets:

- ✔ Episcia *(Episcia cupreata)*
- ✔ Mother-of-thousands *(Tolmiea menziesii)*
- ✔ Orchids (many kinds) — their plantlets are called *keikis*
- ✔ Spider plant *(Chlorophytum comosum)*
- ✔ Strawberry begonia *(Saxifraga stolonifera)*

Multiplication through cuttings

Many houseplants are popular because they multiply so well through cuttings. In the sections coming up, I describe some of the best known methods of propagation via cuttings.

Tip cuttings

Tip cuttings are the most popular means of reproducing plants that are grown in culture. You can use almost any plant that produces branches to harvest tip cuttings. Stemless plants are obvious exceptions to the rule but, oddly enough, so are palms. (Although you can reproduce clumping palms by division, you must use seeds to multiply most palms.)

There's one born every minute

You may have heard other gardeners complaining about *suckers*, secondary growths that they love to hate. What's the difference between a sucker and an offset or plantlet? The answer: not much. Basically, any undesirable new plant development growing off a stem or at a plant's base is called a *sucker*.

African violets, for example, produce suckers that use up the pot's real estate and cause the plant to grow crookedly. Some people welcome such growths on bromeliads and spider plants and call them *plantlets* and would never refer to them as suckers.

To take a tip cutting, do the following:

1. **Study the plant's stem. Each cutting should have at least three *nodes* (the point where a leaf joins the stem), although it can also have many more.**

2. **Cut the stem off with a sharp knife just above the bottom node.**

   Cutting near but not into a node helps the mother plant heal without leaving an ugly stub.

3. **Remove any leaves still attached to the two lower nodes of the cutting and insert the cutting into a pot of moistened potting mix.**

   When you work with a woody plant, use a cotton swab to apply *rooting hormone* (available in liquid, gel, or powder form) to the cut end before you insert it into the mix to help rooting.

4. **Cover the plant with a clear plastic bag and put the cutting in a warm, brightly lit spot out of direct sun.**

The speed at which cuttings take root varies according to the plant. Coleus often start producing roots within days, whereas some woody plants take months to root. You can tell that the plant has rooted when it starts to produce new leaves. At that point, open the plastic bag gradually over a period of several days and then remove it entirely after about two weeks. The plant is now fully independent and can be treated like any adult plant.

Treat plantlets that you cut off of spider plants, mother-of-thousands, or episcias, and unrooted or poorly developed pups and offsets from bromeliads and other plants, just like tip cuttings.

Stem section cuttings

You can raise a few thick-stemmed plants, such as dracaenas and dieffenbachias, from stem sections. You can do so after removing the top of the plant after air layering (see the section "Propagation by air layering" later in this chapter) or after removing a tip of the plant to make a cutting. Then do the following:

1. **Cut what remains of the plant's now leafless stem into 2-inch (5-centimeter) sections that contain at least one or two nodes.**

   Be sure to keep track of which part of the stem section is the "top" (nearest to where the plant's leaves originally grew) and which is the "bottom" (closest to the plant's roots). As you cut, lay the pieces on a table with the top edges pointing away from you.

Sod the old rooting-cuttings-in-a-glass of water routine

The traditional way to root houseplant cuttings was to plop them into a glass of water, but that technique simply isn't very effective. When plant roots form in water, those roots adapt to strictly aquatic conditions. Then when you pot up the plant, the aquatic root often rots away entirely and the poor cutting has to produce an entirely new root system. Quite often, it simply doesn't have enough energy left to do so and dies. Plants that root in potting mix or any other solid medium (perlite and vermiculite, which I cover in Chapter 13, are also good media for rooting plants) immediately produce *terrestrial roots* and suffer little shock when you move them into a larger pot. If you insist on rooting your cuttings in water, pot up the cutting as soon as you first see roots on the stem (they look like pale bumps). The roots have begun to grow but haven't yet fully adapted to an aquatic environment and, therefore, can still quickly grow into healthy young terrestrial roots.

2. **Insert the bottom of each section into a pot of moist growing medium and cover with a plastic bag.**

   Placing the stem section into the mix with the bottom end in the potting mix is essential. If you plant the cutting upside down, with the top buried and the bottom exposed to the surrounding air, it will never root.

You just dropped your stem sections all over the floor and can no longer tell which side is up? No problem! Just plant them on their sides, half burying the cuttings in the mix, as shown in Figure 16-2. The roots can find their way down and the new stem will find its way up!

Figure 16-2: You can multiply a plant with a stem section cutting planted on its side.

Healing time for cacti

Most cuttings root best when you keep their growing mix moist and furnish them with extra humidity by covering them with a clear plastic bag, but cactus and other succulent cuttings do not. In fact, let the cut end of their stems heal over before you insert them into a dry potting mix. Some succulents can take weeks before they heal, and some thick-stemmed succulents can take months, so place the plants in a dry, sunny spot until the cut completely heals over. Even after the cut is healed and you insert the upright cutting into its mix, refrain from watering until the first roots form. Give the cutting a light tug after a few weeks. If it resists being pulled out, it has rooted and can be watered.

Leaf cuttings

New plants can form from a *single leaf.* In fact, many thick-leafed plants, including many leaf succulents (donkey's tail, jade plant, and echeveria, among them), as well as African violets, episcias, peperomias, streptocarpus, snake plants, and many rhizomatous begonias, root quite easily through leaf cuttings.

To take a leaf cutting, simply snap off a leaf at its base and insert the cut part into a moist growing mix to about ¹/₂ inch (1 cm) deep. Soon, new plants will spring up out of the mix around the base of the leaf.

To multiply a succulent leaf through a leaf cutting, place the leaf onto the surface of the mix without covering any part of it, especially its base; otherwise, the cut end may rot if it is covered with moist mix. Don't bother covering succulent cuttings with a plastic bag. The leaf eventually roots in the open air and the roots find their way down into the mix on their own.

Some leaf cuttings produce only one young plant per cutting while others, especially the African violet, produce many. If you get multiple plants from a cutting, separate them when you pot them up for the best results.

You can even cut leaves into sections and each section will produce a plant. This approach works with snake plants, florist gloxinias, streptocarpus, and some begonias. Just be sure to insert the leaf section into the mix, with, of course, the end closest to the plant pointing down into the soil.

Propagation by layering

Layering is one of the more common types of vegetative reproduction in the wild, but is an uncommon practice indoors. *Layering* occurs when part of a plant touches the soil and takes root. Eventually, the stem linking it to the mother plant dies away and it becomes an independent plant.

Most climbing and creeping plants root in this fashion, as do most plants that produce *plantlets* (see "Propagation through plantlets" earlier in this chapter). These plants layer themselves when the leaf or *stolon* on which the plantlet grows touches the ground. Even shrubs and trees often layer naturally when a bent or broken branch touches the ground.

Some plants are self-layering:

- ✔ The nerve plant, for example, roots as it creeps about its pot.
- ✔ The long, fuzzy rhizomes of the Boston fern also seek out spaces in which they can sprout.

Most other plants need help with layering. Just place a pot of moist soil next to a creeping or climbing plant, such as the heartleaf philodendron or English ivy, and pin a section of a branch to the mix using a V-shaped hair pin. You also can pin the plantlets of any stolon-producing plants (such as spider plants, episcias, and strawberry begonias) or plantlets that grow on a plant's leaves (such as on those on the mother-of-thousands plant) to a neighboring pot, as shown in Figure 16-3. You can even layer indoor shrubs, such as crotons or jade plants, if they have any branches that droop toward the ground.

Figure 16-3: To layer an episcia, just pin its plantlet to a new pot and the plantlet roots on its own.

Propagation by air layering

Air layering is the most improbable plant multiplication technique of all. You actually force a plant to root way up in the air, near the crown of the plant. Now *that's* something you don't see very often in nature.

Air layering is really just a smart way of multiplying upright plants that have stiff stems. Such plants are nearly impossible to bend to the ground, so you simply bring the ground to them. You can use this technique on many indoor trees (other than palms), especially when they get so tall that they become ungainly and unattractive. Jut follow these steps:

To encourage a stem to form roots, make an upward-slanting cut into the stem at a point just below the lower leaf.

1. **Cut one-third to one-half of the way into the stem.**

2. **To keep it from healing over and closing, insert a sliver of wood or a match into the opening (see Figure 16-4).**

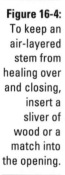

Figure 16-4:
To keep an air-layered stem from healing over and closing, insert a sliver of wood or a match into the opening.

3. **Apply a dusting of rooting hormone with a cotton swab.**

4. **Have someone else wrap the stem in two handfuls of moist sphagnum moss, after which you wrap the moss in a sheet of clear plastic (so that you can see when new roots form).**

   Use a sheet that's large enough to wrap around the moss, leaving no part exposed. The plastic both holds the moss in place and keeps it from drying out too quickly.

5. **To hold the moss in place, attach a twist tie to either end of the sheet, wrapping it firmly around the stem.**

6. **Check the moss weekly, opening the sheet at the top to add water if necessary.**

   After a few weeks, roots begin to show through the moss.

7. **Remove the plastic and cut right through the stem just below the ball of moss.**

8. **Pot up the new root ball, moss and all, and keep the plant in a warm, humid spot out of direct sunlight for a few weeks.**

   You can then treat it as an adult plant.

The mother plant usually looks pretty sorry at this point, with its long bare stem and no leaves at the top. But, don't despair. A number of shoots will soon form just under the cut. If you let them grow, the plant will have several new branches at the top of its stem. If you think the plant will look unattractive with that length of bare stem and branches only at the very top, cut the plant back to near soil level. It soon sprouts new branches at its base, forming a more attractive plant. You can slice the stem that you just cut off into sections and root them separately (see "Stem section cuttings" earlier).

Chapter 17

Conquering Houseplant Pests and Diseases

....

In This Chapter

▶ Spotting potentially harmful insects and diseases

▶ Nipping problems in the bud and preventing them before they happen

▶ Using safe methods to control pests and diseases

....

I wish I could say that the odds are you'll never experience any problems with plant invaders — unwelcome insects and ailments that torture your plants and threaten their good health. The fact is, most indoor gardeners eventually have to deal with houseplant pests and diseases. If you want to find out how to ward off diseases and pests, and fight those problems when they do develop, read on.

The source of most plant problems isn't insects or disease, it's poor *culture* (that is, poor care). If a plant seems listless, the problem usually boils down to insufficient lighting, too much or not enough water, air that's way too dry, or a combination of all three. Plants that are grown under ideal conditions are far more resistant to pests and diseases when they do fall victim to them.

An Ounce of Prevention: Controlling Pests and Diseases from the Start

You can sit back and wait for various pests and diseases to attack your plants, or you can take action to prevent problems from happening. Warding off houseplant problems is fairly simple to do.

✔ Inspect all plants thoroughly before you bring them home from the store. Some of the worst houseplant pests can be traced back to the source.

✔ Always put new houseplants in *quarantine*. Quarantine is a French term that originally referred to a 40-day period, which is an appropriate amount of time to keep your new arrivals away from the rest of your plants. Any pests, diseases, or other problems should surface by then. Carefully inspect any short-lived plants, such as florist plants, which may last only a few weeks and can't be quarantined.

If you have the space, you can quarantine new arrivals by putting them in a room of their own. If that's not an option, place a new plant inside a plastic bag (dry cleaner bags will do the trick) and seal it. Then put the plant somewhere out of direct sunlight. If later you do find pests, you have two choices: Ditch the plant immediately or treat the problem until all the symptoms are gone.

✔ Isolate any plants that show signs of weakness, insects, or disease. (Later sections of this chapter tell you how to spot those problems.) Quarantine them as you would any plant just home from the store.

✔ Keep your plants clean and remove all yellowing or dead leaves and flowers. Rotting material is the perfect host for diseases and yellow leaves are a magnet for pests. That's because healthy plants react to the presence of pests by producing chemicals that make their leaves unpalatable. Weak plants don't have the energy to do so, and so pests find their leaves very tasty.

✔ Wash your plants every every four months or so. Sticking them under the shower is often all they need. This removes dust, grime, and any insects and disease spores hidden among the leaves.

Always wash your plants early in the day so that they can dry off by evening. Foliage that's left moist or wet overnight is an open invitation to disease.

✔ Screen any open windows, especially during the growing season. Unscreened windows say "Welcome" to any insects or disease spores that happen to be hanging around outside. Ordinary screens don't keep all pests out, but you can buy special anti-insect screening from a greenhouse supplier.

✔ Don't immediately tend to your indoor plants after working outdoors in the garden. Spores and pests can hitch a ride on your clothes, hands, and hair, especially during the outdoor growing season. Before even watering your houseplants, take a shower and change clothes. Keep a separate set of tools for your indoor and garden plants.

Yellow or orange-colored clothing also attract insects that are only too glad to hitch a ride into your home.

✔ Hang "sticky traps" (glue-covered yellow cards available in garden centers) before you spot any insects. If you do trap some insects, do a thorough search to determine which plants are hosting them. You can then remove or quarantine them before the problem spreads. (Sticky traps are not the same as *pest strips,* which may contain harmful chemical products.)

✔ Avoid "boosting" plants with high doses of fertilizer, especially fertilizers rich in nitrogen. Extra fertilizer tends to stimulate large, abundant, pale green leaves and long but weak stems that insects just love to munch. Instead, fertilize lightly at all times. And cut back the fertilizer dosage drastically during the winter or whenever a plant is growing under reduced light levels because new growth that appears under poor lighting tends to be weak and, therefore, attractive to insects.

✔ Avoid growing plants known for their susceptibility to insects. If you do, inspect the plants regularly, and be ready to act. Palms, hibiscus, impatiens, and scheffleras are irresistible to spider mites, and fuchsias, geraniums, and most indoor edibles are magnets for whiteflies.

✔ Maintain good air circulation at all times. Run a small fan, if necessary, to keep the air around moving a bit. Most diseases can develop only in stagnant air.

✔ Always wash pots thoroughly before reusing them to eliminate any lingering pests. Soak them overnight in warm water (adding a few spoonfuls of vinegar also helps dissolve mineral salt accumulations). Then wash them in a hot, soapy solution of ten parts water to one part household bleach, and scrub them well with a wire brush.

✔ Take precautions with any plant that you bring inside from the outdoors. Before they enter the house, spray their leaves and stems thoroughly with insecticide and immerse the root ball in soapy water for several hours. And after that, quarantine them for six weeks.

✔ Whenever you treat sick plants, always use gloves and sterile tools to keep from spreading the problem. You can sterilize knives and pruning shears by dipping the blades in rubbing alcohol between each cut.

✔ Give your plants the best overall care possible, including ample lighting and ideal watering and fertilizing routines. Healthy plants attract pests and diseases far less often than weak ones do. And, when weak plants introduce pests into your home, those unwanted guests can reproduce and spread to your healthy ones.

They Crawl, They Fly, They Multiply: Knowing the Enemy

The secret to controlling houseplant pests is getting to know the enemy. The more information you have about a pest that's invaded your home, the more likely you are to conquer it. In the following sections, I tell you about the most common indoor plant pests — what they look like, their life cycles, the damage they cause, and the types of plants they seek out. I also tell you the best treatment for each plant. Later on in this chapter, I tell you about some general methods to prevent bug infestations and rid your plants of pests.

Aphids

Aphids (see Figure 17-1) are pudgy green (or brown, black, yellow, red, or gray) insects that colonize plants, especially young stems and the undersides of leaves. Aphids are usually wingless, although some winged individuals occasionally appear. When they do, you have a battle on your hands because the winged ones spread very rapidly. Aphids line up single file with the oldest female at the head of the queue. As she moves forward, she produces one baby aphid after another. The line formation breaks up when the babies start having babies of their own. All of this happens in a matter of days.

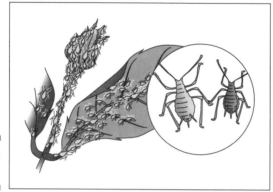

Figure 17-1:
Aphids.

Although they multiply rapidly, aphids spread to other plants relatively slowly and attack neighboring plants first, so you can prevent aphids from getting all of your plants if you act quickly. Aphids are not selective — they attack just about anything that's green. They also transmit viruses and secrete a sticky substance, called *honeydew,* that coats leaves and can cause *sooty mold* (which is described in more detail later in the chapter). Infested plant parts turn pale or yellowish and often twist or curl under.

Treatment: You can control aphids through a program of weekly pesticide treatments. Even simply spraying infected plants with water, directed at the undersides of the leaves, is often enough to knock them off the plant and control the problem. Plus it washes away the honeydew.

Cyclamen mites

Cyclamen mites and their close cousins, *broad mites,* are among the least common houseplant pests, but they're the hardest to control. Part of the challenge is that they're virtually microscopic. A problem with cyclamen mites usually isn't spotted until the plant is so infested that it's on the brink of death. New growth is twisted, brittle, or doesn't happen at all, and any open flowers are discolored. Close inspection will reveal that much of the new growth on an infested plant is covered with small scabs. Fortunately, they attack relatively few indoor plants, notably begonias, African violets, and cyclamens.

Treatment: Throw away any severely infested plants. Insecticides offer some control, but the "hot water treatment" works better (see the section "Environmentally Safe Treatments to Rid Your Plants of Pests" later in this chapter).

Fungus gnats

Fungus gnats and their close relative, the *shore fly,* look a lot like fruit flies except that they're black and tinier. They have an annoying habit of fluttering about your face, even in rooms far away from the infested plant. The adults are quite harmless, but the *larvae* — which are tiny white grubs with dark-colored heads — sometimes chew on plant roots or their very favorite food, organic matter (that is, your potting mix).

Fungus gnats do little damage to adult plants, but can harm seedlings. To prevent them from attacking young plants, always use a fresh bag of pasteurized potting mix when you sow seeds.

With fungus gnats, you never really know for sure whether your treatment worked or whether the gnats just ran through their natural life cycle. Sometimes just when you think you've gotten rid of them for good, they suddenly return. Letting the surface of your potting mix dry out between waterings helps to limit grubs because they need damp soil. This treatment at first may not seem to work because the adults hang around and flutter about for weeks after all the larvae are dead and gone.

Treatment: Pouring insecticide solution over the soil on a weekly basis can help control fungus gnats; *nematode* treatments are also highly efficient. (See the section "Not an Oxymoron: Beneficial Insects" later in this chapter.)

Mealybugs

Mealybugs (see Figure 17-2) seemingly have no houseplant preferences, attacking all with equal enthusiasm. They are, however, among the easiest of all insects to control because the females do not fly and therefore can't get into your home unless you bring them in on a gardening tool or infected plant. Once you have them, you can control them fairly well, but only for a short time. You can expect mealybugs to crop up from time to time, when and where you least expect them.

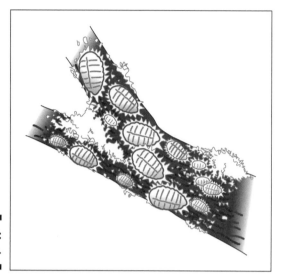

Figure 17-2:
Mealybugs.

Mealybugs are small, oval insects, usually pink or gray, but so heavily overlaid with a white, waxy substance that they look like little tufts of cotton batting. They seem immobile, but will move slowly if you disturb them. Their egg masses are cottony, too. They're especially common on leaf axils, the undersides of leaves, and stems. Like aphids, they give off honeydew that can lead to sooty mold. Infected plant parts weaken, wither, and yellow.

Treatment: You can kill mealybugs by touching them individually with a cotton swab dipped in rubbing alcohol or by spraying the plant with insecticide. Also, inspect nearby pots, shelves, and other fixtures for insect eggs. If you see any, wipe them away.

Red spider mites

Red spider mites (see Figure 17-3) are not actually insects. They are spider-like creatures barely visible with the naked eye. They are generally located on the undersides of leaves. The most common of all indoor pests, they thrive in most home environments and especially in hot, dry air. Increase the air humidity and they become much less of a problem.

The first symptom of their arrival (and they are small enough to waft indoors through a screen) is a yellowish tinge on leaves that turns out, upon close inspection, to be pale yellow spots. As the mites increase in numbers, the leaf turns yellower and appears dusty. To test whether you have spider mites, hold a sheet of white paper under a leaf and tap on it. If tiny particles of moving "dust" fall to the paper, your plant has spider mites.

Figure 17-3:
Red spider
mites.

When they're in large numbers, spider mites produce silky webbing much like a spider's web. Infested leaves eventually dry up and fall off. Most plants are susceptible to spider mites under hot, dry conditions, but they most often attack palms, crotons, hibiscus, English ivy, impatiens, fuchsias, miniature roses, and scheffleras.

Treatment: Prune back heavily infested parts and rinse the whole plant with water. Then begin treatments every three days with an appropriate pesticide. Even just spraying the plant (and especially the underside of its leaves) with water is often sufficient treatment.

Root mealybugs

Root mealybugs, also called *soil mealybugs,* are close cousins of the common mealybug and, like them, are covered with a waxy white coating. Root mealybugs live underground, which makes them especially pernicious because they can invade your plants without your noticing them. The first symptoms of root mealybugs are subtle — slow, stunted top growth, with possibly some yellowing. If in doubt, remove the pot and inspect the roots. You can find soil mealybugs on most plants, but especially African violets and cacti and other succulents.

White, cottony masses in the growing mix or on the roots are sure signs of root mealybugs. Be aware that *perlite,* a common potting mix additive, is also white. To tell which is which, crush any suspicious particle. If it crunches, it's perlite; if it squishes, it was a soil mealybug.

Treatment: To control this pest, wash the potting soil off the roots and spray or soak the roots with insecticide before repotting and sterilize the pot by soaking it overnight in a solution of ten parts water and one part bleach. Root mealybugs move about most freely when plants share a tray with other plants. Growing plants on individual saucers is one means of control.

Scale insects

Scale insects, also called *scale* (see Figure 17-4), are close relatives of mealybugs, so much of what I say about mealybugs also applies to scale. Scale insects, however, wear a shell-like *carapace* (a protective outer covering) and others also produce a cottony covering. Adults are immobile, but nymphs (which are invisible to the naked eye) can move to new plants before they settle down.

Some scale insects attack just about any plant, but many attack only specific varieties: Bromeliads, orchids, and citrus are among the lucky plants that attract their own species of scales. Scale insects pose a particular problem for ferns because they often look like fern spore cases. If in doubt, give the case a flick with your fingernail. Spore cases will stick to the leaf, whereas scale insects take off flying. Infected leaves turn yellowish and sooty mold may form.

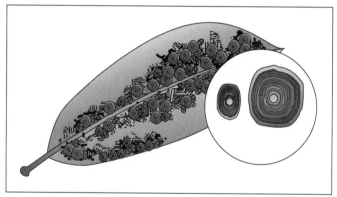

Figure 17-4:
Scale
insects.

Treatment: Start any treatment by scrubbing off the adult scales with a toothbrush dipped in soapy water. The carapace prevents insecticide from reaching the insect and any larvae that it might harbor, but old carapaces of long-dead scales remain on the plant. If you don't remove the old carapaces, you may end up treating a problem that's long dead.

Springtails

Springtails are more of a nuisance than a real problem. These ubiquitous insects live in moist soil all over the world and probably already thrive, sight unseen, in the more humid corners of your house. They're easy to spot on houseplants because the tiny wingless insects jump away from the plant when you water it. Springtails live mostly on decaying vegetable matter, including the peat moss and soil in the potting mix, and they like damp surroundings. They do only minimal damage to plants, sometimes gnawing on young seedlings or leaves that touch the soil.

Treatment: The best treatment is to ignore them, but if the thought of having *any* insects in your home really bothers you, simply let the surface of the potting mix dry out between waterings and springtails will eventually pack up and leave.

Thrips

Thrips are fast moving insects about the size of a comma on this page. The nymphs are wingless and pale in color; the adults have fuzzy wings and are sometimes darker. They seldom fly; instead they get around by jumping from plant to plant. When frightened, they run for cover under nearby plant tissue.

Try breathing gently on a plant if you think it has thrips. If they are present, watch 'em scurry out of their hiding places as fast as their six skinny legs can carry them.

Thrips come in a couple of different varieties: *flower thrips* and *foliar thrips.* Flower thrips usually attack only flowers, and foliar thrips attack both foliage and flowers. Thrips are *raspers*, that is, they scrape the protective coating off cells in order to suck up the plant sap. A thrips invasion results in mottling or streaking on soft plant parts and flowers.

Sometimes the wounds that thrips inflict appear silvery or translucent. Leaves and flowers turn sickly and small black dots of excrement appear. Flower thrips also feed on pollen. If you see yellowish powder spread all over your flowers, you probably have thrips. They attack a variety of plants, including chrysanthemums, African violets, begonias, azaleas, and cyclamens.

Treatment: The treatment for thrips requires removing all infected parts of the plant and spraying the rest with insecticide. If your plant has *flower thrips,* be especially careful to remove all flowers and buds throughout the treatment period, because they feed on pollen deep inside the flower and the insecticide never reaches them. Repeat the treatment weekly for at least a month. Most thrips *pupate* (pass through their pupal stage) either deep inside plant tissues or underground, which puts them out of range of pesticides for a week or two during each cycle.

Whiteflies

Whiteflies (see Figure 17-5) are among the easiest to spot of all the insect pests. These tiny white pests rise up off their host plant at the slightest touch, then book out as fast as possible to another plant, which makes them look exactly like flying dandruff. They lay their eggs underneath leaves where both the adults and the scale-like larvae suck out sap. Both larvae and adults produce sticky honeydew that can lead to sooty mold. They're extremely mobile and can spread rapidly.

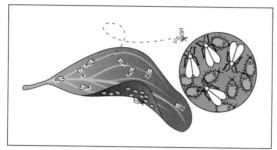

Figure 17-5:
Whiteflies.

Although they attack most plants, they especially love herbs, indoor vegetables, geraniums, and fuchsias. Infected leaves turn yellow and wither. Also, whiteflies can carry dangerous plant viruses.

Treatment: Always treat whiteflies at night, because they tend to fly away when sprayed or disturbed during the day. Start by running a hand vacuum over the leaves to pick up the adults, then wash the plant thoroughly with a damp cloth dipped in soapy water. Leave out sticky traps to pick up stragglers. After the first treatment, vacuum your plants and spray weekly (vacuum first, otherwise they all scatter) with insecticidal soap, concentrating on the undersides of the leaves.

Narcissus flies

Narcissus flies only appear on bulbs you bring in from the garden. Because narcissus plants are forced annually from fresh bulbs, this insect is rarely a problem for its namesake indoors. But, it can wreak havoc on amaryllis (*Hippeastrum*) that you put outside for the summer. A single narcissus fly larva, which looks like a large grub, can hollow out a bulb entirely. Although the bulb usually sprouts again from the base, it may not bloom again for many years.

Treatment: After you notice the damage, it's too late. All you can do is unpot the bulb and remove the soil to see where the insect's entry hole is, then try to dig the fly out of the bulb with a piece of wire. Or try the hot water treatment (see "Environmentally Safe Treatments to Rid Your Plants of Pests" later in this chapter), and extend it to a 40-minute bath.

Not-so-mellow yellow

Are whiteflies giving you a hard time? If the temperature outside is below freezing, you can trick them into following you to their death. Wear a bright yellow outfit and then wander among your plants, giving each plant a good shake along the way. The whiteflies will find your yellow garb far more enticing than the plants and will flock to it. Now head outside and take a 20-minute walk. The poor whiteflies that followed you will catch their death of cold.

The easiest solution is to keep your amaryllis indoors until the last narcissus fades because the adult narcissus fly (it looks and sounds like a bumble bee) lays its eggs only during narcissus flowering season.

Nematodes

Some varieties of these microscopic, worm-like creatures are actually beneficial, but the concern here is for the bad guys. *Rootknot nematodes* are the harmful variety you're most likely to encounter indoors, but even they are rare. Nematode-infested plants look unhealthy and wilt for no apparent reason. If you unpot them, the abnormally swollen roots are a dead giveaway.

Treatment: Don't bother treating infested plants — insecticides have no effect on nematodes. Destroy both the infected plant and its pot, although you can take cuttings first of healthy stems from the upper parts of the plant. Fortunately, this pest does not tend to spread under home conditions, but you still want to check nearby plants for signs of infestation, just in case.

Other insects and arthropods

Other insects and arthropods occasionally wander indoors, but rarely cause much damage because they don't usually reproduce indoors. Those critters include ants, caterpillars, centipedes, earthworms, earwigs, leaf miners, leafrollers, millipedes, pill bugs, and sow bugs. Some already live in basements and can find their way into pots from there. Others move indoors with indoor/outdoor plants that don't receive proper pretreatment before coming inside in the autumn.

Treatment: If you see any of these bugs (and they're usually solitary), simply pick them off the plant and toss them outdoors. You can drown those inhabiting a plant's root ball by immersing the entire pot in a bucket of soapy water for two to three hours.

A Cure for the Common Mold: Treating Plant Diseases

Plant diseases are more of a problem outdoors than indoors because most diseases require high humidity to spread and the air in most homes tends toward the dry side. In addition, many diseases spread to plants with wet or damp leaves and sheltered plants generally don't get wet leaves. But, don't think your plants are entirely immune to diseases. In the following sections, I cover the most common houseplant diseases, their symptoms, and the recommended cures.

Although you can stop plant disease in its tracks by improving growing conditions (rather than spraying), you cannot undo damage already done. The only way to rid your plants of spots, streaks, discoloration, or other affects of disease is to remove the infected part.

Rot

Rot (see Figure 17-6) is probably the most common disease in indoor plants. It's not really a disease, but a symptom of many different diseases. The infected part of the plant becomes soft and black, then decays. Rot can occur on any part of the plant, but mostly near or below soil level, on tubers, roots, stems, or at the crown of the plant.

Cut away the affected part and hope for the best. An application of sulfur spray or powder may help. Take a cutting from a healthy part of the plant, just for insurance. That way, you can keep at least part of the plant going.

Figure 17-6: An example of one type of rot — stem rot.

Rot near the soil level

Rot usually occurs in plants suffering from stress due to poor culture, such as low light or overly moist soil. If your plants don't get proper care, fungi or bacteria that would otherwise be harmless move into weakened plant tissue and rot sets in.

Leaf spot

Leaf spot, like rot, is a symptom of many different diseases. It usually results from an attack to weakened tissues by a microorganism that would be otherwise harmless to a healthy plant. Water left on leaves is usually a contributing factor, so keeping plant leaves dry is half the battle against leaf spot. Depending on the cause, leaf spots may appear round or irregularly shaped; black, brown, gray, or yellow in color; and either localized or spread over the entire leaf, which eventually kills it. Removing damaged leaves is the best solution.

Damping off

Damping off is a disease that afflicts seedlings. Damping off was a major problem back when gardeners still used "real dirt" to start seeds, but peat-based potting mixtures seem pretty much immune to the problem. Affected seedlings blacken or shrivel at or near their base, then topple over.

You can't really cure plants that are afflicted with damping off, but you can prevent it by using a freshly opened bag of soilless mix when you sow seeds and by thinning out seedlings before they become overcrowded.

Gray mold

Gray mold is caused by the fungus *botrytis* and covers leaves, stems, or flowers with fluffy gray mold. Infected parts eventually turn black and die. You rarely get gray mold indoors, where air is dry, but must watch out for it in greenhouses. To prevent gray mold, increase air circulation and avoid getting water on leaves.

Mildew

Mildew is a fungal disease (or, to be more precise, one of many fungal diseases with similar symptoms) that occurs mostly in stagnant, humid air and therefore is rarely a problem indoors. When it does occur, however, it spreads quickly. Literally overnight, it attacks a wide range of plants growing under the same conditions. Typically, a white powdery mold covers the entire leaf surface. This substance is called *powdery mildew* (see Figure 17-7). If the mold is white and fluffy and grows mainly on the underside of the leaf, it is *downy mildew*. You can combat both types by increasing the air circulation around your plants.

Figure 17-7:
Powdery
mildew.

Sooty mold

Sooty mold is a black mold that forms on *honeydew*, a sugary liquid that many sucking insects excrete. Although unsightly, it doesn't directly harm a plant. It does, however, decrease the amount of light that leaves can absorb and blocks their breathing pores. Wipe off sooty mold when you see it, and concentrate your efforts on whichever insect is producing the honeydew.

Viruses

Viruses are microscopic organisms that infect a particular type of plant. A virus that typically attacks an orchid, for example, is unlikely to harm a geranium. Viruses are usually carried by sucking insects, but viruses can also be spread by gardening tools and your own fingers. Unfortunately, plant viruses are incurable.

People who smoke should always wear gloves when touching plants because their fingers often harbor tobacco mosaic virus.

Treating plant viruses is exceptionally difficult because, short of laboratory testing, you can't identify which virus your plant has. Infected plants lack vigor, and sometimes develop yellow streaking or mottling, and stunted or disfigured growth. Often the only way to determine whether your plant has a virus is to eliminate all other possible causes. Then, you can figure that the problem owes to a virus. When a virus strikes, all you can do is destroy the infected plant.

Rules to Remember about Insecticides, Pesticides, and Other Treatments

The use of chemical insecticides on your outdoor plants is a matter of choice, but applying them on indoor plants is completely unwise. Chemical products remain in the air for long periods, sometimes even days, for you, your family, or anyone else who steps in your home to breathe in. Using biological controls to fight unwanted pests is far safer.

Garden center employees see it all the time: Worried houseplant owner buys $15 worth of pesticides to treat a plant that he or she can replace for $3.99. If you have only one or two plants with problems, just treat them with home remedies or toss them and get new ones. (And, remember the first rule of prevention: Give every plant a thorough once-over in the store *before* you buy it.)

- Start any insect control program by putting infected plants under your bathroom shower or take them outdoors and hose them off. The water pressure alone is enough to knock most insects off a plant, which gives you a head start on the treatment.

- Before applying any kind of pesticide, give your plants a thorough watering and wait at least 24 hours. Even biological pesticides can burn leaves if the plants lack water.

- Always read the label *every time* you use a pesticide. Not only does reading the label help you to avoid accidentally increasing the dosage, but it ensures that you don't use the pesticide on plants that cannot tolerate that specific product (the label usually lists the plants to avoid). Also, many products can cause damage to your plants if you apply them under certain conditions, such as at extremely warm temperatures.

- Buy concentrates rather than ready-to-use pesticides. You get many more applications for your money.

- Some pesticides, including insecticidal soaps, are less effective if diluted with hard water. If your tap water is hard, use distilled water.

- Unless the label says otherwise, don't store pesticides after you mix them; they often loose their strength within a short period of time. If you do store them, label the bottle clearly and put it out of reach of children. Otherwise, prepare just enough pesticide for immediate use.

- It's safe to reduce the concentration of a pesticide, but *never* to increase it. Most pesticides are toxic to plants in excessive concentrations.

Environmentally Safe Treatments to Rid Your Plants of Pests

All of the following treatments to rid your plants of insects and other damaging pests are environmentally friendly and pose relatively little danger to humans or pets.

✔ **Insecticidal soap:** This is of the safest insecticides for humans and pets, yet one of the most efficient against insects and mites. Spray it evenly on all surfaces of the plant and repeat weekly for at least one month. Insecticidal soap works faster, always gives good results, and isn't that much more expensive than other household soaps if you buy it in concentrated form. It is best to apply it in cool weather or at cool times of day to lessen possible damage to foliage.

✔ **Soap and water:** An old home remedy that works — but be careful, it can also burn leaves. (A safe ratio is one tablespoon of liquid soap per gallon of water.) Many commercial soap manufacturers change their recipes regularly, depending on which ingredients are cheap and available at the time of manufacture. A soap that provides excellent results one time can burn the plant the next. Look for a brand that advertises itself as a "pure" soap, rather than one that has loads of additives (grease-cutters, bleach, and so on). Hand and body soaps tend to be safer for plants than dishwashing detergents.

✔ **Hot water:** A dip in water at a temperature of about 107°F (43°C) can kill most mites, but puts the plant's health at severe risk. Reserve this method for ridding your plants of cyclamen mites, and the only reason you use such a drastic measure is because these pests are hard to control by any other means.

Submerge the plant for 15 to 30 minutes, maintaining a constant temperature the whole time. Hot water also works for ridding plants of narcissus flies, but leave the plant under water for 40 minutes.

✔ **Horticultural oil:** This product works like insecticidal soap and is applied the same way. Be sure to find an oil that's registered for indoor use on green foliage. So-called "dormant" horticultural oils can harm green plants.

✔ **Rubbing alcohol:** Although not designed to be used as a pesticide, a number of houseplant growers swear by using rubbing alcohol to control plant pests. Apply it by dipping a cotton swab into the alcohol and daubing each insect one by one. If you find that approach agonizingly slow, you can add the alcohol to water (seven parts water to one part rubbing alcohol) and apply it as a spray or plunge the infected plant into the mixture. Spray only in a well-ventilated spot.

✔ **Garlic spray:** You can concoct a pesticidal spray by soaking mashed garlic cloves overnight in a solution of insecticidal soap. It helps repel some insects, but do you really want your home to smell of garlic?

✔ **Sulfur spray or powder:** One of the few biological products for disease control (it is an organic fungicide) safe enough for indoor use, you can get sulfur sprays and powders at garden centers. Never combine sulfur and horticultural oil or apply sulfur sprays or powders within ten days of spraying with oil; otherwise, you may end up with a case of leaf burn.

✔ **Homemade sticky traps:** You can create an inexpensive version of commercial sticky traps by coating yellow cardboard with an adhesive. Most flying insects are drawn to the color yellow (thrips prefer pink or blue, but go for yellow as well), and end up getting caught in the glue. Replace the traps monthly or whenever the strip gets full. These sticky traps rarely prevent insect problems, but they function as early warning signs that you have insects in your home.

Not an Oxymoron: Beneficial Insects

So-called beneficial insects and other helpful microorganisms are becoming popular means of pest control in commercial greenhouses, but they're a hard sell to the average indoor plant owner. For one, most homeowners don't want *any* insects in their homes, not even helpful ones. Also, these insects generally are less effective in homes than in greenhouses because they need specific conditions in order to thrive that most homes with their dry air rarely provide.

Pest control bugs can be prohibitively expensive. The smallest quantity you can buy is enough to treat your houseplants 20 times over (at least). Plus, bugs, as a rule, don't store well over long periods of time so you can't just go to the corner garden center and buy them — you have to order them by mail as the need arises.

Suit up for safe spraying

I don't advocate the use of potentially harmful chemicals, but if you do choose to use them, make sure you wear long sleeves, long pants, gloves, goggles, a hat, and a mask when you spray. And get the family and pets out of the house for at least half a day. When you finish, take a *cold* shower (warm water actually helps the pesticide penetrate your skin). Finally, keep all clothes that you wore while spraying wrapped up and set them aside to wear again for future spraying. If you spray safe pesticides (such as the ones recommended in this chapter), protective clothing is optional but you may still want to wear goggles.

The surgeon general probably already knows about this one

You may have heard about the old home remedy for ridding plants of pests that involves soaking cigarette butts in water. This mixture creates a strong nicotine brew that knocks down almost any pest — and quite possibly you, too, because nicotine vapors are highly poisonous. *Never* use this dangerous, highly toxic mixture on any indoor or outdoor plant (proof that not all home remedies are safer than chemical pesticides).

The only beneficial insect currently suited for use in the average home is the *nematode (Heterorhabditis heliothidis)*, which controls fungus gnats. It has a shelf life of about three months and works invisibly in the plant's potting mix, killing fungus gnats and shore fly larvae as they hatch. Because the nematode can live for years in ordinary potting soil by feeding on other soil organisms, a single treatment sometimes does the job for the entire life of the plant. Someday, such long-lasting natural treatments will definitely help control a wide range of insects and diseases.

In the future, as storage methods improve and the industry finds or develops tougher and smaller beneficials (many are already invisible to the naked eye), I predict that beneficial insects are destined to become *the* treatment option of choice for controlling not only insects and mites but many plant diseases as well.

Part V
Houseplant Settings

"Something's about to die in your cactus container."

In this part . . .

*N*ow that you're equipped with that gorgeous green thumb, you probably want some pointers on where you can display all those lush houseplants you're so proud of. That's what this part of the book is all about. Here, I tell you how to choose houseplant containers that are not only functional but also attractive, and reveal some techniques that designers use to integrate houseplants into a home's decor. And, if you want to give your growing collection of plants a home of their own, check out the chapter on installing your own greenhouse.

Chapter 18

Grow Pots, Cachepots, and Terrariums

*P*lants grown in containers have one big advantage over those grown in an outdoor garden — *mobility*. If a plant gets light from just one direction, you can just swivel it around to make sure the back side of the plant gets its fair share of the rays. Do you have a corner of a room that just begs for a tall and leafy plant, but the spot is too dark for anything that relies on photosynthesis to keep going? Just rotate two plants between a sunny spot and that dark corner on a weekly basis and everybody's happy. Is your entire family paying you a weekend visit? You can't move the flower bed out of the way before it's trampled, but you can move your plants out of the living room to create extra space.

The varieties of houseplant containers are as numerous as your uses for them. In this chapter, I tell you about the various kinds of houseplant housing including the humble grow pot, terra-cotta cachepots, hanging planters, and intriguing terrariums, some of which are planted in a space as small as a bottle.

If you've been an outdoor gardener all your life and are just now discovering the joys of indoor container gardening, you should be aware that pots severely restrict root growth. Plants rarely grow as fast indoors as they do outdoors, and one reason is the lack of room for their roots to spread out. Plants in pots also run out of water reserves much more quickly than plants in gardens (there's just so much moisture in a little pot). Therefore, vigilant watering practices are of the utmost importance.

Pot Wars: Clay versus Plastic

In the late 1940s, plastic pots and planters began to encroach on the solid market share held by clay pots since the time that people began potting plants. Thus began the battle that rages to this day over which pot material is superior — clay or plastic?

Make mine plastic

For many indoor gardeners, the convenience associated with plastic pots makes them the clear choice. Plastic pots are stackable, usually cheaper, and easier to handle than *terra-cotta* (fired clay) pots. They're also light-weight, which makes them a practical choice. Potted plants are heavy enough without weighing them down even more with a heavy container.

Even serious clay pot fanatics have begun to change their minds about plastic pots ever since the introduction of plastics that have the look and feel of terra-cotta. These pots come in a clay-like reddish-brown color and a matte finish — many look exactly like clay pots from a distance.

Because plastic pots are nonporous they lose water more slowly than clay pots, which means that you don't have to water your plants as often. Most foliage and flowering plants prefer some level of moisture at all times. Plastic holds moisture better, which is why most foliage and flowering plants do better in plastic.

Small plastic pots typically have three drainage holes (unlike clay pots that just have one) and larger pots have many more. Furthermore (especially in larger sizes), their drainage holes often extend part way up the side of the pot or have ridges on the bottom to hold the drainage holes off the tray, not only improving drainage, but increasing air circulation through the bottom of the pot.

Plastic pots aren't as fragile as clay pots. They may crack or split open when you drop them, but they rarely shatter into dozens of pieces. In addition, plastic pots don't easily stain and are easy to clean up. Just soak and scrub them like any other pot.

Because plastic is nonporous, these pots don't "breathe." Air circulates through the top of the potting mix only. A well-aerated potting ensures that the plant's roots receive ample oxygen. Therefore, plants that require excellent root aeration, such as orchids and air plants, rarely thrive in plastic unless a particularly well-aerated potting mix is used to compensate for the nonporous plastic.

Because plastic is lightweight, it doesn't have the heft to stabilize a top-heavy plant, such as a large cactus. The majority of the plant's weight is above the rim of the container, so you run the risk of having a heavy plant topple over if it doesn't have a solid foundation.

Make mine clay

Clay is very porous, which allows for both ample air and water circulation. This factor makes terra-cotta the ideal pot material for both plants that need well-aerated roots, such as many epiphytes, and those that can't tolerate constant moisture, such as succulents and many orchids. Clay pots dry out rapidly, so these plants do best in clay. In fact, it's hard to imagine having success with certain arid climate plants (the living stones [*Lithops*], for instance) when planting them in anything but clay pots.

The weightiness of clay makes terra-cotta containers ideal for tall, heavy plants like the cereus *(Cereus peruvianus),* and the rich, reddish-brown color of clay is more suited to classic or modern home decor — more so than pots in "horticulture green."

Clay pots are easily stained by mineral salts from tap water and fertilizer that seep through their sides. Even if you manage to remove the stains entirely, they return as soon as you water again. Plus, clay pots allow for fast evaporation, which means that you have to water your plants in clay pots more often — sometimes twice as often — than your plants that are grown in plastic pots.

New clay pots are so dry that they steal water from the plants you place in them, leaving the plants dying of thirst. Before potting a plant in a clay container, soak the pot in water for 15 minutes.

Shapes, Sizes, and Styles of Pots

The basic shape of a pot is no accident: Plants simply are easier to remove from a pot that's wider at the top. Give the pot a sharp rap against a hard surface and the plant practically leaps out. (If you've ever tried to remove a plant from a pot that's wider at the middle than at the top, you know what I mean.)

Standard-size pots traditionally are as tall as they are wide. In recent years, however, *azalea pots* or *half-pots* (which are actually three-quarters the height of a standard pot), have become as common as standard-size pots (see Figure 18-1). The lower profile of azalea pots makes them easier to hide within *cachepots* (decorative pots designed to hold other pots). In addition, you can find true half-pots, known as *bulb pots* or *tubs,* which are twice as wide as they are deep, although they aren't nearly as widely used as azalea pots.

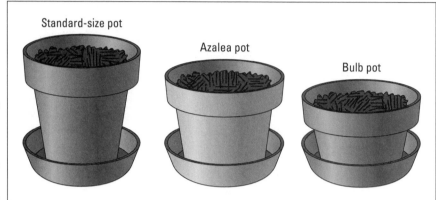

Standard-size pot

Azalea pot

Bulb pot

Grow pots and cachepots

Besides the typical clay and plastic pots, a wide range of other pots are available on the market — glazed pottery, Italian clay pots, fiberglass pots, bonsai pots, wooden containers, and much, much more.

Despite the wide range of containers designed for growing plants, sticking to clay or plastic standard-size and azalea pots is probably wisest. You can then simply slip them inside a slightly larger decorative container without having to unpot them.

The container into which a plant is potted directly is called a *grow pot.* If you slip a grow pot into another more-attractive container for decorative purposes, that second container is called a *cachepot* (see Figure 18-2), which can be pronounced *cash-pot* or *cash-poe.*

Besides their obvious aesthetic value, cachepots make life easier at repotting time. For example, what happens when a plant growing in a decorative pot isn't doing well? You don't want to have to move the pot (the container looks fine, it's just the plant that's suffering). If you use the decorative pot as a grow pot, you have to unpot the plant, pot it up in another container, then repot a new plant into the decorative pot. Instead, simply use the decorative pot as a cachepot and just exchange grow pots. Plus, you never have to move a fragile or super-heavy decorative pot if it's only the grow pot that travels.

Using decorative pots as cachepots instead of as grow pots also means that you can use pots with no drainage holes (an absolute no-no as far as grow pots go). A cachepot that lacks drainage holes can serve the same function as a saucer, holding any excess water that drains out of the grow pot.

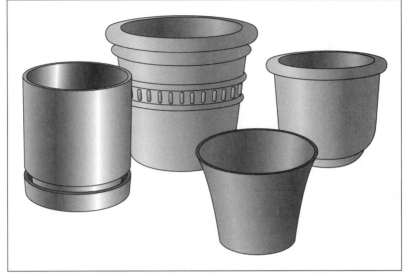

Figure 18-2:
Cachepots
are
available in
a variety of
shapes,
sizes, and
materials.

If your cachepot *does* have a drainage hole, no problem — just slip a saucer inside the cachepot and under the grow pot to catch any drainage. You can also hide the pot and its soil by placing a layer of decorative mulch, such as dried Spanish moss, bark chips, or river stones, on top of the soil at the base of the plant. These are basic designer's tricks: Whenever possible, hide the mechanics!

Many different types of decorative pots can serve as cachepots. The following are some of the more common ones:

- ✔ **Glazed ceramic pots:** These pots are available in a wide variety of shapes, colors, and styles, and combine the weight of clay pots with the sturdiness of plastic ones.

- ✔ **Italian terra cotta pots:** With striking motifs ranging from cherubs to zinnias done in relief, these are quickly becoming *the* cachepots to own. If you grow plants directly inside of them, they'll stain from the minerals in soil and water, so use them strictly as cachepots.

  If you want to keep terra cotta pots (or any porous clay pot) from staining, paint the inside and bottom with a coat of shellac or waterproof paint.

- ✔ **Woven baskets:** Baskets make great cachepots, but they rot away in short order after they come in contact with damp potting mix. To prevent rotting, line the interior with plastic before slipping a grow pot into them.

✔ **Plastic pots and containers:** Plastic pots are now available in just about every imaginable shape, size, and color. Some of them are self-watering, which is a real boon to those who find regular watering a chore.

✔ **Window boxes:** These containers are popular outdoors but work well inside, too. Although you *can* plant your houseplants directly into them if they have drainage holes (a matching drainage tray is a nice feature in this case), they work better if you use them as large cachepots. Otherwise, removing an ailing plant from a tangle of mixed roots is next to impossible. Also, root competition in mixed plantings is fierce.

Line wood window boxes with plastic not only to help preserve them, but to keep them from leaking.

✔ **Tubs and boxes:** Wood, plastic, or fiberglass tubs or boxes are ideal for larger plants or group plantings. A whiskey barrel cut in half, for example, can add to a rustic setting, as well as contain an indoor garden. Put tubs and boxes on casters or a tray with wheels to make them easier to move.

Hanging pots

Hanging pots are a popular fixture in home decoration. In just about any department store or garden center you can find plant hangers that convert an ordinary plastic, clay, or decorative pot into a hanging basket. Just make sure that any container you put in the hanger has a built-in saucer or allows for adding a saucer to it.

Most hanging pots come with clip-on saucers that are supposed to catch drainage, but they're really more for appearances than for practicality. The saucers are typically smaller in diameter than the pots, when instead they should be larger. So water plants in hanging pots carefully to make sure your floors stay dry.

Wire baskets with plants growing from the top and sides can be gorgeous — outdoors! Indoors, watering them is a real problem because they drip from their entire surface. You can water them in a sink, but a better plan is to limit these containers to spots where dripping water won't present a hazard. (For ideas on how to water hanging baskets, which are usually always in need of water, see Chapter 9.)

To maintain uniform growth in a hanging plant, rotate the plant 90 degrees every time you water it. In order to do that, hang the plant from a swivel hook affixed to the ceiling.

Terrariums: Growing Minigardens under Glass

Ever since horticulturist Nathaniel Ward created his glass-covered Wardian case back in 1836, terrariums have fascinated plant enthusiasts. A *terrarium* is simply a glass-sided container used for growing plants. You can fashion a terrarium out of nearly any glass container, from a large aquarium to a pill bottle.

With the humid, pollution-free air and stable temperatures found in a terrarium, many delicate or otherwise impossible-to-grow plants thrive nicely and almost entirely on their own in a terrarium. A well-planned terrarium, in fact, needs less care than any other type of indoor planting.

Most houseplants small enough to fit inside a terrarium do wonderfully there, but not all plants find terrariums heavenly. Plants that tend to dislike high humidity, such as cacti and other succulents, are out of place in a terrarium. And plants that prefer good air circulation — such as many types of orchids, bromeliads, and other epiphytes — languish in stagnant air.

Clear choices for containers

You can use any clear or lightly tinted glass or plastic container as a terrarium. You also can use leaded-glass cases, candy jars, brandy snifters, bottles, and wine glasses — basically, any glass container. Fish aquariums are the most popular choices because their ample size allows you to create entire miniature landscapes inside of them (see Figure 8-3).

You can also grow tiny plants in a narrow-necked bottle, which results in a type of terrarium known as a *bottle garden.* To maintain your bottle garden, you need to fashion the right kind of tools. Just tape a plastic spoon and fork, a cloth, and a razor blade separately to long wooden dowels to create, respectively, a tiny planting trowel, planting fork, cleaning tool, and pruning tool.

Open and shut cases

You can leave your terrariums open to the air surrounding them, or you can keep them closed off to the outside air.

Figure 18-3:
The ideal terrarium container — an ordinary aquarium.

✔ *Open terrariums*, although more humid than the surrounding air, demand a bit more care than closed ones. They require careful attention to watering because they can dry out in only a few weeks.

✔ *Closed terrariums* are covered with a pane of glass, a glass stopper, or other lid that's preferably transparent to allow light to get in from above as well as from the sides. Sealed terrariums lose no humidity to the outside air and rarely need watering. Some terrarium environments have been kept going for decades without the addition of a single drop of moisture! Plants grown in terrariums recycle everything. They give off water vapor, which then condenses and waters their roots, and they create the air they breathe by absorbing carbon dioxide and giving off oxygen during the day, and absorbing oxygen and giving off carbon dioxide at night.

Most closed terrariums are not completely sealed, however. In fact, for faster growth (fresh air is a great stimulant), and to let out excess humidity that can cause the glass to fog up, leave the top open just a crack. If you decide to cover an aquarium with a pane of glass, have it cut to size with one corner cut to create a small opening. Not only does this allow a bit of air to circulate, but it makes the cover easier to pull up when you want to remove it.

Providing the right growing conditions

A terrarium can create its own *microclimate* (a mini-climate of its own apart from the climate surrounding it), but first requires some enviromental conditions to be in place:

✔ Avoid intense sun at all costs, even for short periods, especially if you have a closed terrarium. Closed terrariums can overheat easily. Medium or even low light, however, is acceptable because the high humidity of a terrarium enables plants to produce energy more efficiently, which reduces the need for strong sunlight. A spot under a fluorescent lamp is an ideal place for a terrarium.

✔ Temperature requirements vary according to the types of plants in your terrarium, and vice versa — the types of plants you can grow depend on your home's temperature range. Terrariums that consist of temperate woodland plants — mosses, ferns, groundcovers, and so on — prefer cool conditions, with the temperature at 65°F (18°C) tops. Tropical plants (which include most houseplants) are less choosy. Any indoor temperature is fine, as long as you don't let them cook in the sun.

Planting a terrarium

Planting a terrarium as not nearly as complicated as you may imagine. Try the following steps:

1. **Pre-moisten enough soil to fill about 2 inches (5 centimeters) of the terrarium.**

   Lining the bottom of the terrarium with a drainage layer of gravel, pot shards, or some other material is strictly optional. Drainage layers aren't necessary, and you may not have the vertical space for them anyway.

2. **Even out the soil mix to create a smooth surface.**

3. **Start with small plants that come in 2¹/₂-inch (6.5-centimeter) pots because it's difficult to hide the root balls of larger plants.**

4. **Insert the foliage plants first by removing them from their pots and planting them in a pleasing arrangement.**

   Instead of planting flowering plants directly in the mix, leave them in their pots and sink the pot into the mix. That way you can easily remove them when they stop blooming and replace them with other flowering plants. Try to center the plants in round or oval containers so that they can be viewed from all sides.

5. **Add some mulch to cover up the soil.**

   Live green or sphagnum moss will do, as will dry sphagnum (it often comes back to life and turns green in a closed terrarium). For added decoration in a large container, you can toss in some rocks or stones (and perhaps a small piece of driftwood).

6. **Do not water your terrarium after you plant it.**

   It probably already contains plenty of water and, like all containers without a drainage hole, adding more water later is far easier than attempting to remove an excess of it.

7. **Look for signs of fogging during the first few weeks after planting.**

   If your terrarium fogs up during the day, it probably already has too much water. Leave the top off so that some water can evaporate. If it fogs up only at night, it probably has just the right amount of moisture.

Ongoing terrarium maintenance

Water a terrarium only when its soil begins to feel dry to the touch. When you do water, a teaspoon (5 milliliters) is enough water for a small container (one that would hold more more than $1/2$ gallon or 2 liters); a tablespoon (15 milliliters) of water is enough for a large terrarium. Wait 24 hours and if the soil still seems dry add a spoonful more. Closed terrariums are unlikely to need watering for several months; open ones may need some water after a few weeks.

Avoid adding fertilizer to terrariums. You don't really want the plants to grow all that much (they were probably already big enough when you planted them), plus plants use fertilizer much more efficiently under high humidity. The little bit of fertilizer that was in the potting mix, in combination with the natural fertilizer that results as dead vegetable matter decays, should supply all the fertilizer that terrarium plants need.

Just because terrarium plants are under glass doesn't mean you can forgo regular pruning and cleaning. Plants grow profusely under glass and even the tiniest houseplant can suddenly become a real space hog. Don't hesitate to prune back plants that threaten to take over or that grow too tall, or to dig up and replace invasive plants. Remove dead leaves and flowers, too.

Smaller is better — Terrarium plants

The most common error that beginning terrarium gardeners make is to use plants that are simply too big for the available space. Few naturally tiny houseplants are available, so the usual practice is to use young plants of average-sized species. That's an acceptable strategy but it increases the amount of pruning you have to do. If you want a minimal-maintenance terrarium, plant only true miniatures.

Planting cacti and succulents in a terrarium, even an open one, is *not* a good idea. You can find "desert terrariums" in department stores and even garden centers, but that doesn't mean that you'll have success with them. If you give these plants the strong light they need, you'll literally cook them in the intense heat that builds up in a terrarium exposed to the sun. In weaker light, as the succulents run out of energy, they stretch toward the light source and eventually rot away.

Tropical plants suited for small terrariums

The following plants are ideal for small terrariums because they rarely grow to more than 5 inches (13 centimeters) high in less than a year and some of them are true miniatures. (You can also use them in large terrariums for a little variety.) Because they are tropical-origin plants, they do well under normal home temperatures.

- Button fern *(Pellaea rotundifolia)*
- Creeping Charlie *(Pilea nummulariifolia)*
- Creeping fig *(Ficus pumila)*
- Earth star *(Cryptanthus bivittatus)*
- Eyelash begonia *(Begonia bowerii)*
- Irish moss *(Selaginella kraussiana* 'Brownii')
- Maidenhair vine *(Muehlenbeckia complexa)*
- Micro-miniature sinningia *(Sinningia pusilla* and hybrids)
- Miniature episcia *(Episcia cupreata)*
- Miniature fern *(Polystichum tsus-simense)*
- Miniature holly *(Malpighia coccigera)*
- Miniature pilea *(Pilea depressa)*
- Miniature sinningia *(Sinningia* 'Cindy-Ella' and others)
- Miniature spider plant *(Chlorophytum bichetii)*
- Nerve plant *(Fittonia verschaffeltii)*
- Norfolk Island pine *(Araucaria heterophylla)* (seedling)
- Parlor palm *(Chamaedorea elegans* 'Bella') (seedling)
- Strawberry begonia *(Saxifraga stolonifera)*
- Watermelon begonia *(Pellionia repens* and *P. pulchra)*

Tropical plants suited for large terrariums

The following plants will stay under 12 inches (30 centimeters) high and wide for at least a year. Most of these plants do eventually become too large for terrarium living, at which point you either need to replace them or prune them severely. (All the plants listed in the previous section, "Tropical plants for small terrariums," also make good choices for large terrariums.) As with any tropical plant, they grow well under normal home temperatures.

- Aluminum plant *(Pilea cadierei)*
- Asparagus fern *(Asparagus densiflorus* 'Sprengeri') (seedling)
- Bird's nest fern *(Asplenium nidus)* (young plant)
- Dwarf schefflera *(Schefflera arboricola)*
- Emerald ripple peperomia *(Peperomia caperata)*
- English ivy *(Hedera helix)*
- Episcia *(Episcia cupreata)*
- False aralia *(Dizygotheca elegantissima)* (seedling)
- Guppy plant *(Nematanthus nummularia)*
- Heartleaf philodendron *(Philodendron scandens oxycardium)*
- Maidenhair fern *(Adiantum cuneatum)*
- Mediterranean brake fern *(Pteris cretica)*
- Ming aralia *(Polyscias fruticosa)* (young plant only)
- Miniature African violet *(Saintpaulia ionantha)*
- Norfolk Island pine *(Araucaria heterophylla)* (young plant only)
- Parlor palm *(Chamaedorea elegans* 'Bella') (seedling only)
- Pothos *(Epipremnum aureum)*
- Prayer plant *(Maranta leuconeura)* (young plant only)
- Rabbit-foot fern *(Davallia fijeensis)*
- Ribbon plant *(Dracaena sanderiana)*
- Weeping fig *(Ficus benjamina)* (young plant only)

Chapter 19

Plant Displays for Every Room in the House

• •

In This Chapter

▶ Using houseplants for dramatic effect

▶ Creating complementary plant groupings

▶ Choosing plants suited to a room's environment

• •

I suspect that one of the main reasons you buy houseplants is not just for the sheer horticultural thrill, but also to add color and variety to your home decor. Most of this book focuses on how to keep your houseplants alive and thriving. This focus of *this* chapter is on how to show off your lush and healthy plants to their best effect.

Just Like in a Magazine (Not)

Decorating magazines are loaded with photographs of beautiful room decors, but have you noticed what the majority of these to-die-for interiors have in common? You guessed it — houseplants — precisely positioned for maximum visual impact.

Like much of what is shown in magazines, a stylist's vision and what nature intended are two very different things. The likelihood of any plant actually being able to grow in some settings shown in photo layouts is slim to none. Just as on a Hollywood set, plants are brought in like any other prop, placed just so, the pictures are shot, and then everything goes back to the store that loaned them out.

Those dreamy magazine settings aren't designed to last more than a day, if that long. The happiest plants live near windows. In magazine pictures, they are usually shown anywhere *but* near a window.

To reconcile the environmental needs of your plants with your desire to use foliage for interior decor, you have two choices:

- Buy plants solely for decorative purposes, then replace them as they fade away, tossing them into the compost heap if they are totally spent.

- Move your plants around periodically, putting them in a brightly lit room for a few weeks, then moving them into your designed setting for a few weeks, then back into the light.

When you do find just the right plant that thrives exactly where it looks best, take extra good care of it. It's a real gem and you don't want to lose it.

Trusting Your Own Decorating Instincts

You don't have to rely on magazines in order to create attractive settings using houseplants. Trust your own instincts for what looks good. Try placing plants here and there — on the ground, on pedestals, in groups or separately — until you achieve a look that you like.

Decorating with plants is more than a matter of aesthetics because you're dealing with a living thing. Given that, the following is some practical advice to keep in mind when you add plants to a room's decor:

- Use rugged plants as the foundation of any arrangements (look for plants listed in Chapters 4 through 7 with the "Tuff 'n' Robust" icon). Those plants will remain attractive for long periods of time with little effort.

- Don't start small. Buy plants already grown to the size you want. You still need to acclimatize them to your indoor environment before you use them, however (see Chapter 14 for more on acclimatizing plants).

- Take scale and proportion into consideration. Generally speaking, large plants look best in spacious rooms, whereas small plants look lost in big spaces. The combination of tall plants and hanging baskets will make a high ceiling look lower.

- Set small- to medium-size plants on tables, pedestals, shelves, or anywhere else below eye level. Put large plants on the floor or elevate them only slightly. Above eye level, use cascading plants.

- Use ornamental containers to improve the overall visual effect. Using pots in coordinated colors is one possibility; a variety of pots in harmonious colors is another. There's nothing wrong with contrast, either, in moderation.

- You can visually double the space in a small room with mirrors. Mirrors reflect light, as well, which helps your plants grow better.

Picking a Plant for That Certain Look

You may have room for only a few plants, or time to maintain only one or two. Either way, choose the plants carefully, looking especially for tough, easy-to-care-for varieties.

Different plants create different decorative effects. Keep that in mind when you go shopping for that one special plant, or couple of plants, needed to round out the look of a room. (If you use just one plant for special effect, it's known as a *specimen plant.*) The following list can serve as a guideline. (Figure 19-1 illustrates the silhouettes of a few different specimen plants.)

Figure 19-1:
A sampling of specimen plants that can be used to suit your design purposes.

 ✔ **Airy, feathery plants** soften the setting, changing a hard-edged, high-tech interior or a stark, modern environment, for example, into something softer and more natural looking. Ming aralia *(Polyscias fruticosa)* and false aralia *(Dizygotheca elegantissima)* make good upright airy plants, as do single-trunked specimens of the weeping fig *(Ficus benjamina)*. Trailing feathery plants that are still large enough to make good specimen plants include both the Boston fern *(Nephrolepis exaltata)* and the asparagus fern *(Asparagus densiflorus* 'Sprengeri').

✔ **Rounded, bushy, indoor shrubs** are a bit too large to pass as table plants and too overwelming to combine with other plants (except in very large rooms). They can do an excellent job of softening the lines around furniture or filling in empty floorspace. They also look great on pedestals and, if you raise them to eye level, they can replace indoor trees. This group includes such varied plants as the cast iron plant *(Aspidistra eliator)*, the Chinese evergreen *(Aglaonema* 'Silver Queen'), and the peace lily *(Spathiphyllum wallisii)*.

✔ **Tall, fan-shaped trees** take up little floor space, yet spread out for maximum visual effect. It only takes one to fill in an entire corner. This category includes large specimens of weeping and banana-leaf figs *(Ficus benjamina* and *Ficus maclellandii)*, most single-stemmed dracaenas, and all the taller palms.

✔ **Columnar plants** are best suited to minimal-styled decors. They're also ideal where space is limited. The rubber plant *(Ficus elastica)* and larger cacti and succulents, such as the architectural-looking cereus *(Cereus peruvianus)*, are in this category. Climbing plants trained onto upright supports also make excellent columnar plants.

✔ **Bold, dramatic plants** can provide architectural ornamentation in places where columnar plants are too narrow. Check out large-sized pony tail plants *(Beaucarnea recurvata)*, the bird of paradise *(Strelitzia reginae)*, multi-stemmed specimens of the Madagascar dragon tree *(Dracaena marginata)*, and spineless yuccas *(Yucca elephantipes)*.

✔ Only the largest **flowering plants** are suitable as specimen plants. The others look best as highlights among foliage plants and as tabletop decorations. Among the few that can stand alone are the hibiscus *(Hibiscus rosa-sinensis)* and oleander *(Nerium oleander)*.

Grouping Potted Plants for Maximum Effect

Not all foliage plants look their best all alone. Most of the smaller ones actually look better when combined with others of the same or similar size. You can combine them by placing them close together in their own individual pots or *cachepots* (pots that hold other pots) on a window sill or table, or in a larger container such as a window box or a tub. (If you use a deep container, fill its base with gravel or perlite to bring the plants up to the desired height.)

Some foliage plants are beautifully variegated and can become the focal point of an otherwise all-green arrangement. Don't hesitate to play around with texture. Contrasting "hairy" foliage with smooth leaves, for example, often brings out the best in both. Or, a harmonious look can be achieved by grouping plants with similarly shaped leaves. A single trailing plant can soften the edge of an otherwise dome-shaped arrangement. An upright plant can add height and contrast to an arrangement composed mainly of low-growing plants.

You can even place large plants in groups when you want to use vegetation as a room divider. A room divider doesn't necessarily have to be made of floor plants, either. You can create a visual barrier with a row of hanging plants as well.

When you place a group of plants in the same container, leave them in their individual pots. That way, the plants can be given the regular quarter-turns necessary for them to maintain a balanced growth pattern (see Chapter 8) and you don't have to turn the entire container. Keeping the individual plants in separate pots also enables you to replace any plants that grow too large or stop performing.

A Room-by-Room Decorating Guide

You don't need to limit your houseplant decor to the living room. Any room of your house can be a haven for houseplants, if you just keep the following recommendations in mind.

The kitchen

Kitchens are mini-environments in and of themselves. A kitchen is usually warmer and more humid than the rest of the house. You boil water there, run a dishwasher, turn faucets on and off, and so on. Plants normally love an environment with extra humidity but they don't always love kitchens because they tend to become grimy from evaporated cooking residues. You just need to wash your kitchen plants more often than the rest of your plants; then they'll do fine in a kitchen.

Although you could grow any kind of plant in a kitchen, edible ones are the most obvious choice. Many kitchens have a window right over the sink, which makes a good spot to hang a pot of mixed herbs or install some small shelves on which to grow herbs or vegetables.

Avoid placing any plants directly above the kitchen range. It's too hot there and the plants dry out instantly.

Whatta dish! A garden on a tray

Somewhat like a terrarium (see Chapter 18) without glass sides, a *dish garden* is a miniature garden planted on a tray or other low container (soup tureen, terra-cotta plant saucer, or large bonsai pot, for example). Cactus dish gardens are particularly popular, but woodland and tropical dish gardens are also easy to make and maintain.

Never mix plants with differing needs in the same dish garden. Cacti do best with other cacti and succulents because they like dry conditions, so don't mix in tropical plants, which prefer moister conditions.

You plant and care for a dish garden the same way you would a terrarium, except that you need to water it as often as any other houseplant arrangement. Some dish-garden containers have drainage holes and must be placed on a large saucer. Others don't have holes and don't require saucers, but you must water plants in those containers with the utmost care.

You can use dish gardens anywhere you choose, but they sure do look great as a dining room table centerpiece!

The living room

The living room, along with the dining room, is often your show room for houseplants. This is where you want to generate the maximum visual effect with a minimum of clutter. Here you can display your most prized plants, as well as the largest ones.

If your living room is spacious, consider using plant groupings or large specimen plants. Put them not only where they look best, but also where they can soften harsh angles or hide unsightly permanent fixtures such as thermostats. A single specimen plant is the ideal choice for an empty space that's too small for a piece of furniture.

The dining room

Dining rooms rarely include much excess space for mass plantings, and the dining table usually hides much of the floor space. Nevertheless, plants that are tall, columnar or fan-shaped, or a medium-sized plant on a pedestal, can help fill in those awkward corners. A plant or two arching out from a china cabinet is a nice touch, as is a frilly fern or small plant group on a sideboard.

The dining room table makes an ideal spot for an attractive small foliage plant or an orchid in full bloom. When you have guests over, avoid using tall plants as table centerpieces. They block the view, and the conversation. Dish gardens or small bonsais, on the other hand, make for charming centerpieces. Or, you can buy a pot of mini-chrysanthemums for special occasions.

The bathroom

Few places in the home can benefit more from the addition of a few plants than the bathroom. The high humidity in bathrooms make them ideal settings for tender plants such as ferns and flowering plants. Many climbing plants really take off in the bathroom's warm, humid atmosphere. Most bathrooms aren't spacious, so opt for smaller plants.

Many bathroom windows are tiny and blocked by curtains most of the time. If your bathroom gets only low light, stick to plants that can tolerate such conditions or frequently rotate the plants in the bathroom with plants from other parts of the house.

The bedroom

If you don't have a spare room, a portion of your bedroom (if it's well lit) can serve as a nursery for young plants and plants that need a bit of sun between stints of decorating other rooms.

In many homes, the guest bedroom *is* the plant room and, as such, the plants sometimes suffer from neglect. If you have a timer set to turn on the lights in the middle of the night, make sure to turn it off for the duration of any guest's visit.

Beware of growing perfumed plants in any bedroom. The most delicious aroma during the day can become sickeningly sweet at night when the bedroom door is shut and the scent is concentrated.

Halls and corridors

Passageways usually leave little room for furniture and often seem stark and barren. Tall plants add just the right amount of filler, preferably fan-shaped or columnar types, and take up relatively little floor space. Smaller plants on pedestals also can fill in the gaps. And, pots designed for mounting trailing plants on the wall are ideal if you have little extra floor space.

In narrow spaces with heavy foot traffic, avoid having either fragile plants or spiny ones. Plants in corridors and hallways must be tough enough to withstand frequent contact, yet shouldn't pierce fingers or tear clothes.

Corridors and halls are often darker than the rest of the house, so rotate any plants you grow in corridors every two weeks with plants from brighter areas of the house.

Conservatories and garden rooms

These rooms are, by definition, plant rooms. Garden rooms feature large windows or are lit with abundant artificial light. For maximum light reflection, paint or paper garden room walls in pale shades. (For more on conservatories and home greenhouses, see Chapter 20.)

Conservatories usually have an entire glassed-in wall and at least part of the ceiling made of glass. The light enters from above and from the side, often making the room extremely bright. Dark paint or wallpaper can absorb some of the glare.

Fill conservatories and garden rooms to the brim with plants of all sorts. Not only are garden rooms stuffed with plants irresistible, but the abundant, healthy greenery helps hide dormant plants going through their "ugly duckling" stages. Conservatories and garden rooms are also ideal places for plants that you've temporarily moved from a dark spot so that they can recuperate some energy in brighter light. You can also use those rooms to start annuals and vegetables for an outdoor garden.

Windowsills in any room

Windowsills are the most widely used indoor garden spots in just about every home. Ordinary windowsills are ideal for small plants and can support medium-sized plants if you widen them with a plant shelf. Windowsills are the brightest places in a room and most plants grow better on windowsills than anywhere else.

But watch out: South and west windowsills often become too hot for plants during the spring and summer. At those times of the year, move your plants a few inches back away from the window or somewhere else entirely.

You can also affix plant shelves in front of windows if your windows don't have sills, or hang multiple pots from the ceiling to make the most of available light. You may want to train climbing plants to grow up and around windows to soften their lines and bring the outdoors inside.

The office

Plants definitely *do* have a job in the workplace. Studies show that people who have plants in their offices are happier, have greater concentration, and are absent less often. And, the small amount of time invested in caring for plants is paid back many times over when you discover you work more efficiently if you have a few plants around. (Houseplants adapt equally well in a home office or other workplace.) So, think about adding a few plants atop a cabinet or on a desk. They'll help to calm your nerves when you accidentally delete that file you spent hours working on.

Chapter 20

The Greenhouse Effect: Building Your Own Controlled Climate

A greenhouse seems like the ultimate houseplant dwelling. Think of it. All the glorious light a plant could want. That delicious humidity. Shelter from the weather. Safe from the family dog and cat and toddler. The company of other plants.

I know what you're going to say next. What a life for the plant, but how can I humanly afford a greenhouse? In this chapter, I tell you a little about greenhouses from the deluxe freestanding kind to window greenhouses that you can install yourself.

Decisions, Decisions

I must warn you up front — a greenhouse is not something you buy on a whim. It takes careful thought, planning, and expert advice. Just deciding where to put a greenhouse, what kind of materials to use to build it, and how to heat, cool, and ventilate it are major decisions. In addition, greenhouses may not be the plant heaven that you envision. Greenhouses do offer plenty of advantages for serious plant growers, but they also involve their own special set of challenges.

The advantages of having your own greenhouse

You may want to invest in a greenhouse for a number of reasons:

- ✔ **More growing space:** If you're becoming a serious houseplant grower, space for your expanding plant collection is probably the main reason you need a greenhouse.

- ✔ **Vastly improved lighting:** The superior lighting opens up a wider choice of plants.

- ✔ **Higher humidity:** Increased humidity allows you to grow a wider range of plants, and your plants grow faster and bloom more profusely.

- ✔ **Faster growth:** Many houseplants grow slowly, if at all. In a greenhouse, most plants grow super-fast.

- ✔ **Climate control:** If you want to grow plants that must have colder temperatures for a certain part of the year, you can keep a greenhouse at a brisk 50°F (10°C) if you wish — something your cacti will especially appreciate.

- ✔ **Healthier plants:** Greenhouse plants tend to be sturdier, require less staking, and do a better job of resisting disease and insects. This superior health is a necessity, however, because higher humidity and greater plant density lead to an increase in pests.

- ✔ **Ideal conditions for starting plants from cuttings and seeds:** A greenhouse can function as a nursery, as well as a show place.

The challenges of greenhouse growing

A greenhouse may seem like a total plant paradise, but it does require that you take into account some important details before you plunge headlong into any greenhouse project.

- ✔ **Space limitations:** Ideally, if you want to build a greenhouse, you should own your home, although condo and apartment dwellers can sometimes obtain permission to add on a greenhouse. If you do get permission from a landlord, be sure it's in writing.

- ✔ **Cost:** You can build an inexpensive greenhouse that can be maintained economically, but it takes plenty of planning — and will be much smaller than a deluxe model.

- ✔ **The need for expert help:** Expert advice can range from casual chats with greenhouse suppliers to consultations with an architect. If you do hire an architect, insist on one who has experience with greenhouses and be sure to ask for references.

✔ **Permits:** Local building codes vary, so exactly which permits you need, if any, depends on your community. Don't forget to take *setback* ordinances (minimal allowable distances between your lot and your neighbor's) into account.

✔ **Insects and disease:** Ideal conditions for plants are also ideal for many insects and most diseases, so you must be on the constant lookout for bugs and plant sickness in any greenhouse environment.

✔ **Too much sun:** You exchange the disadvantage of having insufficient light (a common situation in most homes) to possibly having excess light during most of the summer.

✔ **Increased watering and fertilizing:** Because your plants are operating at maximum efficiency, you probably have to water more than once a week and fertilize more often throughout spring and summer.

✔ **Trial-and-error temperature and humidity control:** Expect to make a few mistakes along the way until you get your greenhouse fully up and running. Don't put any valuable plants in your greenhouse until you're sure you know how to operate it properly during every season of the year.

Do the pros outweigh the cons? It all depends on you and your situation. I built my greenhouse 3 years ago, after hemming and hawing over it for nearly 20 years, and now I wouldn't dream of giving it up.

Basic Greenhouse Types

The word *greenhouse* applies to any kind of glassed-in structure that houses plants. You can build (or buy) a freestanding greenhouse, or you can incorporate a greenhouse into your home.

Freestanding greenhouses

A *freestanding greenhouse* is a structure that's independent from the rest of a house, and usually located in a backyard. This type of greenhouse often requires less effort to build than a *lean-to*, or, *attached greenhouse* (one that is built up against an existing building). It isn't part of the house, which means that you don't have to worry about integrating it architecturally with the rest of your home. Also, if it's considered a temporary structure, its construction may not be regulated by local building codes.

Building materials
You can build the frame of a freestanding greenhouse out of wood (treated or untreated), metal, or rigid plastic. A wide variety of shapes is available besides the traditional *span roof* (rectangular with a pointed roof), including A-frame, arched, hexagonal, and geodesic greenhouses.

You can cover your freestanding greenhouse with glass, fiberglass, or various types of plastic including acrylic or polycarbonate paneling, or one of a wide variety of plastic films. In cold climates, consider using double or even triple layers of covering to reduce heat loss. Clear glass is perhaps the most attractive and long-lasting of all coverings and also lets in more light than any other, but your budget may force you to use a cheaper plastic film or fiberglass panels that are more translucent than transparent.

Size

No minimum size exists for a freestanding greenhouse. I've seen tiny structures built out of old window frames that are good for only two or three plants and others that would fill most of an average backyard. A structure 8 feet by 10 feet (2.4 meters by 3 meters) with enough headroom to work in comfortably is a decent size. Many commercial greenhouses are designed to allow you to expand them by adding sections as your plant collection grows.

Cost

A freestanding greenhouse can cost almost nothing to build if you use recycled materials, such as old window frames, and do all the work yourself. Greenhouse kits for moderate-sized structures using inexpensive coverings start at $1,000 and go up from there, not including the cost of installing a foundation.

In warm climates, you can simply lay lengths of 4-x-4 planks flat on the ground and those will suffice for a foundation. In areas where winters bring heavy frost, you need a more solid foundation that reaches below the frost line. Expect to pay at least $5,000 to $10,000 for a solid freestanding greenhouse with two layers of double-strength glass on a permanent foundation installed by a team of experts. Luxury models start at $30,000 on up.

If you want some help in deciding how much to spend, look up "Greenhouse Builders" in the yellow pages and visit a few showrooms. You can also check out the resources listed in Appendix B of this book.

Heat and cold

Ideally, you should place a freestanding greenhouse where it gets full winter sun but some protection from summer sun — you *can* grow beautiful plants in a semi-shaded greenhouse. Many freestanding greenhouses have no electrical outlets or plumbing. (Hoses and extension cords serve as the lifelines for any necessary irrigation, heating, and humidifying.)

In milder climates, freestanding greenhouses are used year-round because they require little heat. The sun coming through the glass keeps the structure sufficiently warm. In colder climes, the expense and labor involved in heating and insulating a freestanding unit exposed to winter winds on all sides and the excessive heat buildup in the summer generally restricts its usage to the spring and fall months.

If your freestanding greenhouse is heated, be sure to install a fail-safe alarm system that informs you if the heat goes off. The temperature inside a freestanding unit can quickly drop below freezing owing to the absence of insulated walls that contain heat. You can find temperature alarm systems through greenhouse suppliers.

You can use all types of heating in a greenhouse — electric, gas, oil, propane, and so on — but electric heaters are the most popular choice for freestanding units. Make sure that your heater is designed for greenhouse use. Some plug-in heaters deteriorate rapidly in the high humidity of most greenhouses.

Lean-to greenhouses

Lean-to greenhouse construction can be just as bare-bones or just as elaborate as a freestanding unit — with only a rudimentary foundation (or no foundation) and plastic or fiberglass covering, or it can feature a laid foundation and glass paneling. Some lean-to greenhouses are closed off from the rest of the house to maintain high humidity, whereas many can be accessed through a doorway (a useful feature in snowy climates).

Lean-to greenhouses are less exposed to the elements than freestanding units. Lean-tos also cost less to heat because they share a wall with your house. Your choice of locations is limited, however. You may find that you have to build your greenhouse on the north side of your home, even if that puts it in the shade most of the day. Expect to pay at least as much for a lean-to greenhouse as you would for a comparable free-standing one.

Some lean-to greenhouses are integrated as part of the home. These greenhouses typically have a solid foundation, share the home's plumbing and heating systems, and nearly always have a glass covering (often double-walled for better insulation).

Window greenhouses

The simplest and cheapest type of lean-to greenhouse is the *window greenhouse,* an easily installed bump-out window designed specifically for growing plants. You can add a greenhouse window to most homes (and even condominiums and apartments) at a small cost and with little effort. Look for an unobstructed window, preferably near a source of tap water, that gets the brightest light possible. (A window under an overhanging roof that keeps out the midday sun is ideal.) Just remove the regular window and attach the greenhouse window. You can do it yourself in an afternoon, preferably with a second set of hands.

Window greenhouse kits usually come complete with everything you need, except caulking. They range from $150 to $500 and come in a variety of sizes. You can also have an architect design a window greenhouse that's integrated with your home's design, but expect to pay thousands instead of hundreds of dollars.

In warmer climates, you don't need to heat a window greenhouse. Else-where, heating a greenhouse window, even on the coldest days, requires little more than running a small fan to blow in heat from your house.

Look for window greenhouses that come with built-in vents that you can open up during the summer. You can use the same fan that blew in heat during the winter to ventilate a non-vented model during the hot days of summer. (If an ordinary south-facing window ledge can become unbearably hot for plants, imagine the heat inside a partially enclosed structure.)

Sunrooms

Solariums and *sunrooms* often function as human living spaces first, but generally include some room for plants (as your level of interest grows, you may find yourself gradually relegating the wicker furniture to the basement to make way for more plants). *Greenhouse additions* typically are smaller rooms, strictly suited for growing plants, and usually extend out of a room, such as a kitchen, and into a yard. Both sunrooms and greenhouse additions require supplementary heating in cold climates.

If you want to install a solarium or greenhouse as a permanent addition to your house, I strongly recommend that you contact a local architect or building contractor. Freestanding greenhouses and window greenhouses, as well as simpler models of lean-to greenhouses, are available as do-it-yourself kits that you can order by mail. For the names of some mail-order green-house kit suppliers, see Appendix B.

Some Basic Greenhouse Construction Guidelines

Before you begin work on any freestanding greenhouse, or any greenhouse-type structure you plan to add to your home, check your local building codes to determine if your community has any regulations concerning size, height, distance from property lines, structural requirements, or anything else that may be regulated. (Try calling information for your city or county and ask for the "building inspection" or "codes compliance" office.)

Some local building codes require that greenhouses be entirely self-contained, which would eliminate the lean-to option described earlier in this chapter. But, if you call your greenhouse a sunroom, it may pass muster. It worked for me!

Non-slip tiles and cement are among the best options for greenhouse floors. Use flooring that can be drenched with water and take dirt and fertilizer spills without sustaining damage or getting stained. Gravel is another flooring option for foundationless greenhouses that's not only relatively inexpensive but also practical because it allows water to drain away easily.

You can place plants directly on the floor of the greenhouse, or you can install waist-high benches made out of rot-resistant wood or rust-resistant metal. Then you can place plants able to thrive in low light underneath the bench and plants requiring full sunlight on top of it. You can also suspend hanging plants from the greenhouse roof. If you have a spare corner and running water, a potting bench with a sink is a nice luxury.

A few electrical outlets and hot and cold (or at least cold) running water are also basic features of lean-to greenhouses (and are easy to set up with the house being nearby), although freestanding greenhouses can make do with a watering hose running from the house and the use of extension cords. You may have to lug water by hand to freestanding units during winter in climates where the ground freezes.

Caring for Greenhouse Plants

Plants grown in a greenhouse require the same basic sort of care as plants grown in any room of the house, just more of it. A greenhouse is much more humid than the rest of your home because of the number of plants giving off moisture through evaporation and it receives much more sunlight. Therefore, your greenhouse plants grow considerably faster and require more regular care — including watering, pruning, and cleaning — than your other plants. Also, because of the need for continuous ventilation in greenhouses, pests and diseases are given ample opportunity to work their way in.

Watering

Water greenhouse plants more frequently than indoor plants, up to several times a week during the spring and summer. If the greenhouse floor allows drainage of excess water, you can water your plants quickly by using a hose with a fan nozzle. Otherwise, use a watering can or watering wand (see Chapter 9).

Fertilizing

Greenhouse plants have a need for increased amounts of fertilizer because of their stepped-up growth. The fertilizing rule for houseplants grown in the home is to always dilute fertilizers with twice as much water (or use half as much fertilizer) as the manufacturer recommends. In a greenhouse, you can use fertilizer full strength, at least throughout spring and summer. If you use the constant fertilization method described in Chapter 11, in which you fertilize each time you water, dilute the fertilizer using $^1/_4$ to $^1/_8$ the recommended dose of fertilizer. Because you're watering frequently and therefore fertilizing frequently, the plants end up receiving a full dose.

To apply fertilizer using a standard garden hose, purchase a *siphon proportioner* (available from greenhouse supply companies listed in Appendix B or at garden centers), which allows you to dispense fertilizer automatically as you water.

Temperature control

You can heat a greenhouse in many ways, including (with small lean-to models) simply using your home's heating system. For other heating options, see a greenhouse dealer. (Look under "Greenhouse Builders" in the yellow pages.)

In cold climates, a backup heating system that does *not* rely on electricity is essential (gas heaters are the popular choice). During a winter power failure, all your plants can be killed in less than an hour.

The flip side of heating is cooling. Because of the exposure to full sun from all directions, greenhouse temperatures can quickly soar to dangerous levels — 120°F (50°C) or higher. In cool climates or cooler months of the year, wall and ceiling vents (screened to keep out harmful insects) may be enough to control the accumulation of heat; otherwise, you may also need to use shading (which I talk about next) and fans.

Shading comes in many forms, including whitewash (now rarely used because of its corrosive properties), spray-on shading compounds, bamboo screens, and shade cloths that you can apply to the inside or outside of the greenhouse. You install shading early in the season and remove it when autumn's shorter days bring cooler temperatures.

Planting a tall deciduous tree (or an evergreen in climates where temperatures remain above freezing most of the year) to the north of the greenhouse to shade the greenhouse at midday is another way to go. Or, you can take advantage of an existing deciduous tree. The tree should be close to the greenhouse without overhanging it to prevent breakage from falling branches.

You may need to equip your greenhouse with fans to ventilate excess heat in the summer. An *evaporative cooler* (basically a fan that draws incoming air through a pad kept constantly moist, thereby cooling the air through evaporation) may be essential equipment during hot summer months.

Humidity control

Low air humidity, a common problem when you're trying to grow houseplants in the average home, is rarely a problem in a greenhouse unless it's not closed off from the house or if it's located in an arid climate. Then, you have to look into rigging up the greenhouse with a humidifier.

In fact, *excess* humidity can be a problem in greenhouses, especially in the colder months. Plants can handle up to 90 percent relative humidity, but humidity levels higher than that encourage the spread of disease. Condensation on cold glass, which becomes water droplets that rain down on the plants, can spread plant ailments. Insulating the greenhouse with a second layer of clear or transparent paneling helps, as does running a fan. Direct the fan upward to keep air near the roof of the greenhouse moving around.

The fact is, greenhouse gardeners may find themselves treating their plants for diseases more often than regular indoor gardeners.

Insect control

A greater amount of outdoor air circulates through during the summer, which results in added problems with air-borne insects (such as, thrips, whiteflies, spider mites, and other pests). Treat greenhouse plants for pests as you would any other kind of houseplant (see Chapter 17 for information on ridding plants of insect invaders).

Part VI
The Part of Tens

The 5th Wave   By Rich Tennant

"I used to get fewer instructions when I looked after these people's children."

In this part . . .

This is the part of the book where I get to share my favorite top-ten lists of houseplant growing tips and tricks, plus other stuff about plants that even seasoned indoor gardeners may not know — such as, how your plants can water themselves so you can take off on that vacation trip guilt-free, and the real truth behind some long-held myths about houseplants.

Chapter 21

Ten Ways to Water Your Plants When You're Not at Home

Many serious indoor gardeners dread the thought of taking any sort of extended vacation. They have vivid memories of returning from a two-week trip to find their lush horticultural treasures looking like candidates for the compost heap. Other folks who frequently travel on business simply give up on growing houseplants because of the hassles involved in making sure their green growing pals are cared for while they're gone.

Good news, faithful reader! You can travel all you want and still enjoy having beautiful plants around the house. You just have to work a out what I call an "absentee care system." I myself travel 12 weeks or so every year — yet my plants are in fine shape because I use a combination of plant-care techniques that don't require my actually being there.

Pick Plants That Store Their Own Water

Cacti, succulents, some orchids, and any other plants that have internal water reserves of some sort make leaving on vacation or business much easier. Just water them thoroughly before you go and you can come back four weeks later (with orchids), or 8 to 12 weeks later (with cacti and succulents), and find them still in perfect shape. You can even leave some cacti and succulents alone for up to 6 months. (Six months without water certainly parches them good, but at least they survive.)

Likewise, plants that you grow in self-watering pots and those that you grow in *hydroculture* (see Chapter 9) can usually last at least three weeks without watering. Just fill the reservoir to the brim before you leave.

Try the Soak-'Em-and-Leave-'Em Method

They say you should never leave plants soaking in water, but what's a rule without an exception? Move your plants at least five feet away from any sunny windows and fill their saucers once until they absorb all the water. Then fill the saucers a second time, right to the brim — and then off you go! If you use this method, most plants can stay in fine shape for a two-week absence.

Try the Hunk of Carpeting in the Water-Filled Sink Method

Cut a piece of indoor-outdoor carpet or a thick piece of acrylic blanket about 2 feet wide by 3 or 4 feet long. Lay the carpet on the kitchen counter with one end of it draped into the sink. Plug the sink and fill it with water until several inches of the blanket or carpet are soaked. Remove the saucers from underneath your plants and place the pots on the portion of carpet that's on the counter. Water the plants thoroughly just once. Thereafter, the capillary action of the roots pulls water up from the sink through the carpeting and to the plants as they need it.

This method is effective only if your kitchen counter receives some amount of sunlight. Figure on this technique holding your plants for about three weeks.

Try the Sheets of Newspaper and Drippy-Faucet Method

All you need to make this self-watering method work is a kitchen sink that gets some light, some sheets of newspaper, and an open faucet.

1. **Start by removing the sink plug. If you leave it in, drowned plants and a flooded kitchen will be there to greet you when you get back.**

2. **Line the bottom of the sink with several layers of newspaper and set your plants on top of them.**

3. **Water your plants thoroughly until excess water drains out of the bottom of the pots and thoroughly soaks the newspaper.**

4. **Open the faucet just enough that a drop falls every 30 seconds to a minute — and off you go.**

You can leave for as long as you want to when you use this method — three months or more — although the plants may be seriously overgrown by the time you get back.

Try the Bricks in the Bathtub Method

Place enough bricks on the bottom of your bathtub to support all your houseplants (one brick per small plant, and up to three across for larger pots) and cover the bricks with 10 to 12 sheets of newspaper. The newspaper should drape over the bricks so that it touches the bottom of the bathtub. Stop up the drain and fill the bathtub with water until it almost covers the bricks. Remove the saucers from your pots and place the pots on the wet newspaper on top of the bricks. Using this method, you can keep the soil moist while your plants are unattended for up to three weeks.

This method works only if you have a brightly lit bathroom. I tried it in a windowless bathroom, hoping that the ceiling light would compensate for the lack of sunlight. It didn't — and most of my plants rotted.

Try the Just Trust Mother Nature Method

When you use this method, you need to begin priming your plants for your absence at least *four weeks* before you leave. First, acclimatize your houseplants to outdoor conditions over a two-week period (see Chapter 1 for information on how to this). Then plant them, pot and all, in a semi-shady spot in your garden. Take good care of them, watering them as needed, for another two weeks. Now you just have to trust Ma Nature to supply regular rain while you're away.

Obviously, this method doesn't work if you don't live in climates where rain can be counted on — unless you have an automatic irrigation system for your outdoor garden. If you live in an area with the right kind of climate but the area suffers a drought while you're gone (or your irrigation system fails), you have some consolation in the fact that your houseplants will be no worse off than your garden plants.

Make a Self-Watering Pot in a Snap

In Chapter 9, I tell you about the handy-dandy self-watering pot. Well guess what? You can build your own using materials you probably already have around the house. Just follow these steps:

1. **Punch a hole in the center of the lid from a margarine container, fill the container with water, and put the lid back on.**

   The container is destined to become a reservoir, with its lid supporting the pot.

2. **Cut a length of wick as long as the distance from the top of the pot to the bottom of the reservoir.**

   You can use actual wicking material, capillary matting (both of which are available at garden centers), a piece of nylon stocking, or acrylic yarn.

3. **Using a knitting needle or crochet needle, push one end of the wick up into the middle of the plant's root ball through a drainage hole in the pot.**

   The tip of the wick needs to reach at least halfway up into the pot. Let the rest of the wick dangle down through the drainage hole into the water in the reservoir.

5. **Water thoroughly from the top before you leave.**

   When you water thoroughly from above, some water will drip down onto the wick. This moistening is necessary to prime the wick — until the wick is moist, it can't start pulling water up from the reservoir below. After it's primed, it pulls water up into the pot as the potting mix starts to dry out, keeping the mix perfectly moist.

This method can be used for more than just a vacation-time watering technique. You can use it all year long on plants that prefer evenly moist soil. Just add water (and fertilizer) whenever the reservoir dries out.

A typical 1-pound (500-gram) margarine container can keep a small- to medium-sized plant moist for two weeks. Use a larger margarine tub or other plastic container for larger pots, or if you plan to go away for extended periods.

Bag It!

The sealed plastic bag technique is particularly effective. It enables you to leave your plants alone for 12 weeks or more without worrying at all about their lacking water.

When you use this method, first clean your plants thoroughly, removing anything that may possibly fall off the plant and rot during your absence — such as dead or yellowing leaves, fresh or faded flowers, and even flower buds.

Next, water your plants thoroughly, place them inside a clear plastic bag, and blow up the bag with air before you seal it off. (Large dry-cleaner bags and twist ties are ideal for this purpose.) Finally, place the bagged plant away from any sunny windows, but in a spot that still receives at least medium light.

When sealed inside a plastic bag after a thorough watering, your plants can't lose water even if they try. When you come back 8, 12, even 16 weeks later, they're just as fresh and green as they were on the day you left.

Never seal cacti, succulents, or other plants from arid climates inside a plastic bag. The "greenhouse effect" that many plants love quickly makes cacti and succulents rot and die.

If you grow plants under fluorescent lights (see Chapter 8), you can modify the "in the bag" method to keep your plants in top shape while you're away. Simply clean up the plants, water them thoroughly, and then surround your entire "light garden" with a large sheet of plastic (transparent or otherwise). Put the grow lights on a timer set to 8 hours of illumination a day to slow your plants' growth to a minimum. You can now leave for as long as 12 weeks without having to worry about your plants' health.

Hire a Professional Plant Sitter

The ideal situation for the absentee houseplant lover is to use the services of a professional plant sitter — if you can find one! They're a rare breed, indeed, especially in smaller towns, but you can find them in the yellow pages for some larger cities (look under "Garden Centers" or "Plants — Interior Landscaping" for some leads) or locate one by asking around (friends, neighbors, garden center employees, other people who keep plants).

Before handing over your house keys to a total stranger, do some checking up. Does the service have references? Is it bonded? What does the Better Business Bureau have to say about it? It's one thing to keep your plants happy, but you do want to see your home still filled with furniture when you get back.

Many pet sitters routinely take care of both plants and pets if you ask them ahead of time (but do check their references — as pet care specialists, they may have rather shaky knowledge of plants). Expect a weightier bill, though, if you have many plants to water.

You can't afford to leave most bonsais alone even for a long weekend, let alone two weeks. Your local bonsai store employees will know of a bonsai sitter and may well offer the service themselves. And, I've never met a bonsai sitter who didn't also care for other indoor plants.

Instruct an Amateur Sitter on Proper Plant Care

Most people ask neighbors, friends, or relatives to water their plants while they're gone, usually with mixed results. Neighbors are perhaps the best choice of the three. They're nearby, so dropping in every now and then shouldn't be a major chore. Friends and relatives who have to drive halfway across town to water a few plants may let your thirsty foliage slip their minds.

The ideal plant sitter is someone who also grows many houseplants. To someone who has never grown plants, the instructions "Just come in one day next week and water my plants" is open to interpretation. That person's idea of watering may be adding a splash to a desperately thirsty plant or drowning an already moist plant until its roots are swimming.

Even if you have the best plant sitter in the world, make his or her life easier by doing the following:

- ✔ **Give the sitter a full plant tour before you leave.** That goes a long way toward ensuring that the sitter doesn't forget any of the plants. Don't forget to point out the hanging baskets; sitters somehow seem to always miss them.

- ✔ **Show the sitter where you keep the watering can.**

- ✔ **Move all plants away from the windows temporarily.** They grow more slowly, use less water, and depend less on outside help.

- ✔ **Group your plants according to watering needs.** Put those plants that usually need weekly watering in one spot, those that can take longer periods of drought in another, and pull together all the touchy plants that need special care (such as daily watering) and put them where the sitter simply cannot miss them. Consider placing a brightly colored sign with each group to help your plant sitter remember which plants need which level of care.

Chapter 22

Dispelling Ten Common Myths about Houseplants

In This Chapter

▶ Some of the (strange) things people say about houseplants

▶ The real truth — and how knowing it can keep your plants alive

*P*eople are prone to say the most peculiar things at times, and some of the strangest stuff I've ever heard is about houseplants. In this chapter, I dispel some persistent myths about houseplants. Like other "urban legends," no one really knows where or when these myths started. These houseplant "facts" obviously sounded credible enough to some people because they've taken on a life of their own. But, to keep your plants alive and healthy you need to know the facts behind the fallacies.

So, want to come along while I explode a few houseplant myths?

None of That Photosynthesis Stuff in the Bedroom!

Myth: Never put houseplants in a bedroom because they steal all the oxygen from sleeping humans.

Reality: This myth is a real oldie, dating back to when removing gift plants and cut flowers from rooms at night was once standard practice in hospitals because hospital workers thought plants would asphyxiate the patients. At the time, it seemed to make sense because plants, after all, *do* absorb oxygen and give off carbon dioxide at night.

In the daytime, however, plants *give off* oxygen and absorb carbon dioxide. Ultimately, plants produce more oxygen than they use up. Put too many plants in a bedroom and it's the carbon dioxide that's likely to diminish, not the oxygen.

Pour on the Fertilizer

Myth: An extra dose of high-phosphorous fertilizer boosts bloom.

Reality: *Never* give plants an extra dose of fertilizer. It's a good way to end up with a dead plant on your hands. The amount of fertilizer that the label recommends is already the *maximum* amount of fertilizer that plants can use under optimal conditions. Indoors, where conditions rarely approach optimal, don't apply fertilizer at even the recommended rate. Dilute it by at least half.

Male Spider Plants Won't Bloom

Myth: If my spider plant doesn't produce babies, it must be a male.

Reality: Spider plants, like most plants, are both male and female. And even if they weren't (some plants produce either male or female flowers but not both), plants that naturally produce plantlets, pups, or offsets do so whether they're male or female. If yours doesn't produce babies, it's probably too young or isn't getting what it needs to truly thrive. The single most common cause of spider plants not producing babies is *lack of light.* Improve the general growing conditions — light, watering, humidity, temperature, and so on — and it should start producing babies before you know it.

Add Egg Shells to the Potting Soil

Myth: Always add a few spoonfuls of crushed egg shells to your growing mix before you pot up a plant. (And why not add tea leaves, coffee grounds, rotting tomatoes, and lawn clippings while you're at it?)

Reality: A pot is a highly artificial environment, and decomposition, which normally frees the mineral elements tied up in eggshells and other organic materials, takes place very slowly (if it takes place at all in a pot). Additionally, the amount of soil in a pot is severely limited as well, furnishing little opportunity for natural decomposition to kick in at a rate that can eventually benefit plants. Adding non-decomposed organic matter to pots can rob plants of the minerals they need because soil bacteria (if present in the right numbers) use up nitrogen as they work to decompose plant wastes.

If you want to add some organic material to your potting mix, use compost. Its elements have already decomposed into a useful state. Otherwise, do your composting outdoors, where natural soil organisms are more numerous and have the space to work.

Keep Cacti in the Dark

Myth: Cacti don't need sun. Grow them in the shade.

Reality: Cacti come from arid environments and most can not only tolerate bright sunlight but actually prefer as much light as you can give them, including full, blazing sun. In fact, the main problem with indoor cacti is a lack of light because what we think of as bright light is equivalent to outdoor shade for cacti.

Cacti, like many tough plants, can survive for ages under totally inappropriate conditions — but surviving is hardly growing. If you want healthy, happy cacti (at least if you have cacti of the desert persuasion), provide the brightest light possible. But make sure, even for desert cacti, that you provide protection from the hot sun during the summer months.

A Rusty Nail Makes for Great Fertilizer

Myth: To supply your plants with a good dose of fertilizer, just plunge a rusty nail into the potting soil.

Reality: Rust makes *terrible* fertilizer.

If you have an acid-loving plant (such as an azalea or indoor citrus) that seems abnormally yellow, it may indicate a lack of iron. Apply an occasional light dose of fertilizer that contains *chelated iron* (check the fertilizer label to see if it does.) Plants can assimilate chelated iron rapidly, unlike the chintzy rust-based iron that gathers on a nail.

Poinsettias Are Poisonous

Myth: The poinsettia (*Euphorbia pulcherrima*) is highly toxic. Always place it out of the reach of children.

Reality: Poinsettias are not toxic (but I wouldn't call them edible either). Eating them can irritate your stomach (plus they taste awful), but you won't be poisoned. Their bad reputation probably stems from the fact that they belong to the genus *Euphorbia* known for its poisonous plants. So, the harmless, holiday-time poinsettia is unfairly blamed for the bad habits of its family members.

Many other houseplants, however, *are* toxic, including dieffenbachias and philodendrons. The safest course of action is to never leave any houseplants within reach of young children or pets.

Pinch Your African Violets to Get More Flowers

Myth: For better bloom, pinch your African violets regularly.

Reality: If there is one plant you should never pinch, it's an African violet! Rosette-type African violets produce a single crown and grow upward, producing new leaves and new flowers from the tip of the plant. If you pinch it, the plant produces a mass of stems at its tip, resulting in a bunch of leaves, a total loss of symmetry, and fewer flowers than you had before.

One type of African violet that you *should* pinch is the trailing type. Pinch a young trailer to stimulate the development of more than one stem. As the plant matures, you occasionally may need to pinch secondary stems to get it to fill out. You want flowers on your African violets? Improve their general growing conditions, but forget about pinching!

There's Always Room for Gelatin

Myth: Gelatin is a great fertilizer.

Reality: I bet the gelatin company told you that one, right? Gelatin does supply a lot of nitrogen, one element that plants do need to grow, but that's all it provides. Supplying gelatin and nothing else to plants tends to stimulate rapid but weak growth that renders the plant highly susceptible to disease and insects.

It is difficult to think of a circumstance when you would want to add only nitrogen to potting soil. Instead, develop a fertilizing program that includes not only nitrogen, but phosphorous, potassium, and all the other minor and secondary elements — and follow it.

Spray Preventatively to Control Insects

Myth: Give your plants a spray of insecticide every now and then to ward off insect infestation.

Reality: An insecticide cannot prevent new insects from feasting on your plants; it can only kill the ones that are already there. If you spray plants with an insecticide when no insects are present, you're wasting time and money. Considering that many chemical pesticides are toxic to humans and pets as well as insects, use them as little as possible, instead of spraying "just in case." To prevent insects, grow your plants under the best possible conditions and keep them clean and free of dead flowers and leaves.

Appendix A
Key to Plant Profile Descriptions

• •

*W*ondering what those pithy plant care descriptions at the close of each houseplant profile in Part II of this book are all about? The following information sheds some light on each of those categories.

Display

Floor: Large plants should be placed on the floor for the best effect and to avoid grazing your ceiling (unless you like that look).

Hanging basket: Trailing and climbing plants can be potted in hanging baskets or in containers mounted above eye level, where they can show off their lengths of greenery.

Table: A medium-size plant works best on tables and pedestals.

Terrarium: Some plants are well-adapted to terrarium culture, and I note them as such.

Bonsai: These plants can be trained to be indoor bonsai.

Requirements

Full sun: Give these plants full sun at least four hours a day, and bright light the rest of the day. (For this lighting category and the three that follow, see Chapter 8 for a test that can tell you what kind of light your home receives.)

Bright light: Give these plants fewer than four hours of direct sun a day and intense light for eight hours or more.

Medium light: These plants prefer good light (enough light to create a shadow) but little direct sun, except perhaps in the morning or at the end of the afternoon.

Low light: These plants prefer moderate to weak light with no direct sun.

Keep moderately moist: Water this plant thoroughly as soon as its potting mix begins to dry out. It cannot tolerate drought.

Drench and let dry: During its growing season, water this plant as soon as its potting mix begins to dry out. When it is not in a phase of rapid growth, water it thoroughly, but allow its mix to become dry for a day or two before watering again. Never allow it to wilt.

Keep on the dry side: Water this plant thoroughly during its growing season, but let the mix go until it is dry to the touch (sink your finger in to the first or second knuckle as a gauge). If the plant is completely dormant, it needs no water at all for a lengthy period, perhaps several months, until it is out of its dormant phase.

High humidity: These plants do best in a very humid environment where a home humidifying system is installed. Chapter 10 describes a test you can use to determine the humidity level in your home.

Moderate humidity: Plants with this rating grow best in a humid room. Some sort of humidifying system is often required. Try the test in Chapter 10 to determine if the room has moderate humidity.

Average home humidity: These plants can tolerate dry air. You don't need to increase your home's normal indoor humidity levels.

Good air circulation: These plants cannot tolerate stagnant air.

All-purpose fertilizer: For plants that need fertilizer of this type, look for chemical ratios, as shown on the fertilizer label, that are equal (for example, 15-15-15).

Flowering plant fertilizer: For plants that need fertilizer of this type, look for the second of the three numbers in the chemical ratio to be higher than the other two (for example, 15-30-15).

Tomato fertilizer: For plants that need fertilizer of this type, look for the third of the three numbers in the chemical ratio to be higher than the other two (for example, 15-15-20).

Acid fertilizer: For plants that need fertilizer of this type, look for the words "acid fertilizer" on the label indicating that it contains special acidifying elements.

Normal room temperatures: These plants tolerate normal room temperatures year-round, from 65°F to 75°F (18°C to 24°C), although they do appreciate a 5°F to 10°F (3°C to 5°C) temperature drop at night, especially in the winter.

Warm temperatures: These plants tolerate normal room temperatures very well during the warmer months, but finding just the right spot for them in winter is critical because they don't like temperatures below 65°F (18°C). In addition, they don't care for air-conditioning.

Cool temperatures: These plants love air-conditioning! They tolerate normal room temperatures during their growing period, but like cooler temperatures, around 45°F to 55°F (7°C to 13°C), during their rest period. Without a cool winter rest, they may produce long, wobbly stems, refuse to bloom, or slowly weaken and die.

Cold temperatures in winter: These plants tolerate normal room temperatures during its growing period, but prefer cold temperatures — 35°F to 45°F (2°C to 7°C) — during its rest period. Although they can often tolerate some frost when planted outdoors, they become more fragile when grown in a pot. Never expose them to freezing temperatures.

All-purpose potting mix: These plants prefer just a standard potting mix.

Cactus potting mix: These plants prefer a potting mix that allows for rapid drainage, but can usually grow in a standard potting mix.

Orchid potting mix: These plants require a mix that drains extremely well, such as a mix largely composed of bark chips or sphagnum moss.

Acid potting mix: These plants require an acid growing mix. Hold off on adding any dolomite limestone when preparing the mix, or add a pinch or two of powdered sulfur to an all-purpose mix.

Propagation

Leaf cutting: These plants can be grown from a leaf cutting. (See Chapter 16 for more information on all the propagation techniques listed here.)

Stem cuttings: These plants can be grown from a stem cutting.

Layering: You can reproduce these plants by layering.

Air layering: These plants can be multiplied by air layering.

Division: These plants can be propagated by division.

Seed: These plants can be grown from seed.

Spores: These plants can be raised from spores.

Care Rating

Very easy: Anyone with basic houseplant skills can grow these plants.

Easy: These plants are generally easy to grow, but cannot stand prolonged neglect. Beginners usually do well with these plants in the short run, but care is needed to keep these plants thriving for many years.

Fairly demanding: These plants have special needs that may be difficult to provide, but anyone with a bit of growing experience should be able to grow them with success.

Demanding: These plants have special needs that are difficult to provide in the average home. Considerable growing skill is usually required to keep them alive and thriving.

Appendix B

Sources for Houseplants and Indoor Gardening Supplies

• •

*Y*ou can find almost all of the plants and products mentioned in this book no farther away than your local garden center, nursery, or florist shop. Most of the plants and supplies even show up occasionally in department stores, hardware stores, and supermarkets. If you're looking for a special variety of plant or indoor gardening tools or products that go beyond the ordinary, you may want to check out the following sources.

African Violets

Belisle's Violet House: P.O. Box 111, Radisson, WI 54867-0111; 715-945-2687; e-mail: BELISLESVH@aol.com. Catalog: $2. Specialty: African violets and gesneriads

Cape Cod Violetry: 28 Minot Street, Falmouth, MA 02540; 508-548-2798; Web: www.vsd.cape.com/~violets. Catalog: $2 (foreign: $3 US). Specialty: African violets and supplies

Lyndon Lyon Greenhouse, Inc.: 14 Mutchler Street, Dolgeville, NY 13329-1358; 315-429-8291; fax: 315-429-3820. Catalog: $3. Specialty: African violets and gesneriads

Tinari Greenhouses: P.O. Box 190, 2325 Valley Road, Huntingdon Valley, PA 19006; 215-947-0144. Catalog: $1. Specialty: African violets and supplies

Beneficial Insects

Nature's Control: P.O. Box 35, Medford, OR 97501; 541-899-8318; fax: 800-698-6250. Catalog: 50 cents

Bonsai

The Bonsai Farm: P.O. Box 1309, Lavernia, TX 78121. Catalog: $1

Cape Cod Bonsai Studio: 1012 Route 28, Harwich, MA 02645; 508-432-8400; e-mail: ccbs@cape.com

Bromeliads

Michael's Bromeliads: 1365 Canterbury Road N., St. Petersburg, FL 33710; 813-347-0349; fax: 813-347-4273

Pineapple Place: 3961 Markham Woods Road, Longwood, FL 32779; 407-333-0445. Send a stamped, self-addressed envelope

Shelldance Nursery: 2000 Hwy. 1, Pacifica, CA 94044; 415-355-4845; fax: 415-355-4931

Tropiflora: 3530 Tallevast Road, Sarasota, FL 34243; 941-351-2267; fax: 941-351-6985; Web: home1.gte.net/tflora. **Catalog:** $2. Specialty: Bromeliads and supplies

Bulbs

Caladium World: P.O. Box 629, Sebring, FL 33871; 941-385-7661; fax: 941-385-5836. Specialty: Caladiums

Cruickshank's, Inc.: 1015 Mount Pleasant Road, Toronto, ON, Canada, M4P 2M1. 416-750-9249; fax: 416-750-8522. Catalog: $3. Specialty: Bulbs and supplies

The Daffodil Mart: 85 Broad Street, Torrington, CT 06790; 800-255-2852; fax: 800-420-2852. Specialty: More than 1,000 different bulbs

Garden Import: P.O. Box 760, Thornhill, ON, Canada, L3T 4A5; 905-731-1950; fax: 905-881-3499. Catalog: $3

Cacti and Other Succulents

Abbey Gardens: P.O. Box 2249, La Habra, CA 90632; 562-905-3520; fax: 562-905-3522. Catalog: $2

Bob Smoley's Gardenworld: 4038 Watters Lane, Gibsonia, PA 15044; 412-443-6770; fax: 412-449-6219

K & L Cactus Nursery: 9500 Brook Ranch Road East, Ione, CA 95640-9417; 209-274-0360; fax: 209-274-0360. Catalog: $3

Lauray of Salisbury: 432 Undermountain Road, Route 41, Salisbury, CT 06068; 203-435-2263. Catalog: $2

Loehman's Cactus Patch: P.O. Box 871, Paramount, CA 90723; 310-428-4501. Catalog: $1

Mar-Low Epi House: In Canada: 31527 Oakridge Crescent, RR 5, Abbotsford, BC, Canada V2S 4N5; in the U.S.: Box 1940, Sumas, WA 98295. Catalog: $2

Rainbow Gardens Nursery: 1444 E. Taylor Street, Vista, CA 92084; 619-758-4290; fax: 619-945-8934. Catalog: $2. Specialty: Epiphytic cactus

Carnivorous Plants

Peter Paul's Nurseries: Chapin Road, Canandaigua, NY 14424-8713. Catalog: free

Herbs and Indoor Edibles

Logee's Greenhouses: 141 North Street, Danielson, CT 06239; 888-330-8038; fax: 203-774-9932; Web: www.logees.com. Catalog: $3

Richters: Goodwood, ON, Canada L0C 1A0; 909-640-6677; Web: www.richters.com. Catalog: $3. Specialty: Vast selection of edible plants

Well-Sweep Herb Farm: 205 Mt. Bethel Road, Port Murray, NJ 07865; 908-852-5390. Catalog: $2

Hydroponic Supplies

Brite-Lite: 2115 Walkley Street, Montreal, Quebec, H4B 2J9; 514-489-3806; fax: 514-489-3805

CropKing Inc.: 5050 Greenwich Road, Seville, OH 44273-9413; 330-769-2002; fax: 330-769-2616; Web: www.cropking.com. Catalog: $3

Heartland Hydroponics: 115 Townline Road, Vernon Hills, IL 60061; 800-354-GROW; Web: www.viasub.net/IUWF/hrt_lnd.html

Indoor Gardening and Greenhouse Supplies

A.M. Leonard: 241 Fox Drive, P.O. Box 816, Piqua, OH 45356; 800-543-8955; fax: 800-433-0633; Web: www.amleo.com. Catalog: $1

Charley's Greenhouse Supplies: 1569 Memorial Highway, Mount Vernon, WA 98273; 800-322-4707; Web: www.charleysgreenhouse.com. Catalog: $2

CropKing Inc.: P.O. Box 310, Medina, OH 44258; 216-725-5656. Catalog: $3

Indoor Gardening Supplies: P.O. Box 527, Dexter, MI 48130; 734-426-9080; fax: 734-426-7803; Web: www.IndoorGardenSupplies.com

Texas Greenhouse Company, Inc.: 2524 White Settlement Road, Fort Worth, TX 76107; 800-227-5447; fax: 817-334-0818; Web: www.metroplexweb.com/tgci

Orchids

Clargreen Gardens: 814 Southdown Road, Mississauga, ON L5J 2Y4, Canada; 905-822-0992; fax: 905-822-7282; Web: www.mississauga.com/clargreen.html. Catalog: $1

Huronview Nurseries: 429 Brigden Road, R.R. 1, Bright's Grove, ON, N0N 1C0; 519-869-4689; fax: 519-869-8518

Klehm Growers: 44 W. 637 State Route 72, Hampshire, IL 60140-8268; 847-683-4761; fax: 847-683-4766; Web: www.orchidmall.com/klehm/

Odom's Orchids: 1611 South Jenkins Road, Fort Pierce, FL 34947; 407-467-1386; fax: 407-465-4479; Web: www.odoms.com. Catalog: $2

Orchid World International: 10885 S.W. 95th Street, Miami, FL 33176; 305-271-0268. Catalog: $7.50, $5 refund on first order

Orchids by Hausermann, Inc.: 2N 134 Addison Road, Villa Park, IL 60181-1191; 708-543-6855; fax: 708-543-9842

Rod McLellan Company: 1450 El Camino Real, S. San Francisco, CA 94080; 800-237-4089; fax: 415-871-2806

Stewart Orchids: 3376 Foothill Road, P.O. Box 550, Carpinteria, CA 93014; 800-621-2450. Catalog: $2

Zuma Canyon Orchids: 5949 Bonsall Drive, Malibu, CA 90265. Catalog $3

Varied Houseplants

The Banana Tree, Inc.: 715 Northampton Street, Easton, PA 18042; 610-253-9589; fax: 610-253-4864; Web: www.banana-tree.com. Catalog: $3. Specialty: Exotic seeds

Brudy's Exotics: P.O. Box 820874, Houston, TX 77282-0874; fax: 713-960-7117. Catalog: $2. Specialty: Houseplants from seed

Exotics Hawaii, Ltd.: 1344 Hoakoa Place, Honolulu, HI 96821; 808-732-2105. For a catalog, send a stamped, self-addressed envelope. Specialty: Houseplants and seeds

Glasshouse Works Greenhouses: P.O. Box 97, Stewart, OH 45778-0097; 614-662-2142; fax: 614-662-2120; Web: www.glasshouseworks.com. Catalog: $3. Specialty: Wide range of exotic houseplants

Harborcrest Gardens: Box 5430, Stn. B, Victoria, BC, Canada V8R 6S4; 250-592-9017; fax: 205-592-9017. Catalog: $2

Lauray of Salisbury: 432 Undermountain Road, Route 41, Salisbury, CT 06068; 203-435-2263. Catalog: $2

Logee's Greenhouses: 141 North Street, Danielson, CT 06239; 888-330-8038; fax: 203-774-9932; Web: www.logees.com. Catalog: $3

Mason-Hogue Gardens: 3520 Durham Road #1, R.R. 4, Uxbridge, ON, Canada L9P 1R4; 905-649-3532. Catalog: $1

Merry Gardens: P.O. Box 595, Mechanic Street, Camden, ME 04843. Catalog: $1

Pacific Southwest Nursery: P. O. Box 985, National City, CA 91951-0985; 619-661-9129; fax: 619-477-1245. Catalog: $3

Southern Exposure: 35 Minor at Rusk, Beaumont, TX 77702-2414; 409-835-0644. Catalog: $5. Specialty: Variegated plants

Southern Perennials & Herbs: 98 Bridges Road, Tylertown, MS 39667-9338; 800-774-0079; Web: www.s-p-h.com

Stokes Tropicals: P.O. Box 9868, New Iberia, LA 70562-9868; 800-624-9706; fax: 318-365-6991; Web: www.stokestropicals.com. Catalog: $4. Specialty: Bananas, bromeliads, gingers, heliconias, and plumerias

Index

∙ ∙

(continued)

• *M* •

FISKARS®

Fiskars Softouch™ MicroTip Pruning Shears

The Fiskars Softouch™ MicroTip Pruning Shears is ideal for accurate trimming of topiary and bonsai, or for snipping off leaf tips and deadheading. Its compact size and profile allows you to get into hard-to-reach areas of your houseplants to make delicate, precise cuts.

For a store near you, call our Customer Service Dept. at **(800) 500-4849.** Find out more about the Softouch™ MicroTip Pruning Shears and the rest of the Fiskars Indoor Gardening product line at the Fiskars HomePage, **www. fiskars.com/indoorgardening**

FISKARS®

Fiskars Potting Sheet

Messy repotting of houseplants is a thing of the past, thanks to the Fiskars Potting Sheet. The vinyl-lined canvas sheet is waterproof, so you can control the soil and water mess when repotting plants. The sheet's corners fold up to form a portable tray, and two corners have handles so you can carry the sheet to the trash or outdoors to shake it out and wash it off.

For a store near you, call our Customer Service Dept. at **(800) 500-4849.** Find out more about the Fiskars Potting Sheet and the rest of the Fiskars Indoor Gardening product line at the Fiskars HomePage, **www. fiskars.com/indoorgardening**

FISKARS®

Fiskars Leaf Shine Mitt

ust and grime can clog plant leaf pores, so keep your plant leaves clean with e Fiskars Leaf Shine Mitt. The soft fleece cloth won't damage tender aves, so you can maintain your plant's natural, healthy ster. Machine washable, with durable overcast stitch-g, the mitt fits large or small hands.

r a store near you, call our Customer Service Dept. at 00) 500-4849. Find out more about the Fiskars af Shine Mitt and the rest of the Fiskars Indoor rdening product line at the Fiskars HomePage, ww. fiskars.com/indoorgardening

FREE six month subscription to **National Gardening** magazine

No other magazine gets to the root of planting and growing like *National Gardening*. That's because here at *National Gardening*, we haven't forgotten what down-to-earth, practical gardening is all about. And we're talking about all kinds of gardening—fruits, vegetables, roses, perennials— you name it and *National Gardening* knows it.

We bring you hands-on growing information you can use to become a more successful gardener. Make smarter variety selections. Time your plantings more efficiently for better results. Extend your growing season. Fertilize your garden more effectively, and protect it from pests using safe, sensible, and effective methods. Harvest healthier, tastier, more beautiful crops of all kinds.

Plus: Swap tips and seeds with other avid gardeners from around the country and around the world. Choose the best, most practical gardening products for your needs. Get expert gardening advice. Let the gardening experts at NGA help you grow everything more successfully!

Special offer to ...*For Dummies*® readers:
For a limited time, you're entitled to receive a six month (3 issue) subscription to *National Gardening* magazine—absolutely FREE. Just fill out the coupon and mail it to the address listed or call **1-800-727-9097**, today! Offer limited to new subscribers only.

❑ **YES** — Please sign me up for a free six month (3 issue) subscription to *National Gardening* magazine. Send the subscription to the name and address listed below.

_____
MY NAME

_____
ADDRESS

_____
CITY/STATE/ZIP   **R8DB**

*Offer limited to new subscribers only. Clip (or copy) and mail coupon today to: National Gardening Magazine, Dept. R8DB, P.O. Box 52874, Boulder, CO 80322-2874

Visit our Web site at *http://www.garden.org*

Discover Dummies Online!

The Dummies Web Site is your fun and friendly online resource for the latest information about ...*For Dummies*® books and your favorite topics. The Web site is the place to communicate with us, exchange ideas with other ...*For Dummies* readers, chat with authors, and have fun!

Ten Fun and Useful Things You Can Do at www.dummies.com

1. Win free ...*For Dummies* books and more!
2. Register your book and be entered in a prize drawing.
3. Meet your favorite authors through the IDG Books Author Chat Series.
4. Exchange helpful information with other ...*For Dummies* readers.
5. Discover other great ...*For Dummies* books you must have!
6. Purchase Dummieswear™ exclusively from our Web site.
7. Buy ...*For Dummies* books online.
8. Talk to us. Make comments, ask questions, get answers!
9. Download free software.
10. Find additional useful resources from authors.

Link directly to these ten fun and useful things at
http://www.dummies.com/10useful

For other technology titles from IDG Books Worldwide, go to
www.idgbooks.com

Not on the Web yet? It's easy to get started with *Dummies 101*®: *The Internet For Windows*® *95* or *The Internet For Dummies*,® 5th Edition, at local retailers everywhere.

Find other ...*For Dummies* books on these topics:
Business • Career • Databases • Food & Beverage • Games • Gardening • Graphics • Hardware
Health & Fitness • Internet and the World Wide Web • Networking • Office Suites
Operating Systems • Personal Finance • Pets • Programming • Recreation • Sports
Spreadsheets • Teacher Resources • Test Prep • Word Processing

IDG BOOKS WORLDWIDE
BOOK REGISTRATION

Register This Book and Win!

We want to hear from you!

Visit **http://my2cents.dummies.com** to register this book and tell us how you liked it!

✔ Get entered in our monthly prize giveaway.

✔ Give us feedback about this book — tell us what you like best, what you like least, or maybe what you'd like to ask the author and us to change!

✔ Let us know any other *...For Dummies*® topics that interest you.

Your feedback helps us determine what books to publish, tells us what coverage to add as we revise our books, and lets us know whether we're meeting your needs as a *...For Dummies* reader. You're our most valuable resource, and what you have to say is important to us!

Not on the Web yet? It's easy to get started with *Dummies 101*®: *The Internet For Windows*® *95* or *The Internet For Dummies*,® 5th Edition, at local retailers everywhere.

Or let us know what you think by sending us a letter at the following address:

...For Dummies Book Registration
Dummies Press
7260 Shadeland Station, Suite 100
Indianapolis, IN 46256-3945
Fax 317-596-5498

BUSINESS AND GENERAL REFERENCE BOOK SERIES FROM IDG

COMPUTER BOOK SERIES FROM IDG